DISCONNECT

THE JULIAN J. ROTHBAUM DISTINGUISHED LECTURE SERIES

DISCONNECT

The Breakdown
of Representation
in American Politics

MORRIS P. FIORINA

WITH SAMUEL J. ABRAMS

UNIVERSITY OF OKLAHOMA PRESS : NORMAN

Also by Morris P. Fiorina

Representatives, Roll Calls, and Constituencies (Lexington, 1974)
Congress, Keystone of the Washington Establishment (New Haven, 1977)
Retrospective Voting in American National Elections (New Haven, 1981)
(with Bruce Cain and John Ferejohn) *The Personal Vote : Constituency Service and Electoral Independence* (Cambridge, 1987)
(ed., with David W. Rohde) *Home Style and Washington Work : Studies of Congressional Politics* (Ann Arbor, 1989)
Divided Government (New York, 1992)
(with Paul E. Peterson) *The New American Democracy* (Boston, 1998)
(ed., with Theda Skocpol) *Civic Engagement in American Democracy* (Washington, D.C., 1999)
(ed., with David W. Brady and John F. Cogan) *Continuity and Change in House Elections* (Stanford, 2000)
(with Paul E. Peterson and D. Stephen Voss) *America's New Democracy : Election Update* (New York, 2003)
(with Samuel J. Abrams and Jeremy C. Pope) *Culture War? : The Myth of a Polarized America* (New York, 2005)

Library of Congress Cataloging-in-Publication Data

Fiorina, Morris P.
    Disconnect : the breakdown of representation in American politics / Morris P. Fiorina with Samuel J. Abrams.
        p. cm. — (Julian J. Rothbaum distinguished lecture series ; v. 11)
    Includes bibliographical references and index.
    ISBN 978-0-8061-4074-2 (cloth)
    ISBN 978-0-8061-4228-9 (paper)
    1. Political parties—United States.   2. Representative government and representation—United States.   3. Culture conflict—United States.
4. Politics and culture—United States.   5. United States—Politics and government—1989–   I. Abrams, Samuel J.   II. Title.
    JK2265.F64 2009
    320.973—dc22

                                                                                    2009020835

Disconnect: The Breakdown of Representation in American Politics is Volume 11 in the Julian J. Rothbaum Distinguished Lecture Series.

The paper in this book meets the guidelines for permanence and durability of the Committee on Production Guidelines for Book Longevity of the Council on Library Resources, Inc. ∞

4 5 6 7 8 9 10

*To Addie
and her siblings
and cousins to come*

CONTENTS

TABLES AND FIGURES

TABLES

FIGURES

FOREWORD

AMONG THE MANY GOOD THINGS that have happened to me in my life, there is none in which I take more pride than the establishment of the Carl Albert Congressional Research and Studies Center at the University of Oklahoma, and none in which I take more satisfaction than the Center's presentation of the Julian J. Rothbaum Distinguished Lecture Series. The series is a perpetually endowed program of the University of Oklahoma, created in honor of Julian J. Rothbaum by his wife, Irene, and son, Joel Jankowsky.

Julian J. Rothbaum, my close friend since our childhood days in southeastern Oklahoma, has long been a leader in Oklahoma in civic affairs. He was served as a Regent of the University of Oklahoma for two terms and as a State Regent for Higher Education. In 1974 he was awarded the University's highest honor, the Distinguished Service Citation, and in 1986 he was inducted into the Oklahoma Hall of Fame.

The Rothbaum Lecture Series is devoted to the themes of representative government, democracy and education, and citizen participation in pubic affairs, values to which Julian J. Rothbaum has been committed throughout his life. His life-long dedication to the University of Oklahoma, the state, and his country is a tribute to the ideals to which the Rothbaum Lecture Series is dedicated. The books in the series make an enduring contribution to an understanding of American democracy.

CARL B. ALBERT
Forty-sixth Speaker of the
United States House of Representatives

PREFACE AND ACKNOWLEDGMENTS

IN THE AUTUMN OF 1964, I enrolled in Political Science I, the first of what would turn out to be a long series of political science courses. Some of our class readings decried the then-current state of American politics, complaining that the Democratic and Republican parties were so similar ("tweedle-dee and tweedle-dum") that the American public was denied a real choice. In particular, some political theorists argued that by practicing "me-too" politics the Republicans were failing in their responsibility as an opposition party. Merely promising to do what the Democrats do—but to do it more efficiently—was not an adequate platform for a responsible opposition. To my young ears this argument seemed persuasive, so during class discussion I ventured the opinion that the ongoing campaign of Barry Goldwater ("a choice, not an echo") was a positive development for American democracy. The professor, a prominent local Republican, responded skeptically that the problem with that argument is that the Republicans were going to lose big, which they did. In the immediate aftermath of the electoral carnage, serious people wondered whether the Republicans could survive as a major party.[1]

Such worries proved short-lived. The next three years saw the disruption of the Democrat Party by divisions over race, the Vietnam War, campus disturbances, urban riots, and the birth of the counterculture—all the troubles later encapsulated in the term, "the sixties." By 1968 the Republicans had regained their political health and nominated former vice president Richard Nixon, an avowed practitioner of centrist politics, who narrowly won in a three-way race that included third-party candidate George Wallace (whose motto was, "There's not a dime's worth of difference between the two parties").[2] In 1972 the Democrats decided it was their turn to offer the American public a real choice with liberal George McGovern and consequently suffered a disaster comparable to the Republican debacle eight years earlier. After these two elections the political science case for the electoral necessity of centrist politics seemed to rest on a rock solid foundation.

Although new to me when I first encountered it, that case was already decades old—taken for granted by mid-century political scientists such as Pendleton Herring and V. O. Key, Jr.[3] Julius Turner, a student of Key, spoke for many empirically minded political scientists in his 1951 critique of a noted academic report, "Toward a More Responsible Two-Party System," which called for two distinct, cohesive parties.[4] Turner argued that in a heterogeneous country like the United States, if there were two such parties, one or the other would have little chance of competing in many areas of the country. As he put it, "You cannot give Hubert Humphrey [a liberal Democratic senator from Minnesota] a banjo and expect him to carry Kansas. Only a Democrat who rejects at least a part of the Fair Deal can carry Kansas, and only a Republican who moderates the Republican platform can carry Massachusetts."[5] In his 1960 book, Clinton Rossiter summarized the conventional wisdom as follows: "In some important respects there is and can be no real difference between the Democrats and the Republicans, because the unwritten laws of American politics demand that the parties overlap substantially in principle, policy, character, appeal, and purpose—or cease to be parties with any hope of winning a national election."[6] Rossiter claimed no original insight—among others he cited Lord Bryce, who first published his classic work about the United States in 1888.[7]

French scholar Maurice Duverger had shown in 1954 that the American case was not exceptional but, rather, part of a broader democratic pattern.[8] Countries whose electoral systems were based on various forms of proportional representation tended to have three or more parties with more distinct identities than countries whose electoral systems were based on plurality rule in single-member districts. Like the United States, the latter tended to have competition between two broadly based parties. Rather than having distinct platforms, parties in such systems tended to be "catch-all" parties. A few years after Duverger, Anthony Downs formalized the abstract logic of two-party and multiparty competition in one of the seminal political science works of the century: *An Economic Theory of Democracy*.[9] In succeeding decades political scientists and political economists extended, adapted, and otherwise relied on Down's formulation.[10]

Thus, the proposition that two-party competition produces convergent politics wherein the parties make overlapping appeals in an effort to capture the center served as a kind of "master theory" for American political scientists for most of the twentieth century. But in the later decades of the century, Rossiter's "unwritten laws" increasingly were being violated. Between 1968 and 1992 the Democrats spent most of the time wandering in the presidential electoral wilderness, in part at least because the electorate viewed their candidates as off-center on important issues of the time.[11] The resulting extended period of divided control of government led me to think about how voters might react to a choice between two parties, neither of which they found very satisfactory.[12] In 1992 Bill Clinton hauled the Democratic Party back to the political center but apparently then forgot the important lesson he had taught, governing like a 1960s Democrat and helping the Republicans take control of Congress for the first time in forty years in the 1994 midterm elections. But when the Republicans, in turn, overinterpreted their 1994 mandate and lurched rightward, Clinton easily won reelection in 1996 by following a strategy of "triangulation" (positioning himself between conservative congressional Republicans and liberal congressional Democrats). Oblivious to what seemed like the relatively clear lessons of those recent elections, however, Republicans continued swimming in currents outside the mainstream. In

1998 appeals to the political center were in short supply as noted by various political commentators:

> Pandering to the ideological extremes would not be necessary if the officeholders thought that moderation and modest achievements would be rewarded by voters who say that limited government and common sense solutions are what they want. But with the prospect of low turnouts, it is the most motivated—and militant—elements at the edges of the ideological spectrum who will receive the most attention.[13]

> Even if there is a backlash against Starr [the Republican prosecutor in the Monica Lewinsky case], Republicans don't really care. They are not focused on swing voters or fence-sitters. Their strategy for the fall is clear and calculating: Appeal to the hardcore Republican base. Get them as outraged as possible. Make sure they give money and vote heavily.[14]

The new strategy proved ineffective as the Republicans lost four seats in the House of Representatives, at the time making 1998 only the second midterm election since the Civil War in which the party of the incumbent president gained seats. Provoked by the apparent refusal of the parties to behave in accord with political science theory, I wrote a survey paper asking, "Whatever Happened to the Median Voter?" pointing out that the master theory that had implicitly underpinned analyses of American politics for a century now seemed less applicable and critically evaluating various explanations in the literature.[15] The 2000 campaign marked a partial return to more traditional politics, as George W. Bush practiced a Republican version of triangulation (he claimed to be a "compassionate conservative," distinguishing himself from congressional Republicans who lacked compassion and from congressional Democrats who lacked, well, conservatism). But meanwhile Democratic candidate Al Gore abandoned Clinton's centrist stance and reverted to the strategy that had proved so ineffective in the 1980s, one of the major factors that contributed to the defeat of an incumbent party candidate during a time of peace and prosperity.[16] And by 2002 compassionate conservatism had been replaced by the idea of "feeding the base." Appeals to centrist voters once again were in short supply and remained so in 2004.

Thus, except for brief interruptions now and then, I have been thinking about the declining electoral status of the political center for almost two decades. *Culture War? The Myth of a Polarized America,* published during the summer of 2004, was a first report.[17] This book, too, is an interim report. I doubt that there is any simple, persuasive explanation of how an interpretation of American politics that prevailed for a century could become outdated in the space of a decade or two. Nor do I think that we can identify, let alone evaluate, the full consequences of the change as yet. I offer this book to my academic colleagues and fellow citizens as an invitation for them to think about these subjects. Reflecting the fact that the chapters that follow are part of an ongoing dialogue rather than the result of a definitive study, I have tried to retain the conversational tone of the earlier lectures on which the book is based.

The choice of title, *Disconnect: The Breakdown of Representation in American Politics,* is deliberately provocative, of course—a bit of hyperbole intended to capture the reader's attention and communicate my own sense of concern about the matters discussed in the pages that follow. In America today there is a disconnect between an unrepresentative political class and the citizenry it purports to represent. The disconnect has three dimensions. First, the political class is considerably more polarized than a generation ago; however, the citizens, whose votes the political class covets, appear to be little changed in their moderate orientation from those citizens of a generation ago. Rather than moderate their appeals to attract centrist voters, many candidates today prefer to hide their real beliefs and intentions by careful use of crafted language and to practice a politics of mobilization of their own partisans and demobilization of the opposition.[18] Second, the rhetoric and activities of the political class reflect a set of issue priorities that are not the priorities of the American public. In particular, whether genuinely felt or merely tactical, the heavy emphasis of the political class on so-called hot button social issues is not shared by the larger electorate. Finally, the dogmatic, divisive, and uncivil style of "debate" engaged in by many members of the political class is not appreciated by ordinary Americans, who are for the most part less certain, more open to compromise, and more polite than their leaders. In the first three chapters of the book, I describe these three dimensions of the disconnect, updating, refining, and extending the analyses and arguments put forth earlier in *Culture War?* and responding to questions about and criticisms of that earlier work. Chapters 4, 5, and 6 are very different. In those chapters I explore explanations of why politics today differs from that described by previous generations of political scientists, suggesting that the sources of contemporary political change lie in sociodemographic changes and the responses of the political order to them. In chapters 7 and 8 and the epilogue, I weigh some of the plusses and minuses of the new politics for representative government; consider what, if anything, might be done to change it; and speculate that new countertrends are now operating to undermine the current disconnect.

Given the lengthy period during which the thinking expressed in the following pages has gestated, I cannot remember all the colleagues who have influenced my thinking in one way or another. But certainly those who have participated most actively in the academic debate deserve, at the least, explicit mention: Alan Abramowitz, Wayne Baker, David Brady, James Campbell, John Evans, Andrew Gelman, Marc Hetheringon, Gary Jacobson, Philip Klinkner, Geoffrey Layman, Matthew Levendusky, Norman Nie, Pietro Nivola, Jeremy Pope, Robert Shapiro, and Alan Wolfe, with apologies to others whom I may have overlooked. Theda Skocpol's earlier Rothbaum Lectures and Robert Putnam's work on social capital were both major sources of inspiration for chapters 5–6 of the book. Ronald Peters and Cindy Simon Rosenthal read the manuscript for the University of Oklahoma Press and provided extensive comments that materially improved it.

When Gary Copeland, then-director of the Carl Albert Center, first invited me to serve as the 2005 Rothbaum Lecturer, I was delighted to accept. Previous lecturers of my acquaintance had nothing but highly favorable reports of their experience, and mine turned out to be as rewarding as they had reported. Superbly organized and well-attended, the lecture series should serve as a model for similar series elsewhere. Much of the credit must go to the center's assistant to the director, LaDonna Sullivan, whose off-the-charts organizational ability and temperamental unflappability are qualities too seldom found in university settings. Cindy Simon Rosenthal and Joel Jankowsky were gracious hosts during my three-day visit, and my session with university president and former senator David Boren was a delight. During his political career, Boren was the kind of elected official who is in tragically short supply today. Last, but most assuredly not least, I thank my longtime assistant/collaborator/friend, Samuel Abrams, who has been a major contributor to this project.

University of Oklahoma Press editors Matthew Bokovoy, Charles Rankin, Jay Dew, and Alice Stanton sheparded the manuscript through the production process, and Kim Kinne provided expert copyediting. I hope the finished project reflects well on their efforts.

DISCONNECT

CHAPTER 1

A DISCONNECT
IN POLITICAL POSITIONS

CLEM MILLER (D-CALIF.) WAS ELECTED to the U.S. House of Representatives in 1958. The pace of political life was much slower in those days, and Miller took time to write a delightful series of letters to friends and supporters describing Congress and the daily life of its members. What follows is an excerpt from his description of the first day of the 1961 session, which happened to be the birthday of Democratic Speaker Sam Rayburn of Texas. Joe Martin of Massachusetts is the former Republican Speaker:

> Joe Martin rises. . . . his words are slow and full, deep affection showing through their formality. The chamber is silent, each of us pondering what is between these two, while Martin talks throatily of long, long ago . . .
> "Mr. Speaker and my colleagues, it is a great privilege to have the opportunity, even for a few moments, to pay my respects to a dear friend, an old friend and a Member whose friendship has lasted over 35 years without a jarring note. It has been my privilege to know Sam Rayburn all these years, and I can testify, as few men can testify, to his rugged Americanism, his loyalty to country, and his intense desire above everything else to maintain the high honor and integrity of the House of Representatives." . . .
> Rayburn's face never flinches, but he shifts his weight heavily from one side to the other, cups his jaw in one and then the other hand, as he looks unblinkingly at his friend Joe Martin.

In his reply Rayburn said (among other things), "I make no promise except to say that every man and woman in this House will be treated like every other Member of the House and have all the rights of every other Member of the House, because you are chosen by the people, you are a selected group." Miller concludes, "When he says this he lines up with every Member of the

3

House personally. He is not an institution. He is not Speaker. He is one of us."[1]

Substitute "Dick Gephardt" (D-Mo.) for "Joe Martin" and "Newt Gingrich" (R-Ga.) for "Sam Rayburn" in 1995, or substitute "Nancy Pelosi" (D-Calif.) for Sam Rayburn and "John Boehner" (R-Ohio) for Joe Martin in 2007 and try to read the foregoing passages while keeping a straight face. Indeed, imagine how many rank-and-file members today would refer to the membership of Congress—Democrats and Republicans—as "us" rather than as "us" and "them." (For that matter how many members today really care about "the high honor and integrity of the House of Representatives"?) The congressional world described by Miller—where Democrats and Republicans generally treated each other with civility during working hours, and many drank, played poker, and golfed together after hours—is long gone.[2]

At the time Miller wrote, congressional leaders were a different kind of people from those who serve today. As leaders of their parties, they compiled partisan voting records, of course,[3] but generally they were not known as ideologues or extremists. Rayburn was succeeded by John McCormack of Massachusetts, a New Deal Democrat who was personally quite conservative.[4] McCormack was succeeded by Carl Albert of Oklahoma, a moderate in both policy views and political style. Thomas P. (Tip) O'Neill of Massachusetts succeeded Albert, and Jim Wright of Texas succeeded him. O'Neill might be considered something of a transitional figure, but with the accession of Wright, the kind of congressional leader familiar today clearly had emerged.

The change was somewhat slower on the Senate side. Mike Mansfield of Montana, a western moderate, succeeded Lyndon Johnson in 1961 and served as the Democratic majority leader for nearly two decades. When the Republicans took control of the Senate after the 1980 elections, well-known moderate Howard Baker of Tennessee became floor leader, followed by Robert Dole of Kansas in 1984. Trent Lott of Mississippi, who took the post in 1996, was the first of the new type of Senate leader, one who more resembled the leadership of the House in terms of strong policy views and partisan behavior than the previous generation of Senate leaders. The changes in leadership were only more visible examples of what was happening in the Congress as a whole. Developments among the rank and file can be described more systematically than via anecdotes about leadership changes. Everyday political commentary divides members into general categories like liberals, moderates, and conservatives. Political scientists have been doing the same thing quite precisely for several decades now, using statistical techniques to construct spatial maps of Congress. The most widely used method is that of Poole and Rosenthal.[5] In brief, they assume that each member of Congress has an "ideal point" in a policy space—a point where he or she is maximally satisfied with public policy. The farther policy is from that point, the less the member of Congress likes it. Assume further that when considering a bill or resolution the member votes aye or nay on the basis of whether he or she prefers the public policy that would come to be if the bill were to pass or the status quo that will persist if it were to fail. With modern computing power all the members and numerous roll calls for a given period can be considered together and a spatial map constructed with members and roll calls positioned to satisfy some summary measure of predictive accuracy.[6]

Perhaps surprisingly, for most of American history a one-dimensional policy space suffices to represent the membership of Congress.[7] The dimension is a left–right dimension dominated by economic redistribution issues, with (illustrating with contemporary senators) people like Russ Feingold (D-Minn.) on the far left, Olympia Snowe (R-Maine) in the middle, and Jon Kyl (R-Ariz.) on the far right. To return to our main concern, figure 1.1 contrasts the Poole–Rosenthal scores for the 1961–62 House of Representatives—the first two years of the Kennedy administration, when Representative Miller was writing—with those of 1999–2000, the first two years of the administration of George W. Bush (the diagrams are representative of their eras, and the Senate looks much like the House at both times).

Figure 1.1 Polarization of Congress since the 1960s

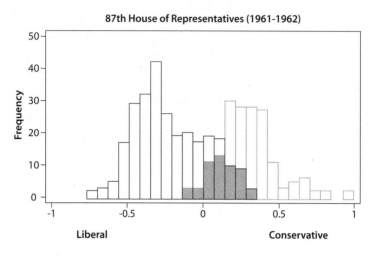

87th House of Representatives (1961-1962)

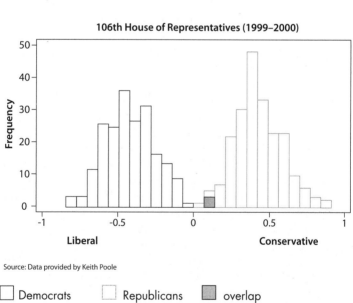

106th House of Representatives (1999–2000)

Source: Data provided by Keith Poole

☐ Democrats   ☐ Republicans   ■ overlap

Two related points of contrast stand out (besides the important fact that there are fewer Democrats and more Republicans now than a generation ago). First, each party has become more internally homogeneous—its members are not as spread out today as previously. Second, each party has moved outward on its side of the continuum—there is no doubt that the Democrats are the left party and Republicans the right. As a consequence of these two developments, the overlap between the parties has all but disappeared: although the distribution of members was bimodal in the 1960s, it is significantly more so today. At mid-century, there was a middle range occupied by both Democratic and Republican members, whereas in most recent Congresses almost every Republican is to the right of every Democrat. As numerous commentators have observed, moderates have largely vanished from today's Congress.[8] These changes appear to have begun in the mid-1970s, and they are the very definition of polarization—both extremes gain while the middle shrinks.

Of course, as I discuss in chapter 5, the realignment of the American South has made a significant contribution to these changes. Democrats have largely shed their conservative southern wing, leaving the party more homogeneously liberal, while Republicans have gained southern conservatives, making their party more homogeneously conservative. But replacement of conservative and moderate southern Democrats by conservative Republicans falls far from a total explanation of the increase in Congressional polarization—probably not much more than one-third of the total.[9] In the 1970s and 1980s, non-southern Democrats and Republicans were *more* polarized than their counterparts in the south. Starting in the 1970s, Republicans in the non-South moved quite a bit farther to the right and non-southern Democrats moved somewhat left in the 1990s.[10]

Polarization within the Congress is the most widely recognized, best measured, and thoroughly studied instance of political polarization, but the academic consensus is that polarization is not limited to the Congress. There is evidence that many state and local government bodies have grown more polarized,[11] that the leaders and activists in the increasing number of cause groups are highly polarized,[12] and that campaign activists and contributors are polarized.[13]

Delegates to party nominating conventions have been the subject of numerous studies, both by the media and by academics. Such individuals are prominent in their parties, some as elected or appointed officials, some as financial contributors, some as leaders of important party constituencies, and many as volunteer campaign workers. Surveys of delegates to the presidential nominating conventions are available since the 1972 campaign. Many of the questions included in these surveys change over time and are thus not comparable, but every survey asks the delegates' ideological self-placement on a five-point scale running from "very liberal" to "very conservative." Figure 1.2 shows that the percentage of Republican delegates choosing the most extreme "very conservative" position has risen from about 12 percent to more than 30 percent in the past generation, while the percentage of Democratic delegates choosing the most extreme "very liberal" position has risen in parallel from about 8 percent to nearly 20 percent over the same period.[14]

Finally, consider a class of people who are active in politics without necessarily holding any kind of official position. National Election Studies (NES) surveys conducted in each presidential year since 1952 allow us to track changing political attitudes and behavior over long periods. The surveys inquire about participation in campaigns, and political scientists typically define a campaign "activist" more or less broadly as someone who reports engaging in a given number of activities, such as trying to persuade someone how to vote, attending a meeting or rally, working for a campaign, giving money to a campaign, wearing a campaign button, or displaying a bumper sticker. In this book I define an activist as a partisan who engages in three or more such activities (there are few such people—more on this in chapter 3). Figures 1.3 and 1.4 show increasing polarization within this activist segment of the country.

The trend lines in figure 1.3 measure the difference between how each party's campaign activists feel about liberals compared with conservatives.[15] Over the course of the past forty

Figure 1.2 Extremism of National Convention Delegates

Data points show the percentage of delegates who rated themselves as "very liberal" or "very conservative" on a 5-point Liberal-Conservative Scale.

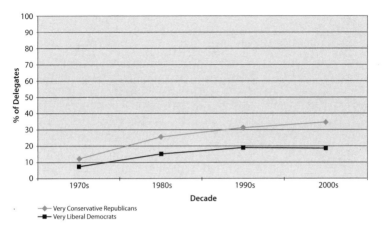

Source: ICPSR, *New York Times*, and Roper Delegate Polls

years, there is a tendency for activists increasingly to like one category and/or dislike the other. With the notable exception of 1964, when ideological feelings ran especially high, Republican campaign activists today express 20–30 degrees more liking for conservatives relative to liberals than they did in the 1960s and 1970s. Self-identified Republican partisans who are not active are less polarized and have become only slightly more so, with little change since 1980. The trend is similar for Democratic activists, although they feel less strongly about liberals relative to conservatives than Republican activists do, and while Democratic identifiers show some evidence of increasingly strong feelings about liberals and conservatives, the difference is much smaller than among Republican identifiers. Self-identified independents, if anything, feel less strongly about liberals versus conservatives than they did a generation ago.[16] Figure 1.4 shows similar trends in feelings about the political parties, although the differences between partisans and activists are smaller.

Figure 1.3 Difference between campaign activists and nonactivists on ideological feelings toward liberals and conservatives.

Data points represent average differences in rating of liberals versus conservatives, and the trend lines illustrate growing ideological distinction between activists and nonactivists.

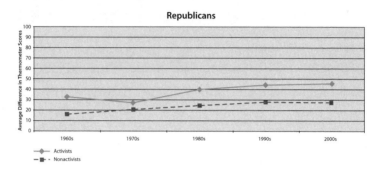

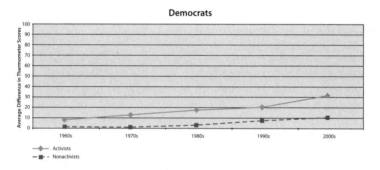

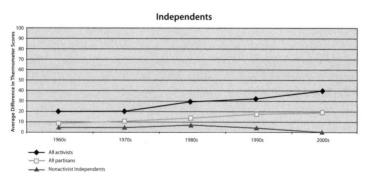

Figure 1.4 Difference between campaign activists and nonactivists on ideological feelings toward political parties.

Data points represent average differences in rating of Democrats versus Republicans, and the trend lines illustrate growing ideological distinction between activists and nonactivists.

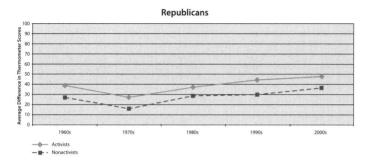

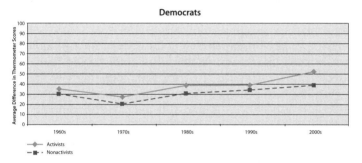

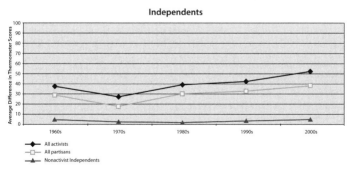

Data from the National Election Studies.

A CENTRIST PUBLIC

The evidence of growing polarization within the political class contrasts with the absence of evidence of any comparable increase among the citizenry at large. For example, contrast figure 1.2, which shows the growing tendency of national convention delegates to choose the most extreme ideological categories, with figure 1.5, which shows the absence of any such increase in the broader public. The top panel of figure 1.5 shows that the proportions of ordinary Americans who choose the most extreme categories are actually lower in Gallup polls conducted in the 2000s than in Gallup polls from the 1970s, and the plurality that prefers the moderate label is about 5 percentage points *higher* in the 2000s than it was in the 1970s.[17] The bottom panel combines the six categories into the standard three-point scale—liberal, conservative, moderate/don't know. The overall picture is fewer liberals, more moderates, and about the same number of conservatives as a generation ago.

James Campbell reported that in the NES version of the ideology measure there was a statistically significant decline in the moderate category between 1972 and 2004, a finding that largely reflects a decline in the number of "don't knows," whom analysts customarily classify as moderates—the percentage of exact middle-of-the-scale placements was 27 percent in 1972 and 26 percent in 2004. In the General Social Survey (GSS) version of the ideology measure, the percentage of "don't knows" is lower and the percentage of moderates higher than in the NES.[18] In the GSS the percentage of Americans placing themselves in the exact center of the seven-point scale or refusing to place themselves at all has stayed remarkably constant over the past four decades.[19] Figure 1.6 shows the proportions of Americans who identified themselves as moderates (or answered "don't know") for each of the three survey organizations from the 1970s to today. Gallup shows a slight increase in moderates, NES a slight decrease, and GSS no change. Clearly, the citizenry as a whole is much less deeply divided between liberals and conservatives than are political elites, and any evidence of increased polarization lies somewhere between nonexistent and slight.

Figure 1.5 Average Americans' Ideological Identification.

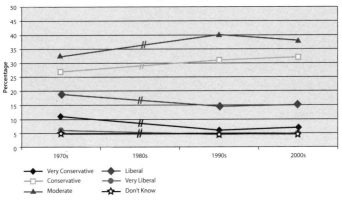

Proportion of Americans who self-identify with specific
ideological categories

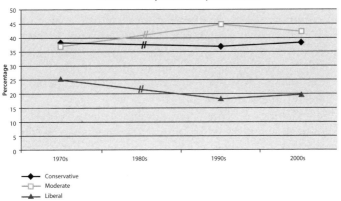

Proportion of Americans who self-identify as
conservative, moderate, and liberal

Data from the Gallup Polls' Liberal-Conservative Self-Identification scale. In the bottom panel "very conservative"
and "conservative" as well as "very liberal" and "liberal" responses have been combined. In both panels, 1980s
data have been imputed.

Figure 1.6 Percentage of Americans who classify themselves as moderates (or answered "don't know") according to three national polls.

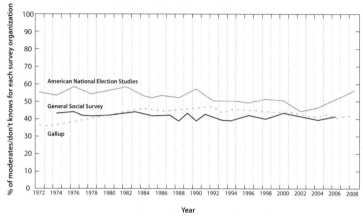

In tune with this objective disparity, the largely centrist American population consistently views the political alternatives that vie for consent to run the country as more extreme than the population—and growing more so. Figure 1.7 depicts where Americans perceive the two major parties on the left–right ideological dimension. Evidently, a majority of the public see themselves as choosing between two parties that are more extreme than they are, with each party moving sharply toward its end of the scale between the 1990s and the 2000s.

While ideology is a convenient summary measure often used by political scientists and political commentators, a simple liberal–conservative self-classification makes voters appear more ideological than they actually are. Consider a recent study by Ellis and Stimson, who examined the economic and social issue preferences of self-classified liberals and conservatives.[20] As the top panel in figure 1.8 illustrates, the minority (about 20 percent) of Americans who categorize themselves as liberals have a reasonable resemblance to what informed opinion would think of as liberal. More than 60 percent of self-classified liberals are liberal on both economic welfare issues and the newer social–

Figure 1.7 How Americans place the two major political parties on the Liberal-Conservative Scale.

Scores range from 1 ("very liberal") to 7 ("very conservative")

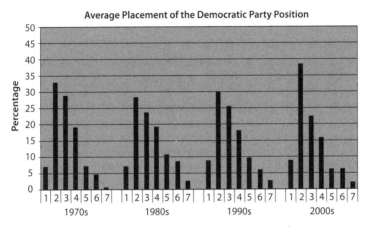

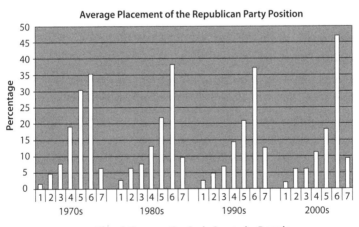

Data from the National Election Studies.

cultural issues. Another 20 percent of them are old-time New Deal liberals who are left of center on economic welfare issues but not on social issues. Self-described conservatives are another matter entirely.

The conservative label has always been more popular in the American context—about 35–40 percent of Americans call themselves conservatives in most surveys. But as the bottom panel of figure 1.8 shows, only one in five of those Americans who adopt the conservative label have issue stances that are right of center on both economic welfare and social–cultural issues. Somewhat more than a quarter of self-described conservatives are social conservatives only (they might be called "Huckabee conservatives" in 2008 terminology), about 15 percent are economic conservatives only, and most surprising, a third of those who adopt the conservative label express conservatives views on *neither* economic nor social issues.[21] Findings like these indicate that Americans are even less ideological than their self-categorizations would suggest.

In a conceptually related analysis, Carmines and Ensley reported that in contrast to members of Congress, whose roll call votes on all manner of issues fall on a single left–right dimension, the positions of voters are spread across all four quadrants created by crossing economic and social issue positions (conservatives, liberals, populists, libertarians).[22] As one would expect from a generation of work dating back to Philip Converse's classic study, American attitudes are multidimensional, and most Americans cannot reasonably be called left–right ideologues.[23] I do not consider this a fault of the electorate; on the contrary, the electorate does not oversimplify and distort a complex reality as political elites do.

What should one make of all this? For at least half a century political scientists have known that the political class (traditionally called "elites") differs from the broader public (traditionally called the "mass public") in a number of ways. Briefly, in addition to being less active, the public is less interested in politics than the political class and is, partly in consequence, less knowledgeable. As I discuss in the next chapter, ordinary Amer-

Figure 1.8 Issue Stances of Self-Described Liberals and
Self-Described Conservatives

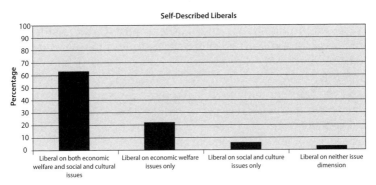

Self-Described Liberals

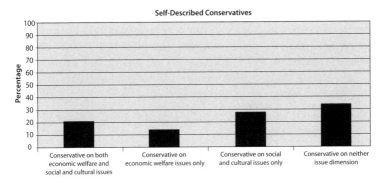

Self-Described Conservatives

Source: Ellis and Stimson, 2005.

icans hold their views less strongly and are more likely to
change their minds than activists, who are more intense and
more stable in their positions. Moreover, as shown by Ellis and
Stimson's and Carmines and Ensley's studies, the political
views of ordinary Americans are not nearly as closely tied
together as the views of members of the political class. The orientation of the public is more pragmatic—far more people position themselves on the issues on a case-by-case basis rather than
deduce their specific positions from some abstract principle.[24]

In the 1970s and 1980s, many social scientists anticipated that the rising educational level of the population would diminish the differences between the public and the political class. In the 1990s the proliferation of information sources further reinforced that expectation. But the evidence indicates otherwise. Better-educated or not, the American public today is no better informed than a generation ago.[25] And although cable television and the Internet may have made more information available, they have also made it easier to avoid exposure to it than it was when there were only three broadcast networks.[26] (Recall the old adage about leading a horse to water.)

Of course, even if the public's ideological positioning has not changed much, and even if their issue positions are not terribly consistent with the ideological labels they adopt, that does not preclude their having polarized opinions on particular issues. So, let us take a closer look. In every presidential election year between 1984 and 2004 inclusive, the NES has asked respondents to position themselves on five issue scales, where each scale offers seven positions running from the most liberal to the most conservative stance on the issue:

- More government services/higher spending—fewer services/less spending
- Government health insurance—private health insurance
- More government aid for Blacks/minorities—should help themselves
- Greatly decrease military spending—greatly increase
- Government-guaranteed job and standard of living—on your own[27]

A sixth question included in each of these studies asks respondents to choose between four positions on abortion, ranging from most to least restricted.

Even in the purportedly polarized context of 2004, the pattern is generally centrist (with the exception of the health insurance issue, which is left-center), with more people toward the center of the scales than at the extremes. The question is how much the distributions have changed. The answer is not much, and there is little indication of increased polarization.

Table 1.1 Percentage Point Changes in Policy Views: 1984–2004

	Liberal			Moderate			Conservative
Left Shift							
Health Insurance	6%	2	3	0 (-9)[a]	0	-2	-2
Spending/Services	5	4	5	-3 (-5)	-3	-3	-2
Right Shift							
Aid to Blacks	0	-2	-5	-5 (-7)	-1	6	8
Defense Spending	-5	-4	-3	-5 (-4)	8	4	2
Polarization							
Jobs/SOL[b]	2	1	0	-2 (-7)	0	1	3
Lib-Con	0	2	3	3(-7)	-1	3	1
No Change							
Abortion		1	-1			3	-1

Source: National Election Study Cumulative Data File
Note: Numbers are percentage point changes in scale position between 1984 and 2004. The abortion item has only four response categories.
[a] Numbers in ( ) are percentage point changes when "don't knows" are treated as moderates.
[b] SOL = Standard of Living.

Table 1.1 shows the percentage point changes between the responses on the five issue items asked in 1984 and 2004 (the rows do not sum to zero because of rounding error and different numbers of "don't know" responses). Ignore sampling error, declining response rates, and other complicating factors, and treat these numbers as exact. On only one scale—government responsibility for jobs and standard of living—is there a bit of evidence of polarization: between 1984 and 2004 there was a small decline (2 percentage points) in the number of people placing themselves in the exact center of the scale and a marginal increase in the number placing themselves on the left (3 percentage points) and the right (4 percentage points).

The other four scales do not show even this slight degree of increasing polarization. On three of the four scales, there was a single-digit decline in the number of respondents who chose the exact middle of the scale, but on none of the scales did the middle lose to both extremes, the definition of polarization. Rather, on government versus private health insurance, the population shifted leftward. In 2004 11 percent more Americans favored government health insurance and 4 percent fewer favored private insurance than in 1984. A similar pattern holds for the choice between more public services versus lower public spending. In 2004, 14 percent more Americans placed themselves on the liberal slide of the scale than in 1984 compared with 8 percent fewer on the conservative side.

Conservatives need not fret, because on the other two scales the population shifted rightward. On aid to minorities, the left and the middle lost to the right—14 percent more Americans favored the two rightmost scale positions (individual initiative and self-help) in 2004 than in 1984. Defense spending showed an even more notable shift: the doves lost 12 percent, and the hawks gained 14 percent.

Finally, on abortion, there was virtually no change in popular opinion over the twenty-year period. The NES abortion item leaves much to be desired, however, and I will treat this issue at greater length in the next chapter.

In sum, when examining individual issues rather than broad ideological categorizations, one can see somewhat more change, but not change that illustrates polarization, namely, middle-of-the-road people moving toward both extremes. Rather, one sees a nonideological public moving rightward on some issues, leftward on others, and not moving much at all on still others. Depending on what problems the country faces and the perceived success of existing policies on solving them, the large pragmatic public opts for more government on some issues and less on others.

SUMMARY AND IMPLICATIONS

There is little doubt that the political class in the United States is significantly more polarized today than it was a generation ago. But a close examination of the general population finds little or no sign of a comparable increase in polarization. As scholars previously have documented, despite vast increases in educational levels and the availability of political information, the American public looks much the same as it did a half century ago—centrist more than polarized in its specific positions, pragmatic more than ideological in its general orientation, and far less attuned to and concerned about politics than the political class. Today, as in earlier decades, most Americans are busy earning their livings, raising their families, and trying to squeeze in a little recreation. For most of them, most of the time, politics and government are not high priorities.

Of course, our elected representatives *should* be closely attuned to politics—that is their occupational responsibility. But rather than greater attentiveness and knowledge contributing to more faithful representation, the positions taken by many representatives distort the views of the public at large. Here is the disconnect that is the title of this book: those who ostensibly represent the American public take positions that collectively do not provide an accurate representation of the public. I emphasize the modifier "collectively" here. The concept of representation is a complex one, which political theorists have explicated, critiqued, and otherwise discussed for generations.[28] *Who* should be represented—voters, citizens, everyone, those in the electoral constituency, or the nation at large? *What* should be represented—values, interests, wants, the short-term, or the long-term? *How* should representatives represent—by faithfully following their constituents or by using their own best judgment? I will make no attempt to grapple with all such questions in this book—they have been posed for generations, and general agreement on the answers remains elusive. But my discussion unavoidably touches on some of them, especially the tension between what Robert Weissberg calls dyadic as opposed to collective representation.[29]

As the parties have become more internally homogeneous and more distinct from each other (Democrats more liberal, Republicans more conservative), it is probable that dyadic or microrepresentation—the correspondence between the positions and actions of an elected official and the legal jurisdiction that elects him or her—has become easier and more accurate, whereas collective or macrorepresentation—the correspondence between what representative institutions produce and the entire public wants—has deteriorated. For example, Jacobson pointed out that in 1998 only about one-third of Americans favored the impeachment of President Clinton, but that support was heavily concentrated in Republican districts and states.[30] Thus, in voting for impeachment many Republican representatives and senators could follow the wishes of the voters in their districts and states even while voting and acting against the preferences of a majority of the country. But in the end, even voters who approved of their own representative's actions were unhappy—Republicans in the electorate were dissatisfied by the failure of the collective Congress to convict Clinton, and the larger majority of Americans were dissatisfied that the collective Congress moved on impeachment at all.

Today when partisan lines are more clearly drawn, it is probably easier for most representatives to please their electoral constituencies than when the parties were more heterogeneous and factionalized. Brunell has gone so far as to argue that redistricting to create safe seats may be a good thing—when most districts are heavily Democratic or heavily Republican, it is an arithmetical fact that more constituents will have a representative of their own party than would be the case if most districts were highly competitive when almost half of each district (the losing party members) would have voted against the winner.[31]

Although such arguments are valid as far at they go, there are reasons not to take too much comfort in them. Most obviously, the country is not composed entirely of Democrats and Republicans. For more than a generation, one-third or more of Americans have classified themselves as independents (at the time of this writing, Pew reports an unusually high figure of 42 percent for 2007).[32] Independents, who are more moderate and ambivalent in their views than partisans, probably are not as happy with their choices today as partisans are. Moreover, only about half of self-categorized partisans report being "strongly" attached to their parties. Some of these weaker adherents undoubtedly are not as happy with today's more polarized choices as with the fuzzier choices of the past.

But most important, as the impeachment example illustrates, voters can be more satisfied with their individual representatives but not more satisfied with what their representatives col-

lectively produce: improvements in microrepresentation may
have come at the cost of a deterioration in macrorepresentation.
In his essay, Jacobson noted that only a minority of Americans
are happy with two-party politics as it stands. A majority prefer
non-partisan elections or a third party. Similarly, a plurality
favored divided party control of the presidency and Congress
rather than unified party control.[33] These were figures from the
late 1990s, a period of divided government. A decade later, after
six years of partisan warfare under mostly unified Republican
control, Gallup reported that support for unified party control of
the presidency and Congress had slipped to 37 percent, and by
a 48 to 40 percent margin, Americans opined that a major third
party was needed to adequately represent the people.[34]

The greater homogeneity and distinctiveness of today's parties is a result of so-called party sorting, a process treated at
length in the next chapter and again in chapter 5. Jacobson and
Sinclair have correctly argued that party sorting is an important
part of the explanation for today's more polarized politics, at
least for Congress.[35] Ironically, some members of an earlier generation of political scientists argued strongly that such party
sorting was an unalloyed political good that the political science
profession should help to foster. That argument has been badly
undermined by developments that were not anticipated. I treat
this more normative argument at length in chapter 7.

CHAPTER 2

_____

DISCONNECTS IN PRIORITIES,
CERTAINTY, AND STYLE

SOME PEOPLE ARE ACTIVE in politics simply because they enjoy
the process; for them, political participation is a pleasant recre-
ational activity not unlike bowling in a league, attending wine
tastings, or working at church picnics. Activities like these provide opportunities to socialize with like-minded people and
may induce pleasant feelings of group identification. But
although identifying people's true motives is a notoriously difficult thing to do, most students of political participation believe
that at least in part, political activism stems from strong feelings
about political issues and public policies.[1] As Verba, Schlozman,
and Brady commented in their magisterial work on political
participation, "activists told us over and over that their participation was founded, at least in part, on a desire to influence
what the government does."[2] This should come as no surprise.
Common sense tells us that Americans who wish to change the
status quo (outlaw abortion, legalize gay marriage) or who
desire to preserve it (keep abortion legal, outlaw gay marriage)
are more likely to be politically active than those who lack
strong feelings about such issues. As discussed in the preceding
chapter, however, the political views of those who are active are
more extreme than the views of the larger but less active public.

In this chapter, I consider two additional ways in which the
views of the political class differ from those of the American
public. First, the concerns and priorities of the political class are
different from those of the larger public. Second, how the political class holds and expresses their beliefs differs from how the
larger public does. The certainty and consistency with which
members of the political class hold their views is greater, and
the manner that many members of the political class adopt to

24

present their views and priorities is different from and unattractive to the broader public.

DIFFERENTIAL PRIORITIES

Killing our babies is the issue of the century . . . cutting taxes or any other issue pales in comparison.

JOHN MCCARTHY, THEN STATE
CHAIRMAN OF THE CALIFORNIA
REPUBLICAN PARTY[3]

When a society comes to believe that human life is not inherently worth living, it is a slippery slope to the gas chamber. You wind up on a low road that twists past Columbine and leads toward Auschwitz.

PEGGY NOONAN, COLUMNIST,
ON THE TERRY SHIAVO CASE[4]

Six million Jews died in concentration camps, but six billion broiler chickens will die this year in slaughterhouses.

INGRID NEWKIRK,
NATIONAL DIRECTOR, PEOPLE FOR THE
ETHICAL TREATMENT OF ANIMALS[5]

[The Massachusetts ruling allowing gay marriage] marks one of the darkest days in the history of American law. Unless the people of the state of Massachusetts rise up with one voice in opposition to this lawless and socially destructive decision, it will destroy society as we know it."

STEVE CRAMPTON,
CHIEF COUNSEL, AMERICAN FAMILY ASSOCIATION[6]

Embryonic stem cell research leads to slaughtering humans. Each of us was once just that—an embryo. We are now grown. But we started out as embryos. That means, that from the start we were humans, real live humans.

PASTOR J. GRANT SWANK, JR.[7]

In a way, we are at war with Mexico, in a way . . . Mexico is aiding and abetting an invasion of this country . . . in fact, they are creating situations along that border using their own military to protect drug trafficking into the United States, pushing their own

*people into the United States for a variety of reasons. It is an
invasion. It is an act of aggression.*

REP. TOM TANCREDO (R-COLO.)[8]

*There is no reason for anyone in this country, anyone except a
police officer or a military person, to buy, to own, to have, to use a
handgun. I used to think handguns could be controlled by laws
about registration, by laws requiring waiting periods for
purchasers, by laws making sellers check out the past of buyers. I
now think the only way to control handgun use in this country is
to prohibit the guns. And the only way to do that is to change the
Constitution.*

MICHAEL GARTNER, THEN
PRESIDENT OF NBC NEWS[9]

*I support a constitutional amendment to protect the American flag
from acts of physical desecration. With all the issues pending
before Congress, like saving Social Security, national security,
education, and the budget, there are those who ask, "Why should
Congress focus any time and attention on a constitutional
amendment to protect the flag?" Because it is the right thing to do.
We owe it to the veterans who defended our flag, and we owe it to
the American people who love our flag.*

SEN. ORRIN HATCH (R-UTAH)[10]

In the preceding quotations political observers would recognize many of the prominent political issues of the past decade.
That much is familiar enough. What may be more surprising is
that none of the issues referenced above is considered very
important by the broader American public. The Gallup organization regularly asks people what they judge to be the most
important issue facing the country. Respondents reply in their
own words and are allowed to give multiple responses. Table 2.1
lists the responses for surveys conducted near the 2000 and 2004
presidential elections and the 2006 congressional elections.

Looking at table 2.1, it comes as no surprise that Americans
were concerned about the war in Iraq and terrorism in 2004. But
notice how often Americans mentioned many of the hot-button
issues referenced in the quotations above: not very often. Abortion barely registered, and gay marriage did not register at all;

Table 2.1 Americans' views of the most important issues facing the country

2000		2004		2006	
Education	17	Issues on the war with Iraq	26	Situation in Iraq/War	26
Ethical/moral/Religious decline	13	Economy (general)	17	Fuel/Oil Prices	15
Health care/hospitals	12	Unemployment/Jobs	14	Terrorism	10
Crime/violence	10	Terrorism	13	Dissatisfaction with government/	9
Government/President Clinton/	9	Poor Health Care/Hospitals	9	Congress/politicians/candidates	
Congress/politicians		Ethical/Moral/Religious Decline	7	Economy in General	8
Economy (general)	8	Federal Budget Deficit/Federal Debt	4	Immigration/illegal aliens	8
Poverty/hunger/homelessness	7	National Security	4	Poor health care/hospitals;	6
Don't Know	6	Social Security Issues	3	high cost of health care	
Social Security issues	5	Foreign Aid/Focus Overseas	3	Ethics/moral/religious/	5
Drugs	5	Government/Congress/Politicians	3	family decline; dishonesty;	
Taxes	5	OTHER (list)	3	lack of integrity	
Children's needs	4	Judicial System/Courts/Laws	3	Unemployment/Jobs	4
International problems/	4	Cost associated with	3	Education/access to education	4
foreign affairs		Health Insurance		Foreign Aid	4
Fuel/oil prices	4	International Problems	3	Energy crisis	4
Unemployment/jobs	3	Education (unspecified)	2	Federal Budget deficit/federal debt	3
Other (list)	3	Medicare Increases/	2	Taxes	3
Race relations/racism	3	Senior Citizen Insurance		High cost of living/inflation	3
Gun control/gun laws too strong	3	Poverty/Hunger/Homelessness	2	Poverty/hunger/homeless	3
Environment/pollution	3	Taxes	2	War in the Middle East	3
Military/defense issues	2	Presidential choices/Election year	2	Wage issues	2
Medicare increase/senior citizen	2	Unifying the country	2	National Security	2
insurance		Other comments	2	Environment/Pollution	2
Judicial system/courts/laws	2	DON'T KNOW	2	International Issues	2
Care for the elderly	2	Immigration/Illegal Aliens	1	Crime/Violence	2
Immigration/illegal aliens	2	Lack of Money	1	Gap between rich and poor	1
Abortion issues	1	Lack of respect for each other	1	Lack of Money	1
Gap between the rich and poor	1	Crime/Violence	1	Foreign trade/trade deficit	1
Federal budget deficit/federal debt	1	Poor leadership/Corrupt	1	Lack of respect for each other	1
Wage issues	1	Fuel/Oil Prices	1	Social Security	1
Honesty/integrity	1	Abortion Issues	1	Unifying the country	1
REFUSED	1	Environment/Pollution	1	Abortion	1
Cost of living/inflation	1	Foreign Trade/Trade Deficit	1	Children's Behavior/	1
Welfare	1	Corporate Corruption	1	Way they are raised	
		Wage Issues	1	Drugs	1
		The media	1	Media	1
		Way children are raised	1	Medicare	1
		Cost of Living/Inflation	1	Welfare	1
		Drugs	1		

Data from *The Gallup Poll*, collected on October 9, 2000; November 10, 2004; and August 10, 2006, respectively.

gun control, stem cells, and flag burning were similarly low or missing from the list of public concerns. Despite the intense congressional debate about immigration during the spring of 2006, even that issue did not arouse concern among the broader public at a level at all comparable to that present in the halls of Congress, in the blogosphere, or on the news pages of the mainstream media. Of course, one might object that the war in Iraq and the prospect of terrorist attacks pushed everything else lower on the agenda of public concerns, as the economy did in 2008. But consider the 2000 data. Even during the hiatus between the end of the cold war and 9/11, at a time of international peace and economic prosperity, many issues that are prominent in contemporary politics did not show up as matters of major public concern. The preceding test is a difficult one for an issue to pass. After all, people could believe that abortion or gay marriage is the second or third most important issue, behind the war in Iraq or health care. Thus, consider another common survey item that provides a test of importance that is as easy as the most-important-problem test is difficult. In this one, the survey presents the respondent with a list of issues that have been selected because they are considered to be prominent political issues. Respondents are asked to rate how important each item is to them as an election issue: very, somewhat, not too important, or not at all. If they so wish, voters could rank every issue on the list as "very important," and abortion and gay marriage would rank as high as the war in Iraq. But that is not the case. When the issues are ranked, the pattern is much the same as with the more difficult most-important-problem question.[11] Relative to general issues of foreign policy and national security, the economy, and social welfare, the so-called hot-button or cultural issues that receive so much media attention and figure so prominently in campaign rhetoric are simply not considered very important by the American public. In 2004, despite all the media attention to gay marriage and despite the presence of gay marriage prohibitions on the ballot in eleven states, a study that asked people to rank sixteen issues in order of electoral importance reported that gay marriage came in fifteenth, behind only tort reform.[12] Table 2.2 reports the results of a June 2006 Pew Poll that asked the public to rate nineteen issues in order of their electoral importance. Despite the fact that Congress had recently debated immigration reform at great length and with great intensity—with the two chambers passing conflicting bills—immigration registered in the exact middle of voter concerns. In the same month that proponents of a constitutional amendment to ban flag burning tried to persuade the U.S. Senate to consider it, the issue ranked fourteenth out of nineteen in terms of electoral importance.

Table 2.2 Americans' rankings of most important electoral issues

Issues and ranking number	Very important (%)	Not at all important (%)
1. Education	82	3
2. Economy	80	1
3. Health Care	79	1
4. Social Security	75	1
5. Situation in Iraq	74	2
6. Terrorism	74	2
7. Taxes	68	2
8. Job Situation	66	4
9. Energy Policy	64	2
10. Immigration (Median)	58	5
11. Budget Deficit	56	4
12. Environment	52	3
13. Minimum Wage	52	8
14. Flag Burning	49	22
15. Government Surveillance	44	11
16. Inheritance Tax	44	13
17. Global Warming	44	11
18. Abortion	43	15
19. Gay Marriage	34	33

Note: Respondents were registered voters.
Source: June 2006 Pew Center for the People & the Press Poll

Abortion and gay marriage came in even lower, taking positions eighteen and nineteen in the poll. What could more clearly illustrate a disconnect between the priorities of the country and the priorities of the political class?

IGNORANCE, UNCERTAINTY, AND AMBIVALENCE

In *Culture War?* we presented data showing that Americans were largely moderate in their political views. "Moderate" literally means not extreme. Moderates are people who hold middle-of-the-road positions, where both "moderate" and "extreme" are defined relative to the political context that prevails in a society at a given time. In the previous chapter, I showed that public opinion continues to be moderate in that sense. But on further reflection, and in light of recent research, I believe an argument that focuses solely on centrist policy positions is too narrow.

Public opinion researchers have long understood that not all so-called moderates are informed citizens who choose an option between two more extreme alternatives. Rather, the moderate category also includes people with little or no information who decline to take any position at all as well as people who have inconsistent beliefs that prevent them from identifying closely with either party or with either end of the ideological spectrum.

In a classic article, Philip Converse made the case that in contrast to political elites, many ordinary Americans (the "mass public") gave responses to pollsters that were "nonattitudes."[13] According to Converse, the average American knew little and cared little about politics; hence, his or her views were poorly informed—when they existed at all. If queried by an interviewer, citizens often would oblige with a response rather than admit ignorance, but on a different day, to a different interviewer, to a somewhat different survey question, that response might well be different. Some interpreted Converse as suggesting that a majority seemed to be responding randomly.[14]

To illustrate, a typical voter might believe that health care, Social Security, or some other issue was very important but know little about the policy alternatives that the political class was debating, let alone the likelihood that the alternative policy options would be effective. In contrast, members of the political class are firm in the belief that the alternatives their side is proposing will work and the ones the other side is proposing will either only make matters worse or benefit the wrong people (or both). They may have no more empirical basis for their beliefs than ordinary citizens, but ideology and partisanship fill the evidentiary gap. In sum, ordinary Americans are more *uncertain* about their political views and how they should translate them into voting than members of the political class. Consider that when asked when they made up their mind about how to vote (figure 2.1), the percentage of activists who replied that they "knew all along" or "as soon as the candidates announced" was twice as high as the percentage of ordinary partisans and three times as high as the percentage of independents, a fact that probably reflects both the extremity of the activists' positions and the certainty with which they hold their views.

Figure 2.1 Timing of Electoral Choice

The question was "How long before the election did you decide that you were going to vote the way you did?" and respondents answered using a six-point scale. The figure shows those respondents who answered either "knew all along" or "when the candidate announced."

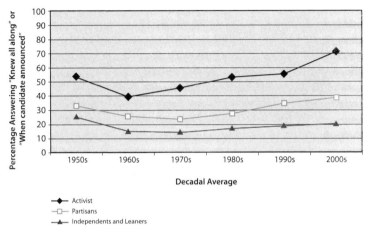

Decadal Average

- Activist
- Partisans
- Independents and Leaners

Data from National Election Studies

Today, most public opinion researchers hold a more flattering view of public opinion than the one Converse painted in the 1960s.[15] They share with Converse the belief that for most people most of the time politics is not a terribly important matter; hence, people walk around with numerous facts, beliefs, and impressions in their heads.[16] These "considerations" come from a variety of sources—most obviously family and friends, schools, personal experience, their everyday environment, and the media. Moreover, these considerations vary widely in importance, and, given their varied sources, many may be inconsistent. When prodded to think about a subject, people sample from the numerous considerations they possess and aggregate them into a response. But if they were prodded at a different time or in a different social context, or if they were prodded in a different way (such as by a differently worded survey question), they would draw correspondingly different samples of considerations and for that reason possibly give a different answer.

For example, when asked about abortion typically somewhere between 35 and 40 percent express the belief that it should always be legal. But when asked whether abortion to determine the gender of the child should be permitted, about one-third of those respondents who believe that abortion "should always be legal" answer "no."[17] I do not consider such people thoughtless or hypocritical; rather, they simply had not thought of a consideration that the second question brought to their attention. Their views are *ambivalent*—because they hold conflicting considerations, how they respond to a survey depends on what considerations are brought to their attention.[18] Members of the political class do not display such ambivalence. Ask a National Abortion Rights Action League (NARAL) activist whether abortion should be legal to choose the gender of the child, and he or she is very likely to answer yes. Similarly, ask a Focus on the Family activist whether abortion should be legal in cases of a serious threat to the mother's health, and he or she is very likely to answer no.

Public opinion researchers have found that to some degree Americans accept conflicting core beliefs and values that underlie their attitudes on specific issues.[19] Thus, Americans who strongly believe in equality hold more liberal views on economic issues whereas those who strongly believe in individual achievement hold more conservative views.[20] But many Americans believe in both equality and individual responsibility. Analogously, many Americans believe both in a woman's right to choose and in the fetus' right to life—they are pro-choice *and* pro-life. The core values of individualism, equality, and traditional values underlie attitudes on gay rights issues.[21] Most generally, and contrary to Professor Schama's stark dichotomy between "godly America" and "worldly America," the research of Wayne Baker shows that many Americans consider themselves to be both godly and worldly.[22] Thus, one of the reasons survey questions that "frame" issues in different ways can produce significantly different findings is that Americans hold beliefs and values that conflict when applied to specific policy issues.[23]

Some new survey items illustrate more fully than before the nuances of public opinion on the hot-button issue of abortion. In

Culture War? we showed that in contrast to the political class a majority of Americans held conditional views—they were "pro-choice, buts," believing in a woman's right to choose, but also that some reasons to have an abortion were not sufficiently weighty to justify it. Thus, in the GSS battery, overwhelming majorities believe abortion should be legal in pregnancies that result from rape or incest, that threaten the mother's health, or when the fetus has a serious birth defect. In contrast, narrow majorities oppose legal abortion because the mother is unmarried, poor, or just does not want more children. In the new battery we explicitly distinguished between threats to a mother's life and to her health and also between rape and incest (in case the latter did not result from forcible rape):

> Should it be legal or illegal for a pregnant woman to have an abortion
>
> - If staying pregnant would hurt her health but is very unlikely to cause her to die?
> - If doctors believe that continuing to be pregnant could cause her to die?
> - If the pregnancy was caused by sex she chose to have with a blood relative?
> - If the pregnancy was caused by her being raped?
> - If the fetus *will be* born with a serious birth defect?
> - If she *learns that the child will* not be the sex she wants it to be?
> - If the child would be extremely difficult for her financially?[24]

These items were included in the Cooperative Congressional Election Study conducted during the congressional campaigns of 2006.[25] Table 2.3 shows the responses

When pregnancy seriously threatens the mother's life, the legal abortion side is as close to unanimity as survey categories ever get, although almost one in ten Americans appear willing to sacrifice the mother to save the fetus. Legal abortion for pregnant rape victims also garners exceptionally high support. Fetal defects and threats to the mother's health garner two-thirds majority support for legal abortion. Abortion because of incest

Table 2.3 Americans' views on when abortion should be legal: 2006

Circumstances in which abortion should be legal	U.S. totals	Red states	Blue states
Threat to mother's life	91%	90%	92%
Rape	84	83	86
Threat to mother's health, not life	68	66	72
Fetal defect	69	67	72
Incest	56	52	61
Financial distress	45	42	49
"Wrong" gender of fetus	22	20	23

Source: 2006 Cooperative Congressional Election Study.

receives a narrower majority, and abortion because of financial problems received a comparable majority in opposition. An overwhelming majority believes abortion for gender preferences should be illegal. The differences between residents of red states and blues states are minor, averaging about 5 percentage points across the seven conditions.

Following the well-known trimester framework laid down by *Roe v. Wade*, the new battery went on to ask about the stage of pregnancy during which abortion should be legal:

Which of the following describes when you think it should be legal for a pregnant woman to have an abortion for that reason?

- Only during the first three months of the pregnancy, before the fetus's major organs have fully formed
- Only during the first six months of the pregnancy, before the fetus can survive outside the mother
- At any time during the pregnancy

Table 2.4 shows the time distribution of the responses. The responses make clear Americans' aversion to third-trimester abortions. Even in the extreme case of a serious threat to the mother's life, only a minority supports legal abortion in the third trimester. In less extreme circumstances support is far lower—between one in five and one in four Americans support legal third-trimester abortion in the cases of rape, fetal defects, and

Table 2.4 Americans' views on stage of pregnancy during which
abortion should be legal

Reason for abortion	Never	1st trimester	2nd trimester	At any time
Threat to mother's life	10	30	14	45
Rape	17	45	17	22
Threat to mother's health, not life	33	27	16	24
Fetal defect	32	26	20	22
Incest	45	25	14	16
Financial distress	56	20	13	12
"Wrong" gender of fetus	79	8	6	7

Source: 2006 Cooperative Congressional Election Study.

threats to the mother's health, and somewhat fewer than one in five in the case of consensual incest. Seven out of eight Americans believe that third-trimester abortions for financial reasons should be illegal. And just as the threat-to-a-mother's life circumstance identifies the strongest pro-life citizens—the 10 percent who would sacrifice the mother—so the gender-selection circumstance isolates the strongest pro-choice citizens—the 7 percent who would permit third-trimester abortions because the fetus was of the "wrong" gender.

When given a stark choice between classifying themselves as "pro-choice" or "pro-life," Americans divide fairly evenly, with a slight edge to pro-life.[26] But as the preceding two tables show, those simple labels make a mockery of the nuanced views that Americans actually hold. Pro-life and pro-choice activists may believe that all questions are settled by a pronouncement that life begins at conception or at birth, but 80 percent of Americans either aren't sure when life begins or don't believe that an answer settles all questions. Whether the typical American is pro-life or pro-choice all depends on why the abortion is needed and when it will take place.

In sum, typical Americans differ from members of the political class not only in taking more moderate positions on most issues, but also in having positions that are more conditional than members of the political class. Their positions not only are less extreme, but also are less certain and more ambivalent. Although this point is largely a clarification of my earlier argument, it adds an important element to it as well. Previously I had observed that activists held more extreme and intense views, which gave them greater motivation to participate in politics. Recent research by Diana Mutz finds that there is another side to this standard finding: people whose social networks expose them to conflicting political considerations are actually discouraged from participation.[27] Their ambivalence creates internal conflict that lowers their motivation to participate and, even more important, discourages them from visible participation that would introduce conflicts into their relationships with others in their work and social circles. Thus, in disturbing feedback loops, Americans who receive heterogeneous messages that in principle might lead to balanced judgments withdraw from politics, while those who receive only one-sided messages are further encouraged to participate.[28]

STYLE

Given that most Americans do not hold extreme views on public issues and are not certain about their views, imagine how they must react to the style of some of today's political commentary:

We should invade their countries, kill their leaders, and convert them to Christianity.
ANN COULTER, SYNDICATED COLUMNIST[29]

I would like to apologize for referring to George W. Bush as a "deserter." What I meant to say is that George W. Bush is a deserter, an election thief, a drunk driver, a WMD liar, and a functional illiterate.
MICHAEL MOORE, FILMMAKER[30]

The abortionists have got to bear some burden for this because God will not be mocked. And when we destroy 40 million little innocent babies, we make God mad. I really believe that the pagans, and the abortionists, and the feminists, and the gays and the lesbians who are actively trying to make that an alternative lifestyle, the ACLU, People for the American Way—all of them

who have tried to secularize America—I point the finger in their
face and say "You helped this happen."

THE REVEREND JERRY FALWELL AFTER 9/11[31]

The empty life of this ugly little charlatan proves only one thing,
that you can get away with the most extraordinary offenses to
morality and to truth in this country if you will just get yourself
called reverend.

CHRISTOPHER HITCHENS
ON THE DEATH OF JERRY FALWELL[32]

How many Americans talk like this in their workplaces and other social circles? Granted, Ann Coulter and Michael Moore are not exactly the norm—even among the political class—but they are not exceptional either. Consider the blogs and the letters to the editor, which often reek of such vitriol. On rare occasions a moderate citizen protests the "take no prisoners" style of politics practiced by many in today's political class: "San Francisco has spawned a cadre of political activists of various points of view who are self-righteous, obsessive and focused on single issues. They have infused the public discussion with acrimony, name-calling and resorting to any means to win. When they lose, they then resort to continuing their fights through appeals, litigation and ultimately revenge on their opponents. Compromise and appeal to the great good is not a concern to these activists."[33]

Small wonder that despite the proliferation of information sources in recent decades, Americans are no better informed than they were a generation ago.[34] Although cable news shows provide 24/7 coverage, and specialized magazines and websites abound, Americans know no more about politics and government today than when their televisions carried only three networks and the Internet was unimagined. Well, if the new information sources have a high proportion of drivel, who can blame Americans for lack of interest in the news? Commentators from comedian Jon Stewart to political theorists have decried the style of much current political discussion—loud, rude, vitriolic, ad hominem.[35] In the cut-throat competition for ratings, the more extreme cable TV shout shows emulate the style of professional wrestling and shed about as much light on politics. Partisans on each side attack their counterparts on the other as ignorant, stupid, corrupt, and unpatriotic. Reasonable compromises are sell-outs and those who arrange them are defectors or traitors. Such people reject Ronald Reagan's dictum that "someone who agrees with me 80 percent of the time is my 80 percent friend, not my 20 percent enemy."

A number of factors have contributed to this unattractive state of affairs. Mary Ann Glendon has emphasized the expansion of the sphere of rights in the 1970s.[36] It is one thing if you and I disagree about a public policy matter, but our disagreement is far more serious if you are denying my right to something. In the latter case your opposition is illegitimate, and you are not only my opponent but my oppressor. And should the courts affirm *my* right, then you may feel that an undemocratic process has imposed an unjust outcome.[37] Even when most people are willing to compromise, rights are inherently more difficult to compromise than interests, because the most committed advocates are likely to believe that to compromise a right is to negate it.[38]

The symbolic nature of many contemporary political issues is another factor that makes compromise more difficult and contributes to the nasty quality of contemporary debate. An old academic saying holds that "the reason academic fights are so vicious is that there is so little at stake." If there is $100,000 on the table that you and I can share if we can come to an agreement, but forfeit it if we cannot, then although it may take some squabbling, the odds are good that we will come to an agreement. If I strongly favor religious symbols in public places, however, and you find this extremely offensive, the odds of a compromise are lower. One or both of us will go to court demanding that our right be upheld.

But as chapter 4 will discuss at some length, the kind of people who dominate political life today may be as important a factor as the nature of the issues or the discourse in which they are discussed. A very wise political scientist once wrote the following:

> Democracy is based on a profound insight into human nature, the realization that all men are sinful, all are imperfect, all are

prejudiced, and none knows the whole truth. That is why we need liberty and why we have an obligation to hear all men. Liberty gives us a chance to learn from other people, to become aware of our own limitations, and to correct our bias. Even when we disagree with other people we like to think that they speak from good motives, and while we realize that all men are limited, we do not let ourselves imagine that any man is bad. Democracy is a political system for people who are not sure that they are right.[39]

The problem is that many of today's political activists are all too sure that they are right. Too many resemble Eric Hoffer's descriptions of the true believer:

> It is the true believer's ability to "shut his eyes and stop his ears" to facts that do not deserve to be either seen or heard which is the source of his unequalled fortitude and constancy.
>
> The fanatic can not be weaned away from his cause by an appeal to his reason or moral sense. He fears compromise and cannot be persuaded to qualify the certitude and righteousness of his holy cause.
>
> Though they seem to be at opposite poles, fanatics of all kinds are actually crowded together at one end. It is the fanatic and the moderate who are poles apart and never meet. The fanatics of various hues eye each other with suspicion and are ready to fly at each other's throat. But they are neighbors and almost of one family. They hate each other with the hatred of brothers.[40]

These are precisely the kind of people who attach greater weight to symbols than normal people; the kind of people who loudly assert their rights, even when they have little or nothing tangible to gain by doing so and doing so inconveniences the larger community; the kind of people who equate compromise with the absence of principle; the kind of people who refuse to lose; and the kind of people who regard their goals as justifying the politics of personal destruction.

Some recent research supports the plausible supposition that the style of political debate affects citizens' attitudes toward politics independently of the issues debated and the contending positions on those issues. Diana Mutz and Byron Reeves have reported striking experimental research aimed squarely at this question.[41] They hired professional actors to portray competing congressional candidates in an unspecified midwestern district. The actors read scripts that Mutz and Reeves had prepared but did so in two different versions. In one, the actors were civil—they spoke in a normal tone of voice, listened respectfully to each other, and did not interrupt or cut off the other speaker. In the second condition the actors spoke the same words but did so in an uncivil manner—raising their voices, interrupting, rolling their eyes, and using other impolite actions (reminiscent of Al Gore's behavior in the first 2000 presidential debate). From initial baselines, people exposed to the civil debate showed increased trust of government and politicians, whereas people exposed to the uncivil debate showed decreases. Holding the substance of disagreement constant, the manner in which the disagreement was expressed made a significant difference. In an intriguing follow-up study, Mutz showed that close-up camera shots heightened the effects of incivility. The in-your-face disagreement emphasized by much of television today likely results in greater dislike of the opposition and delegitimation of their arguments than more distant shots of civil disagreement.[42]

Experimental research by Brooks and Geer has provided a refinement of Mutz and Reeves's finding: citizens viewed incivility most negatively when directed at personal traits, not at issue positions.[43] People did not like personal attacks—whether expressed in a civil or uncivil manner. They did not mind incivility when it was expressed at the positions of the political opponent. But they reacted negatively against incivility directed at the opponent's person. In contrast to Mutz and Reeves's finding, however, Brooks and Geer did not find that the negative reaction to incivility led to any increase in negative attitudes toward politics and government.

On the other hand, to date survey-based research has found little or no evidence that negativity per se demobilizes Americans. On the contrary, exposure to negative ads that are policy based enhances interest and participation, and even when negative ads focus on the personal qualities of the opponent there is no evidence of lower interest or lower voter turnout.[44] Still, campaign ads for national candidates rarely approach the level of negativity cited above and to which citizens are exposed in ways other than national campaigns. Moreover, cross-sectional evidence does not rule out the possibility that the long-term decline in voting by independents and ideological moderates is related to the growing negativity of contemporary politics.[45] The subject clearly requires further research, but it still seems reasonable to worry that over and above the fact that the political class advocates more extreme policy alternatives than majorities would prefer, ordinary Americans are turned off by the uncivil manner of many members of the political class, their emphasis on issues of limited importance to most people, and the dogmatic style with which political activists present their views. As the late Molly Ivins humorously put it: "People who genuinely care about politics . . . are apt to get all red in the face, to carry on until the tendons stand out on their necks and to shake their wattles like turkey gobblers—a phenomenon so alarming it scares off many another citizen who might otherwise get involved. 'Geez, if that's what politics does to you, count me out!'"[46]

HOW BIG IS THE POLITICAL CLASS?

My use of the term "disconnect" implicitly assumes that the political class constitutes a relatively small part of the American body politic. After all, if half the population held more extreme positions than the other half, had priorities different from the other half, and engaged in a conflictual style unattractive to the other half, we would worry about the condition of our politics but probably not describe it as a disconnect between the public and a (comparably sized) political class. In fact, a few scholars do claim that the political class has grown much larger than presumed in *Culture War?* and in this book, so, just how big is the political class?

Naturally, the answer to this question depends on how the political class is defined. If we take all the candidates for public office, the people who contribute to or work in their campaigns, the people who staff the myriad advocacy groups and their most active members, plus the stratum of people who follow politics closely and feel intensely about political issues, we are surely talking about millions of Americans. But we should not let the absolute magnitude of this number blind us to the fact that the eligible electorate numbers more than two hundred million people, of whom more than one hundred and twenty million voted in the 2004 presidential election and about eighty million in the 2006 congressional elections. Even a political class of ten million members would be less than 10 percent of the presidential voters and less than 5 percent of the eligible electorate.

In a recent article, James Davison Hunter, whose book *Culture War* reportedly stimulated Pat Buchanan's 1992 remarks at the Republican Convention, observed that his thesis applies to 15 percent or so of the population, a qualification he did not make in the original.[47] This is a quite reasonable estimate and a rather far cry from the 80–90 percent cited by Matthew Dowd as a reason not to appeal to the center in the 2004 presidential campaign.[48]

Recently, some have suggested that with increasing education levels in the American population, the appearance of new communications technologies, and the increased polarization of national politics, the political class has grown much larger than previously. Alan Abramowitz has argued that Converse's 1960s portrait of a politically disengaged public is seriously outdated: "In 2004, however, the proportion of active citizens reached 45 percent and the proportion of campaign activists reached 23 percent. Both of these figures were all-time records."[49] In addition, he cited record numbers of voters who perceived party differences in 2004 and who cared about the outcome. If the political class truly included somewhere between a quarter and one-half of the eligible electorate, the case for a disconnect would be much weaker.

But the case is far less clear than Abramowitz asserts. Consider his claim that in 2004 "the proportion of active citizens reached 45 percent and the proportion of campaign activists reached 23 percent. Both of these figures were all-time highs." The first thing to note is the special nature of the 2004 data.[50] Without the 2004 observation, there is no increase in activity lev-

Figure 2.2 Campaign activism of Americans I

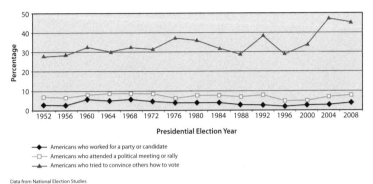

— Americans who worked for a party or candidate
--□-- Americans who attended a political meeting or rally
—▲— Americans who tried to convince others how to vote

Data from National Election Studies

els. In fact, there appears to be a very small downward trend in campaign activism that reversed only in 2004. But, for purposes of argument, set that point aside.

How does one rise from the category of mere voter to "active citizen" according to Abramowitz? By engaging in one campaign activity beyond voting. So, what precisely did Americans do to set an all-time record for political engagement in 2004? Did they go out and ring doorbells, distribute leaflets, and in other ways work for a party or candidate? No. As figure 2.2 shows, the number of people engaging in such acts in 2004 was in the same low single-digit range that it has been for the half-century history of the NES. Did these suddenly newly engaged citizens give up a work day, an evening, or a Saturday afternoon to attend a meeting or rally? No. As figure 2.2 shows, the number of Americans who did so fell in the same high single-digit range typical of the past half-century. Figure 2.2 indicates that the record increase in the size of the active public arose nearly entirely from talk—the number of people who reported trying to convince others how to vote rose 14 percentage points in 2004. In sum, a husband and wife discussing Bush v. Kerry was sufficient to gain admission to "active citizen" status under Abramowitz's definition.

Figure 2.3 Campaign activism of Americans II

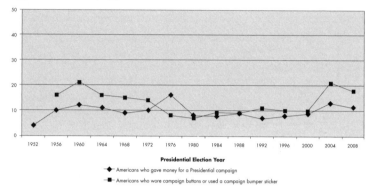

Presidential Election Year

◆ Americans who gave money for a Presidential campaign

■ Americans who wore campaign buttons or used a campaign bumper sticker

Now consider how such "active citizens" ascend to the even more rarified category of "campaign activist." This ascension required one more activity. For a few people this meant writing a check. As shown in figure 2.3, the number of Americans who reported giving money to a campaign rose about 4 percentage points in 2004, the first time the percentage of contributors hit double-digits since the not-so-polarized 1976 election between "Jerry" Ford and "Jimmy" Carter. Figure 2.3 indicates that most campaign activists achieved their exalted status by wearing a button or putting a bumper sticker on their car. The number of Americans who publicly expressed their political preferences in these ways rose about 11 percent from the norm since 1984 to reach a level not seen since 1960.

But does such participation necessarily signify increased engagement on the part of ordinary citizens? The party organizations have been much more active in the past three elections, mobilizing grass roots supporters and rediscovering the virtues of old-fashioned GOTV (get out the vote) activities. Such increased party activity shows up clearly in the party contact reports among NES respondents. As figure 2.4 shows, there has been a steady increase in party contact reports since 1992, breaking the 1972 high in 2000 and jumping an additional 8 percent-

Figure 2.4 Rates of party contact (party mobilization)

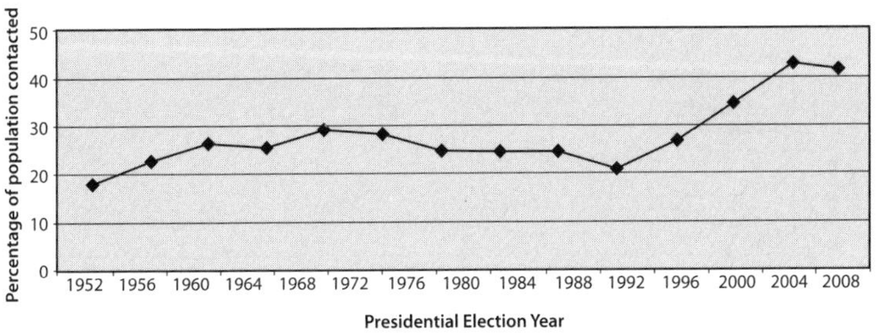

Data from National Election Studies

age points in 2004. Party workers may simply have passed out more buttons and stickers in 2004. The 5 percentage point increase in turnout that occurred between the 2000 and 2004 elections may have the same explanation. It does not necessarily indicate increased psychological engagement among citizens; it may only reflect an increase in mobilizing activities by the parties.[51]

This is not the place to make an extensive argument about psychological engagement versus party mobilization in 2004, but additional data bear even more directly on the question than the preceding figures. According to the NES, although a record number of Americans reported that they cared about the outcome in 2004, the percentages who reported reading about the campaign in the newspapers and following it on TV were down; in addition, as shown in figure 2.5, interest in the campaign was about the same as in 1992, well within sampling error of 1976 and about the same as in 1960–68 (and, as Converse points out, it is a reasonable presumption that declining response rates yield a somewhat more politically interested NES sample today than in previous decades.)[52] Increased activity with no corresponding increase in interest is consistent with a mobilization argument. Contrary to what Abramowitz argues, a record number of Americans may not have jumped into the political arena in 2004; they may have been pushed.

Figure 2.5 Americans' reported interest in Presidential campaigns

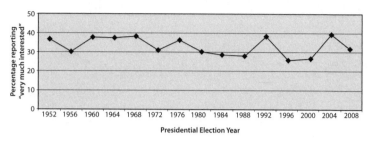

Data from National Election Studies

Abramowitz further contends that counter to Converse's portrait of a nonideological electorate, "the American electorate today is far better educated than the public of the 1950s. . . . As a result of this dramatic rise in education levels, a much larger proportion of today's electorate is capable of understanding and using ideological concepts."[53] Whether Americans today are more "capable" than earlier generations is not the issue, however. As noted earlier, Delli Carpini and Keeter reported that despite "this dramatic rise in education levels," contemporary Americans are no better informed than they were a generation ago.[54] A recent Pew Center report reaffirms that conclusion as of 2007: "But . . . the coaxial and digital revolutions and attendant changes in news audience behaviors have had little impact on how much Americans know about national and international affairs."[55] And in a recent book, Wattenberg reported that it is precisely younger, better-educated cohorts of Americans who are the least well-informed.[56] The communications revolution has generated an explosive increase in the number of information sources but at the same time has made it easier for people to avoid them.[57] As Kohut and Doherty wryly commented, "The good news is that at least Americans do not know any less than they did two decades ago."[58]

Thus, a close examination of recent data finds little indication of any dramatic increase in the size of the political class. Impressions to the contrary are probably a reflection of the 24/7 news cycle and the Internet, which greatly magnify the visibility of such people even in the absence of any increase in their number.

SUMMARY AND IMPLICATIONS

The political class is a relatively small proportion of the American citizenry, but it is the public face of politics—the face that the media portray as an accurate image of the American public. It is not. Not only is the political class more extreme in its positions, as shown in chapter 1, but its priorities do not mirror those of the larger public. Whether its priorities are genuine or tactical, the kinds of narrow "wedge" issues emphasized by the political class rank relatively low on the public's list of concerns. Moreover, the certitude with which members of the political class express their views and the uncivil style often displayed by members of the political class is off-putting to many normal Americans, with possible negative consequences for political participation and beliefs about government.

But in no way does the small size of the political class, its unrepresentativeness, and its incivility diminish its importance. On the contrary, its members are largely responsible for the multifaceted disconnect between the American people and their government. This pronounced minority of unrepresentative Americans who have an inordinate interest in politics and an exceptional certainty that their cause is right heavily influences what policy issues dominate the political agenda, what policy alternatives receive consideration, and how the debate is conducted. And their choices do not closely resemble those that a representative sample of Americans would make.

How has this happened? Discussions of representation traditionally assume that the representative genuinely wishes to represent a constituency, however he or she defines it and whatever the characteristics of constituents he or she thinks are the proper objects of representation. This desire to be "faithful" to constituents need not have an exalted motivation; it can be something much more mundane, such as the desire to be reelected by constituents. Through much of American history, most American elected officials did make a serious effort to be good, or at least acceptable, representatives. But institutional and social changes in the past half century or so have changed the mix of people who seek public office, bringing into influential positions far more people who wish to advance certain principles or ideologies than to represent their constituents. As Jacobs and Shapiro have argued, many of today's politicians do not wish to follow public opinion, but to change it, or at least to evade its influence, and they are willing to distort and de-legitimate it in pursuit of their ideological ends.[59] How and why this has happened is the subject of chapter 4.

Politician don't Pander.

CHAPTER 3

POPULAR MISCONCEPTIONS
OF POLARIZATION

CHAPTER 1 SHOWED that contrary to what is often claimed, and in contrast to much of the political class, the American people by and large are not divided into hard-left liberals and hard-right conservatives. Rather, whether one examines their general ideological stances or their positions on particular issues, normal Americans' views fall between the more polarized positions advocated by contending factions of office-holders and candidates, party and issue activists, and others in that active minority who constitute the political class.

Chapter 2 showed that the disconnect between the American people and the political class is not limited to ideological leanings and positions on specific issues. Rather, it extends to priorities and behavior. By and large Americans are not fixated on the kinds of cultural issues so prominent in our recent politics—abortion, gun control, gay marriage, stem cell research, flag burning, and the like. Rather, the general public is concerned with broader questions of peace and war, domestic security, the economy, education, and health care. Furthermore, Americans are more uncertain and more ambivalent about political issues than are members of the political class, who see the political world in black and white terms and have no doubts about which is which. Moreover, most Americans do not like the contentious, uncivil style in which the political class so often conducts contemporary political debate.

The preceding findings obviously contradict the prevailing view of a country more divided than at any time since the Civil War. What explains such gross misperceptions? Numerous factors contribute, but three of these together probably explain the lion's share of inaccurate beliefs about the American people. The first is a collection of statistical mistakes, each of which leads us to exaggerate the extent of political division and conflict. The second consists of a common tendency to confuse people's easily visible and measurable *choices* with their less visible and more difficult to measure *positions*. The third consists of mistaking the party sorting and realignment that have taken place within a relatively unchanged electorate for change in the aggregate electorate itself. Each of these is discussed in turn.

STATISTICAL FALLACIES

In the summer of 1972, I moved from upstate New York to southern California just before the two presidential nominating conventions. Shortly after arriving I was walking through a parking lot when a slow-moving Volkswagen van passed by. The young adult male driver wore a tie-dyed T-shirt and had long bleached-blond hair pulled back in a ponytail. The van itself sported various psychedelic patterns. "No doubt a McGovern supporter," I mused. But as the van pulled into a parking place a bit ahead of me I was taken aback to see old bumper stickers reading "Reagan for Governor" along with brand new "Nixon—Agnew" bumper stickers. I realized then that patterns of dress and personal appearance popularly associated with liberal sympathies were not always accurate guides to political positions.[1]

Human beings are natural statisticians: we notice patterns in our environment and draw inferences about them. But we are by nature not terribly good statisticians, and many of the inferences we draw may be far from accurate. There are probably good evolutionary reasons for this. If early hominids died after being bitten by snakes with a particular color pattern, then learning to flee from or kill all similar snakes had survival value, even if a trained herpetologist today knows that most such snakes are nonpoisonous. In a similar manner, if some primitive hominids died after eating white mushrooms, their comrades probably were more likely to survive if they avoided all white mushrooms, even if mycologists can identify numerous perfectly edible white mushrooms. From an evolutionary standpoint it made good sense for our progenitors to observe correlations relevant to life and death and act on them, even if such correlations were weak or spurious. Today, millions of years later, we still instinctively observe our environments and make inferences from those observations. Much of the popular impression of polarization comes from media contrasts of easily observed or measured demographic or sociological characteristics. Red state residents are more likely to be White and Protestant, to own guns, to be "born again," to go to church weekly, to listen to country music, and to vote Republican. Blue state residents are more likely to be racial minorities, Jewish, and Catholic; to rent porno movies; to be agnostics; to frequent Starbucks on Sunday mornings; to listen to National Public Radio (NPR); and to vote Democratic. Such correlations between observed characteristics and political choices certainly are real but are much weaker than often assumed. If you pass a Black woman on the street, the odds that she is a Democrat rather than a Republican are about 9:1, but few such observables are so closely related to the vote. If you pass a White woman on the street, the odds that she is a Democrat rather than a Republican are only a little better than 50:50. The correlations often cited in media portraits of divisions among the American people fall at various point in between but are generally closer to 50:50 than to 90:10. For example, according to the exit polls, more than 35 percent of gun owners voted for John Kerry in 2004—not everyone who owns a gun is a card-carrying member of the National Rifle Association angry at "jack-booted federal thugs." In a similar manner, more than one in four born-again Christians voted for John Kerry—not every evangelical Christian is a Bible-thumping theocrat.[2] In the interest of an entertaining discussion, the pressure of limited airtime, or the allure of a colorful story, there is a general tendency to exaggerate the strength of correlations between sociocultural characteristics and political views (a special case of the general journalistic maxim, "first simplify, then exaggerate"). Americans differ much less in their political views than in their social characteristics.

The exaggerated picture of American polarization also reflects a common tendency to draw inferences from bad samples—bad in the sense of unrepresentative. In contrast to reputable survey firms, the media do not draw random samples of American adults and describe their political views and activities. The media cover those who are active participants in politics, and these participants are seriously unrepresentative in several different ways, as described in chapters 1 and 2. The political actors featured in the newspaper and news magazines, on radio and television, and over the Internet are more extreme, more strident, more certain, and care about different things than normal Americans, but they are portrayed as the norm.

For example, in a particularly inaccurate segment on ABC's 20/20, George Stephanopoulos asserted that the United States was more divided than at any time since the Civil War.[3] Among the bits of "evidence" cited was the figure that "about 8 million people log on to political blogs or partisan web journals every day, creating virtual communities of like-minded partisans who demonize each other." Well, assume contrary to fact that those are 8 million *different* people—that no one visits more than one such political blog per day. Furthermore, assume contrary to fact that every political blog is the kind of liberal or conservative blog that demonizes the other side—that none take centrist, reformist, or nonpartisan stances.[4] Under those favorable assumptions, less than 4 percent of the eligible electorate (currently 200+ million Americans) are members of such "virtual communities of like-minded partisans."[5] Given the inaccuracy of the preceding assumptions, the proportion of Americans who hit polarized blog sites every day is probably closer to 1 percent.[6] Civil war? Evidently the criteria for classifying political conflicts as civil wars have become looser in recent decades.

A good illustration of the tendency to exaggerate evidence of political conflict was provided by a Connecticut Democratic primary election held in September 2006. The election attracted heavy national media coverage as incumbent senator Joe Lieberman campaigned to save his seat from a challenge stimulated by bloggers who aroused the "netroots" in support of an insurgent candidate, Ned Lamont. The national media and the blogosphere both portrayed the outcome as an important indicator of

Table 3.1 Connecticut 2006 Democratic primary election

Variable	Number	Percent of VAP
Voting age population (VAP)	2,565,991	
Registered voters	1,989,913	77.5
Registered Democrats	670,356	26.1
Democratic primary voters	283,055	11.0
Lamont voters	146,587	5.7

political sentiment in the country and a demonstration of the power of the netroots. After his narrow loss, Lieberman antagonized Lamont supporters by refusing to accept his defeat and retire gracefully from the field, deciding instead to run in the general election as an independent. Outraged sympathizers of Lamont attacked Lieberman as defying the wishes of the people of Connecticut. Table 3.1 suggests a different interpretation.

The voting age population of Connecticut is a bit in excess of 2.5 million people, of whom almost 80 percent are registered. A large plurality of registered voters eschew both the Republican and Democratic labels, however, choosing no party: only about a third of the registered voters are Democrats eligible to vote in the closed Democratic primary. About 40 percent of the eligible Democratic voters actually voted in the primary, giving Lamont a bit under 52 percent of their vote. Thus, the "voice of Connecticut" amounted to something less than 6 percent of the voting age population of the state. In the general election Lieberman won an absolute majority in a three-way race, suggesting that he had a reasonable understanding of the true voice of his state.

Not only does the public face of politics in America reflect an unrepresentative sample of Americans, but it also reflects an unrepresentative sample of developments, situations, and events. After all, the media cover what is newsworthy, and what is newsworthy is by definition what is uncommon or unrepresentative. Erikson's comment a generation ago is even more true today: "A considerable portion of what we call 'news' is devoted to reports about deviant behavior and its consequences."[7] Conflict has news value as well, especially unusually severe or episodic conflict. Something in human nature makes us more likely to take note of disagreement and division, polarization, battles, and war than agreement and consensus, moderation, cooperation, and peace. If we pass two people chatting on the street, we barely notice. If they are yelling at each other, we pay them some attention as we pass. If they are rolling around on the sidewalk pummeling each other, many of us will stop and watch—but that does not mean that we would want to elect either of the combatants to Congress—providing that we had a more reasonable choice.

Unrepresentativeness pervades contemporary media coverage of politics. The standard story describes a newsworthy event or development that has given rise to political conflict or division and quotes a spokesperson on each side of the issue. Generally these spokespersons will be members of the political class heavily involved with the issue, who assure the viewer or reader that the conflict is very serious and not subject to compromise or resolution.

On a personal note: I heard through the grapevine that after reading *Culture War?* a well-known pundit commented that I needed to get out more, apparently implying that I did not have a good read on the current disconnect situation. On the contrary, I think it is that pundit who needs to get out more. Ronald Reagan was correct—Washington, D.C., is an island surrounded by unreality, as are many of our state capitals, not to mention Manhattan, Hollywood, and the campuses of our colleges and universities. Members of the national media need to get out more. Instead of sitting through a coveted interview with a high-ranking government official, they need to spend several days walking the aisles of Wal-Marts, standing outside megachurches, and sitting in minor league baseball stadiums having conversations with normal Americans. When they follow the campaigns out in the country, they should tune in their car radios to country stations rather than NPR. Instead of following the candidates and their entourages into rural diners, they should sit in the diners and converse with the locals when no candidates are around and no campaigns are in progress. And instead of getting a quotation from the leader of an advocacy group, they should call their distant relatives in the hinterlands and ask about their opinions, or whether they have any opinions at all.

I hasten to emphasize once again that nothing in the preceding discussion is meant to deny the importance of the unrepresentative minority of Americans who are highly active in politics and who constitute the public face of politics. On the contrary, as chapter 4 explains, through a mixture of accident and intention we have constructed a kind of politics that gives disproportionate political influence to such people. The argument here is only that we should not make the mistake of assuming that the influence and importance of the political class stems from their representation of the broad swath of the American public. It does not.

CHOICES AND EVALUATIONS ARE NOT THE SAME AS POSITIONS

In the 2004 presidential election the NEP exit poll reported that more than 90 percent of Americans who classified themselves as Republicans voted for George W. Bush, and nearly 90 percent of Americans who classified themselves as Democrats voted for John Kerry. During the months preceding the 2006 congressional elections, polls consistently reported that about 90 percent of Republicans approved of the performance of President Bush while about 90 percent of Democrats disapproved. Some commentators point to numbers like these as unambiguous proof that Americans are polarized.

Indeed voters' choices and evaluations at times appear highly polarized, but that does not mean that their positions are. We addressed this misconception at some length in *Culture War?* but its continued appearance shows that additional explanation is necessary. Votes are *choices* that people make, and approval ratings are *evaluations* people offer. But such choices and evaluations are not simple expressions of voters' *positions*; rather, they reflect *comparisons* of voters' positions with the candidates' positions or the officials' actions. For example, a voter who cares about abortion and nothing else approves or disapproves of a candidate by comparing the candidate's position to his personal position. And the voter decides which candidate to vote for by comparing the positions of both candidates to his personal position. Knowing the voter's position alone is not nearly enough to predict his vote choice or his evaluation of a candidate. For example, single-issue pro-life voters and single-issue pro-choice voters may both disapprove of an official, the former because she is too liberal on abortion, the latter because she is too conservative. Votes and approval ratings depend equally on where voters stand and where candidates stand and what they do.

Given this complex conditional nature of performance evaluations and voting decisions, votes and approval ratings by themselves can tell us nothing about whether the political positions of voters are polarized. If a hard-core conservative Republican runs against a knee-jerk liberal Democrat, the voters can only choose between those two possibilities, even if every voter is a moderate who would prefer more middle-of-the-road choices. Alternatively, if a squishy moderate Democrat runs against a RINO (Republican in name only), a moderate will be elected even if all the voters are hard-core ideologues who find both candidates unsatisfactory. Voters can only choose between the alternatives on the ballot.

Consider figure 3.1. In the top panel of the figure, the electorate actually is polarized, but if they have to choose between two moderate candidates (D_M and R_M, who perhaps are desperately competing for the few moderate voters in the middle), they will elect a moderate. In the bottom panel of the figure, the electorate is centrist, but if forced to choose between extreme liberal (D_L) and extreme conservative (R_C) candidates (who perhaps emerged from low-turnout primaries) who locate equidistant from the median on opposite sides, they will elect an extremist. In sum, whether an election winner is moderate or extreme does not tell us anything about whether the electorate is moderate or extreme. We need data on the positions of the voters as well as that of *both* candidates.

Figure 3.1 Electoral Choices May Reveal Nothing About Voters' Positions

D_M = moderate Democrat, R_M = moderate Republican, D_L = liberal Democrat, and R_C = conservative Republican.

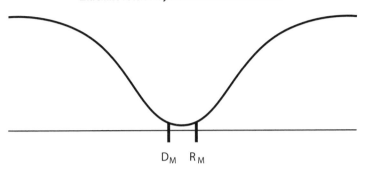

Extremist Voters May Elect Moderate Candidates

D_M R_M

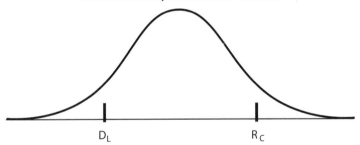

Moderate Voters May Elect Extremist Candidates

D_L R_C

As we showed in *Culture War?* presidential performance evaluations can polarize while voters do not change their positions at all.[8] In figure 3.1 Democrats are arrayed on the left, Republicans on the right. If the president moves from a position near the center of the entire electorate to one at the center of his base, he has moved closer to most of his own party and consequently his approval ratings among his own party rise. At the same time he has moved away from everyone in the other party so their approval of him falls. Gary Jacobson has shown that President Bush's approval ratings are more polarized by party than any president in the half century since presidential approval has been measured, and Jacobson correctly attributes the causation to where it belongs: President Bush.[9] Love him or loathe him, President Bush governed as a divider not a uniter. The historically unprecedented level of party polarization in his approval ratings largely reflects the actions and positions he has taken rather than any sudden sharp polarization of the positions held by the electorate.[10]

Recent research by Philip Klinkner on the way the Iraq War issue affected the 2004 presidential voting nicely illustrates the distinction between people's positions and their evaluations.[11] Klinkner contrasted the views of self-classified Democrats and Republicans on U.S. foreign policy *goals* (e.g., to advance human rights, to combat terrorism) and found that although Democratic and Republican partisans' views are significantly different in a statistical sense, the differences are not substantively large. Contrasting the views of partisans on the *means* that the United States uses to carry out foreign policy (e.g., military power vs. diplomacy), Klinkner again reported differences that are statistically different but not substantively large. The same is true for partisan attitudes on specific national defense *issues*, like the importance of a strong military, and again on partisan attitudes on *values*, like patriotism and national pride. But when it comes to partisan attitudes toward George *Bush,* Klinkner found the huge partisan divide that Jacobson has described. The underlying values and positions of Democratic and Republican partisans are not nearly as divided as their evaluations of President Bush.

Jonathan Rauch came to a similar conclusion after examining 2005–2006 public opinion data.[12] Although partisan differences certainly exist, they are not at a level that justifies claims that foreign policy has become the defining difference between Democrats and Republicans today. Rauch concluded, "Encouragement comes from the underappreciated fact that America's partisans agree on much more than the conventional wisdom would suggest." As Jacobson and Klinkner found earlier, the polarization comes from Bush: "Questions about *President Bush* send both parties rushing to their respective corners" (italics in original).

But, "Judging by public opinion, once Bush and the Iraq war—the two great foreign-policy polarizers—cease to dominate the agenda, a bipartisan swing toward a less confrontational, more multilateralist foreign policy appears likely." According to journalist Thomas Edsall, Karl Rove abandoned the "compassionate conservative" strategy that the Bush campaign used in 2000 after campaign pollster Matthew Dowd produced analyses showing that swing voters had largely disappeared.[13] The result was adoption of the base strategy and a president first elected as a uniter, not a divider, who will go down in history as the great polarizer.

The problem with analyses such as that attributed to Dowd is that voters are not born as hard-core partisan loyalists or moderate independent swing voters.[14] True, many enter the electorate with a partisan affiliation that predisposes them one way or the other, and a few are so highly predisposed that they will not break party lines except under the most extreme circumstances. But in any given election most voters mark their ballots at least in part on the choices the political order offers them. When party elites take relatively similar positions, voters will not see a lot of difference between the candidates—having seen little difference, voters will be more likely to be undecided about whom to vote for and more likely to vote for attractive candidates of both parties. Conversely, when party elites are polarized, voters will see significant differences between the candidates, and seeing those differences they will be less likely to be undecided and less likely to vote for a personally attractive candidate who takes positions distinct from the ones they hold. Thus, the proportion of independent or undecided voters waxes and wanes over time depending on the positions the candidates take. Contrary to 2004 lore, there was nothing historically unprecedented about the 2004 voting:

> Never in modern election history has there been a presidential campaign in which each party was so certain that the other had drifted to the fringes of the political spectrum. . . .
>
> "The world has become bipolar," says [A], a Republican pollster and political consultant. "You're either for [Republican nominee] or you're going to go out there and beat the heck out of him. The

same with [Democratic nominee]. We just don't have as much middle ground." . . .

A polarized campaign is one in which the undecided vote is likely to be relatively small as the candidates reach October. . . . .

Four years ago at this time polls by both parties showed nearly a quarter of the voters undecided between [Republican nominee] and [Democratic nominee]. This time, according to [Republican] pollster [B], the same surveys place the undecideds at less than 9 percent of the electorate.[15]

Were these passages written by reporter Thomas Edsall quoting Republican pollster Matthew Dowd discussing the Bush— Gore race in 2000? No, these passages were written by reporter Alan Ehrenhalt quoting Republican pollsters Lance Tarrance and Richard Wirthlin discussing the Reagan—Mondale campaign in 1984—way back in the good old days before America was polarized.

Estimates of the number of swing voters in 2004 were as low as 5 percent according to some pollsters, as high as 20 percent using weaker identifying criteria.[16] Compared to 1984 ("less than 9 percent"), that does not seem especially unusual; it only seems unusual compared with 1992 when the Democrats nominated an apparent centrist and Ross Perot roiled the electoral waters (19 percent of the popular vote), and, to a lesser extent, with 1996 when a "triangulating" President Clinton, Ralph Nader, and Perot added uncertainty to the contest. Imagine the following hypothetical rough analogue to 1992: in 2008 what if the Republicans had nominated a candidate who held many positions different from those of the party base (say, Rudy Guiliani); a well-known, well-funded independent had entered the race (say, Michael Bloomberg); and the Democrats nominated a candidate outside the traditional mold (say, Barack Obama). In such a scenario would not the sharp partisan lines drawn in 2004 have blurred? During the campaign the polls would register a sharp rise over 2004 in the number of undecided voters, and the final outcome would show an increase in partisan defections over 2004. I return to this possibility in the final chapter.

PARTY SORTING

To claim that Americans are polarized is to claim that the distribution of public opinion has a U-shape rather than the familiar bell-shape: when public opinion is polarized, the middle is smaller than the extremes. To claim that public opinion has become *more* polarized is to claim that the distribution of public opinion is becoming more U-shaped: when public opinion is polarizing, the middle is losing and the extremes are gaining. Chapter 1 reports that there is little evidence for either claim.

What many observers mean by polarization is what we call party sorting[17]—the development of a tighter fit between party affiliation on the one hand and ideology and issue positions on the other. A generation ago both parties contained a sizable minority of ideological "misfits." In 1972 more than a quarter of self-identified Democrats placed themselves right of center on an ideological scale, and a little more than 10 percent of Republicans placed themselves left of center. By 2004 various social changes discussed in chapters 4–6 of this book had rendered the two parties considerably more ideologically homogeneous: only 12 percent of Democrats and a mere 4 percent of Republicans reported the "wrong" ideology. So, the relative numbers of conservatives and liberals in the electorate may not have changed, but their party affiliations have.[18]

The hypothetical electorates depicted in table 3.2 illustrate the distinction between party sorting and polarization. The electorate consists of 100 liberals, 100 moderates, and 100 conservatives. In period 1, liberals are somewhat more likely to be Democrats and conservatives are somewhat more likely to be Republicans; however, both parties contain significant numbers of liberals and conservatives. Knowing a voter's party affiliation in period 1, then, provides only a little information about his or her political ideology. Between period 1 and period 2, the parties sort along ideological lines. The great preponderance of liberals now affiliates with the Democratic Party, and a similarly large proportion of conservatives affiliates with the Republican Party. The result is that the period 2 parties are far more ideologically

Table 3.2 Party sorting without increasing polarization

Period	Democrats	Independents	Republicans
Period 1	60 liberals,	100 moderates	40 liberals,
	40 conservatives		60 conservatives
Period 2	80 liberals,	100 moderates	20 liberals,
	20 conservatives		80 conservatives

homogeneous than the period 1 parties. Knowing a voter's party affiliation in period 2 provides a great deal of information about her ideology. Notice, however, that in both periods the ideological distribution is the same: 100 liberals and 100 conservatives (along with the 100 moderate independents). Despite declines in the numbers of conservative Democrats and liberal Republicans, the aggregate level of polarization in the electorate is unchanged.

Some analysts prefer to call the party sorting depicted in the preceding example "partisan polarization." But this terminology confuses the discussion—partisan polarization also calls to mind intraparty conflict, such as that between the Democratic old guard and new politics activists in the late 1960s. I prefer the term "party sorting," reserving the term "polarization" for when more citizens locate themselves at the extremes on an issue than locate themselves in the center, or when they are moving from centrist positions toward the extremes.

Given the political changes that have occurred in the United States since the mid-twentieth century, it would be extremely surprising if there had *not* been some party sorting. Consider the political realignment of the South. Forty years ago, the Democratic Party had a much larger proportion of adherents in the South—many of whose racial and social attitudes and views on national defense were more conservative than those of the national Democratic Party. As Democratic strength in the South fell (particularly among White men), one would logically expect the Democratic Party as a whole to become more homogeneously liberal.

Surprisingly, however, these political changes do not leave as big an impression on public opinion as one might expect. For example, between 1987 and 2007 according to surveys by the Pew Research Center, the average difference between Republicans and Democrats on 40 survey items asked repeatedly over the twenty-year period increased by 4 percentage points (from 10 percent to 14 percent).[19] This seems like a surprisingly small increase.

Matthew Levendusky has conducted the most extensive analysis of party sorting during the last quarter of the twentieth century.[20] In addition to analyzing the increasingly strong correlation between party identification and liberal—conservative ideology, Levendusky has examined changing correlations between party identification and issues, both aggregated into broad categories and disaggregated into individual issues. Although there is a general tendency to see greater differences between ordinary partisans over time, the differences and changes are less than one might have expected and there are some surprises along the way.

Each election year, the NES surveys Americans' attitudes within a number of policy areas. Any general discussion of American politics would include these four prominent policy areas: New Deal economic and social welfare issues, social and cultural issues, racial issues, and defense and military policy issues. On the basis of contemporary political commentary, one might expect that the correlation between New Deal issue positions and party identification has declined over time in the direction of less party sorting. One prominent line of argument is that the Republican Party capitalized on racial resentment among working class Democrats to break up the New Deal Democratic majority, and a best-selling book in 2004 argued that Republicans use social and cultural issues to distract Americans from voting their true economic interests (represented by Democrats).[21]

Conversely, one would expect that Democratic and Republican partisans have become better sorted on racial issues, as the images of the two parties became increasingly associated with race (Democrats sympathetic to minorities, Republicans less so). In their classic work, Carmines and Stimson showed that party elites became increasingly differentiated on racial issues after the 1958 elections, and they suggested that the sorting of ordinary voters followed elite separation.[22]

Social issues such as equal rights for women, abortion, school prayer, and the like were in some cases (gay marriage) absent from the national agenda a generation ago or in other cases (abortion) independent of party positions a generation ago. Today, such issues have moved to the center of disagreement between party elites.[23] Thus, one would expect these issues to have little or no relationship to partisanship in the early years of the NES data but to be strongly related to party identification today.

Finally, since the Democratic Party splintered over the Vietnam War in the 1960s, the Republican Party on balance has been the more hawkish of the two parties on matters relating to defense and military policy. So, a strong correlation between defense-related issues and party identification should exist over the entire three-decade period, and if anything, the correlation may have increased in the past few years as a Republican administration waged war in Iraq.

Figure 3.2 displays the correlations between partisanship and voter positions in the four policy areas.[24] Evidently, Americans today report party affiliations more consistent with their issue positions than they did a generation ago. But it is surprising to find that (1) over the entire thirty-year period the correlations between party identification and New Deal issues are stronger than those between party identification and other issue categories, and (2) the correlations between party identification and New Deal issues have increased, not decreased. This is rather clear evidence that popular commentators have overstated the diminished importance of these issues to the electorate.[25] On both racial issues and cultural issues, party sorting has gone from almost none to significant levels. For defense-related items, there is little change in the relationship until 2004, suggesting a direct response to the contentious debate over the Iraq war and the war on terror.

But although all of the areas show some sorting, one should not exaggerate the extent of the change. Even in 2004, correlations

Figure 3.2 Party Sorting in Four Issue Areas

Higher correlations signify greater relevance of the issue to party affiliation as measured by the Party Identification scale and the Issue Index.

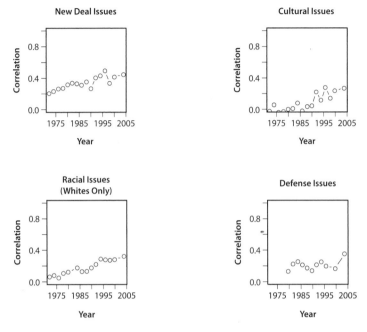

Source: Figure created by Matt Levendusky from National Election Studies data.

between partisanship and the racial, social, and defense policy areas were still much closer to zero than to one—numbers that seem somewhat shy of "The Great Sorting-Out" discerned by Democratic Party intellectuals William A. Galston and Elaine C. Kamarck and by political columnist Ronald Brownstein.[26] Significant numbers of American partisans stubbornly continue to take positions that are at odds with the national stances of their party's leaders.

Even if evidence of massive sorting on the level of general ideology or broad issue areas is absent, it is possible that voters have sorted on one or two important issues. For example,

Democrats and Republicans could be quite far apart on abortion yet have very muted differences over women's equality.[27] Sorting could be occurring on different issues, at different times, and among different groups, and averaging everything together may obscure significant trends and differences.

To check that possibility, Levendusky carried out detailed analysis of six issues in the NES surveys—three economic and social welfare issues (whether government should provide health insurance, whether it should ensure jobs and a good standard of living, and how government should balance spending and services), two cultural issues (whether abortion and school prayer should be legal), and a race issue (whether the government should provide economic assistance to Blacks and minorities). Given the trends observed for each of the broad policy areas, positions on some of these issues must be more strongly related to partisanship today than a generation ago. Figure 3.3 plots the percentage of respondents who shared their party's national position on each issue.[28]

The most notable feature of the graphs is the lack of clear patterns. On some issues, there appears to have been little sorting, and on other issues the sorting appears to be limited mostly to one party. On the issue of government-provided health insurance, for instance, there is not much sorting going on in either party—in the aggregate, the mass parties look more or less as they did thirty years ago. But on the issue of whether the government should ensure jobs for its citizens and provide a social safety net, Republicans have become somewhat more inclined to agree with their party's view that government should let each person get ahead on his or her own whereas Democrats have not exhibited a trend toward greater party sorting (unless 2004 marks the start of one). On the issue of how government should balance spending and services, Democrats have become better sorted and Republicans somewhat less well-sorted.

On the long-standing issue of whether the government should help minorities, White Republicans have become better sorted on the issue, with a large majority now in agreement with the party position that Blacks and other minorities should help themselves. But White Democrats have changed little over

Figure 3.3 Party Sorting on Specific Issues

▲ = Republican, and ○ = Democrats

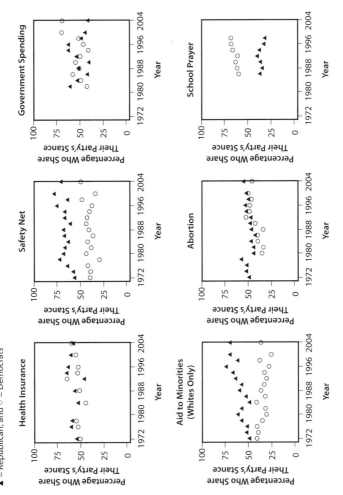

Source: Figure created by Matt Levendusky from National Election Studies data.

the thirty-year period. Even as White Southerners left the party, White Democrats who stayed did not become any more liberal; in fact, most Democrats today remain out-of-step with the party position that government should provide more assistance.

From the standpoint of this book, the results for abortion and school prayer are the most interesting. Arguably, other than the Iraq War there has been no single issue in American politics during the past generation that has attracted so much attention and created so much controversy among party elites as abortion. Indeed, for approximately two decades abortion served as a litmus test for presidential candidates, with the NARAL and similar pro-choice groups exercising a veto on the Democratic side, and Focus on the Family and similar pro-life groups exercising a veto on the Republican side. It is thus not surprisingly that the graph for the abortion issue indicates that as the national parties became more clearly identified with pro-life or pro-choice positions, ordinary partisans followed suit, albeit with a lag of more than ten years.[29]

Party sorting on abortion today still has a long way to go, however. Sorting among rank-and-file partisans falls far short of that among party elites, as illustrated by table 3.3. In the 2004 NES, more than 40 percent of self-described "strong" Republicans and "strong" Democrats (each group comprises about one-sixth of the population) did not support the stated positions of their party leadership on abortion—and virtually the same percentage of strong Republicans say abortion should *always* be a legal personal choice as the percentage who said it should *never* be legal.[30] Democrats are less divided than Republicans (a majority of strong Democrats say abortion should always be legal), but more than one-third of them believe that abortion laws should be more restrictive than those favored by the national party. Even among citizens who claimed the strongest attachments to their political parties (and thus were very likely to know their party's position), there remains considerable heterogeneity.[31]

The new abortion battery introduced in chapter 2 further illuminates the nuances of party sorting on abortion. Table 3.4 shows

Table 3.3 Imperfect party sorting on the issue of abortion

Circumstances in which abortion should be legal	Strong Democrats	Strong Republicans
Never permitted	10%	22%
Only in case of rape, incest, or when the woman's life is in danger	23%	37%
For a clear need	13%	18%
Always as a personal choice	54%	23%

Source: 2004 National Election Study.
Note: Percentages of self-described "Strong Democrats" versus "Strong Republicans" on legality of abortion under
    different circumstances.

the party breakdown on the new battery. Responses to the seven justifications for abortion fall into three categories. First, there is consensus across parties on three justifications. Large majorities of every partisan category favor legal abortion in the cases of pregnancy that threatens the mother's life or pregnancy that results from rape. Strong Democrats and strong Republicans differ considerably to be sure, but even three-quarters of strong Republicans favor legal abortion if the mother's life is in danger and more than three-fifths do if the pregnancy resulted from rape. On the other side, all partisan categories overwhelmingly reject legal abortion for the purpose of gender selection. There is a thirty-percentage-point difference between strong Democrats and strong Republicans, but even two-thirds of strong Democrats believe gender selection is not a sufficient justification for legal abortion. Second, on two other justifications for abortion, strong Republicans are isolated. They are the only partisan category in which a majority opposes legal abortion where a mother's health but not her life is threatened and where the fetus has a serious birth defect. Finally, on the remaining two conditions, the parties are split. In the cases of pregnancy resulting from incest and pregnancy that would hurt the mother's financial condition, majorities of Democrats and Republicans oppose each other, with independents leaning toward the Democrats. In sum, partisans differ, but the divisions are far more complicated than the black—white choice offered by party activists.

Table 3.4 Partisan differences on abortion

Circumstances under which abortion should be legal

Partisan Category	Cause Mother's Death (%)	Rape (%)	Hurt Mother's Health, No Death (%)	Serious Birth Defect (%)	Incest (%)	Financial Difficulty (%)	Sex of Fetus Undesired (%)
Strong Democrat (18%)	98	97	89	89	79	74	35
Weak Democrat (13%)	94	92	83	84	65	57	28
Independent (36%)	95	84	71	73	60	55	24
Weak Republican (12%)	87	81	61	61	44	31	11
Strong Republican (20%)	74	62	34	34	23	11	4

Source: 2006 Cooperative Congressional Election Study.

As for other social issues, school prayer is interesting because here, a countertrend emerged (see figure 3.3). Levendusky found that over time, Democrats became more accepting of their party's position (opposition to mandatory school prayer), whereas Republicans became less accepting of their party's position (support for school prayer). In each presidential election survey, a majority of respondents—including a majority of Republicans and a near-majority of Democrats—supported a moderate position: "The law should allow public schools to schedule time when children can pray silently if they want to." Even if party elites remain sharply divided over school prayer, ordinary partisans are not. The issue of equal rights for women exhibits a similar pattern. By 2004, support for equality for women had become the clear position among the adherents of both parties—by huge majorities. In other words, over the past 25 years or so, Americans have moved toward a consensus on this once-contentious issue.

Finally, consider the issue of gay rights. In 2004, same-sex marriage in Massachusetts and San Francisco was a hot-button issue in the campaign. Although survey organizations have begun to ask about gay marriage only recently, the GSS has long included a series of questions on the public's attitudes toward homosexual relations. Figure 3.4 plots the percentages of Democrats and Republicans who stated that same-sex relations are "only wrong sometimes" or "not at all wrong." An interesting finding is that the parties are sorting—Democrats and Republicans are becoming more different. But that sorting takes place against a background of increasing tolerance for homosexuality—Republicans are just not changing as rapidly as Democrats (and independents). Gay marriage and other gay-related issues remain controversial, and partisans now are more distinct than they used to be, but the disagreement results from different rates of change in the same direction, not changes in opposing directions.[32]

In sum, abortion is the only consistently measured social issue that exerts a strong push on party sorting. Other cultural issues—school prayer, women's rights, and gay rights—are

Figure 3.4 Level of acceptance of homosexuality among Democrats and Republicans

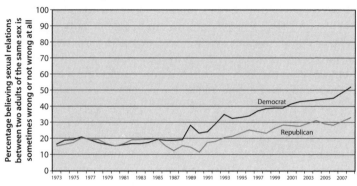

Data from the General Social Survey

ones on which the partisan attitudes of ordinary citizens seem either to be converging rather than diverging or to be moving in the same direction but at different rates. Rather than party sorting contributing to a culture war organized around these issues, increasing numbers of ordinary Americans appear to be separating themselves from the conflict that characterizes the party elites.[33]

SUMMARY AND IMPLICATIONS

For a number of reasons, Americans think our country is more divided than it is. First, whereas the sociological and cultural characteristics of Americans differ in highly visible ways, their political positions differ far less. But the former are easily observed; hence, casual observation leads us to exaggerate our political differences. The media do not correct such exaggerations; on the contrary, news practices and values, along with their own unrepresentative social contexts, lead journalists to reinforce distorted impressions and portray an atypical political class as typical of Americans generally. Second, the evaluations people form and the votes they cast are not direct indicators of the positions they hold; an equal component of their choices and evaluations are the candidates' and office-holders' positions and actions. Even moderate voters will make polarized choices if that is all they are offered. Third, a complex process of party sorting has rendered today's Democrats and Republicans more internally homogeneous and more distinct from each other than the parties of a generation ago. That is, the electorate as a whole shows little change, but within that largely stable electorate partisans have sorted themselves more neatly than in the past. Thus, when Americans compare contemporary Democrats and Republicans, they see greater differences than in the past but fail to realize that in the larger population there are about the same proportions of liberals and conservatives as there have been for a generation. And on specific issues that national surveys have measured consistently over time, there is no more evidence of polarization today than there was in the early 1980s.

In large-scale societies direct democracy is infeasible. If such societies are to be governed democratically, it must be through some form of representative democracy. Some democratic theorists make a virtue out of this necessity, arguing that representative democracy dampens popular passions and brings greater expertise and superior judgment to the process of governing. Such assumptions may have been more true than not for most of the American past—certainly most of the framers of the U.S. Constitution accepted such arguments. But these arguments look much less persuasive today. Historically, the job of the representative was to find common ground and negotiate the compromises necessary to solve societal problems with some acceptable allocation of benefits and costs. But many of today's representatives minimize common ground, deny that there is any acceptable middle ground, and insist that a victory for their side is the only acceptable solution to a problem. Facts give way to ideology. Facts consistent with one's position are emphasized, and those that are inconsistent are ignored or denied altogether. And if inaccurate or distorted information makes ordinary people believe such claims of no common ground, the potential for positive political action declines.

Responsibility for correcting popular misconceptions and exposing those who spread them lies primarily with two sectors of our society: the media and academia. Unfortunately, the economic incentives of the former lead them to reinforce or even create popular misconceptions much of the time, whereas the career incentives of the latter lead them to place relatively little value on efforts at popular education.

CHAPTER 4

INSTITUTIONAL CONTRIBUTORS
TO THE DISCONNECT

IN THE FIRST THREE CHAPTERS of this book, I have summarized the results of a relatively straightforward research effort—to describe the state of American public opinion and contrast it with the opinions held by members of the political class. Anyone with a spreadsheet program and some familiarity with the data sources can replicate the tables and figures reported in the preceding chapters, and although different analysts might reach marginally different interpretations in particular cases, the general conclusion is clear: the American public is not very polarized today and has not become appreciably more polarized in recent decades, whereas the political class is polarized and has become more so.[1]

In chapters 4–6, I take on a more difficult task—to explain how and why the political class has become disconnected from the larger public. The number of potential explanatory factors is large, and the ways in which the factors fit together are myriad and probably complex. Thus, interpretation—even speculation—plays a larger role in these chapters. In that light much of what follows should be viewed as a suggested research agenda rather than as an empirically supported account. In this chapter I argue the following: (1) the political class that developed in the generation that came of age between the 1960s and 1990s differs in an important way from the political classes that existed for much of American history prior to the 1960s, (2) that difference makes the contemporary political class less representative of the broader public than the political classes of earlier generations, and (3) changes in political institutions and procedures during the past half century have magnified the importance of this new political class for determining the conduct of political life in

75

America. The result is a political process that is less responsive to the broader citizenry than it has been during much of American history. This chapter proceeds in reverse order, beginning with the third component because it suggests a puzzle to which the first and second components provide a solution.[2] My argument, however, is insufficient to account for how the distortions of representation cumulated and reinforced each other. The two chapters that follow suggest how some major social changes interacted with these institutional changes to organize the new political class in ways that increased polarization.

POLITICS THEN AND NOW

The American polity of 1930 was far closer to that of 1900 than to that of 1960.

MORTON KELLER, HISTORIAN[3]

In one specific sense this claim by historian Morton Keller is too conservative. Keller sees the history of the American polity as consisting of three regimes, with the middle one—the party regime—lasting about a century, from the 1830s to the 1930s, after which it was replaced by a populist and bureaucratic regime. I would extend Keller's argument as follows: If we could transport people through time, then technological advances aside, an American politician taken from the 1840s and plunked down in the early 1950s would find the conduct of politics more familiar than would a politician taken from the 1950s and transported into the 1980s. To be sure, political scientists and historians have documented massive changes—in the electoral, institutional, and policy realms—in the four-generation-long era of American political life that ended in the 1960s. Burnham, Brady, and others have identified three electoral realignments, which occurred in the 1850s, the 1890s and the 1930s.[4] McCormick has broken this four-generation span into two periods, (1) a "party period," extending from the administration of Andrew Jackson to that of Theodore Roosevelt, during which policy making was largely distributive and political participation widespread and enthusiastic; and (2) a more regulatory, more redistributive, and less participatory politics beginning in the second decade of the twentieth century.[5] McGerr has argued that the old nineteenth-century politics of partisan mobilization was replaced by a new politics of advertising in the first quarter of the twentieth century.[6] And Skowronek has described the development of a professional administrative apparatus between the 1870s and 1920s that replaced the old "state of courts and parties."[7]

Politics changes continually, of course, and there is no denying either the changes in electoral fortunes that altered the balance of political forces or the major changes in how government is structured, what it does, and how it does it. But my claim is more limited. As McCormick writes, "It would be misleading to exaggerate the extent of political change at the beginning of the twentieth century. Despite election laws designed to weaken party machines, the structure of party organizations remained traditional, and in the year-in-and-year-out choice of men for public office the parties yielded to no one."[8] This is my argument—that more change in the *conduct* of electoral politics (i.e., how parties and candidates constructed and maintained supporting coalitions) took place during the past generation than during the four generations that preceded it, even though those generations saw the Industrial Revolution, the growth of the United States into a world power, and two world wars. Readers whose lives do not span the old and new politics will need some explanation of this contention.

Put simply, American democracy has evolved from a more responsible form at its founding to a more participatory form today. At some risk of offending colleagues who devote their professional lives to the nuances of democratic theory, briefly consider two ideal types of democracy (see table 4.1). Call these alternative types "popular democracy" and "responsible democracy."[9] In general, the popular form is a more active form of democracy that demands more of the ordinary citizen than the responsible form. The latter incorporates a more passive notion of democracy in which citizens are more reactive than proactive (sympathizers of popular democracy sometimes refer to responsible democracy as "elite" democracy).[10] Thus, popular democ-

Table 4.1 Two models of democracy

Popular democracy	Responsible democracy
Elections express popular will	Elections grant popular consent
Elections determine policies	Elections determine leaders
Citizens vote prospectively	Citizens vote retrospectively
Direct democracy is preferred	Representative democracy is preferred
Popular participation is necessary for effective democracy	Clear accountability of leaders is necessary for effective democracy
Democratic politics should advance citizen development	Democratic politics should produce effective governance

racy regards the decisions and actions of government as legitimate only if they are expressions of the popular will, which in turn reflects active and widespread participation on the part of the citizenry. In contrast, responsible democracy contends that legitimacy requires only that governments be held accountable—that their decisions and actions receive or fail to receive popular consent, as expressed in free elections.

If government actions are to express the popular will, then citizens must offer specific guidance about what policies should be adopted and implemented—they must be knowledgeable about issues and policy alternatives. And if popular elections are to determine the policies the winners should follow, citizens must engage in prospective voting, comparing the alternative platforms the competing parties offer and choosing the one they prefer. Responsible democracy regards such requirements as unrealistic and asks only that citizens freely choose between competing cadres of leaders.[11] Moreover, responsible democracy requires only that citizens retrospectively ratify or reject what leaders have done by voting to continue them in office or to replace them with new leadership. During the 2006 congressional elections campaigns, these two notions clashed in the debate over the war in Iraq. Republicans tried to frame the election as a "choice" election, repeatedly asking: what is the Democratic policy for ending the war? Failing to hear any clear response, they asserted that there was no reason for dissatisfied voters to vote for Democrats. In opposition, Democrats tried to frame the election as a "referendum" election, replying that even if Democrats have no credible alternative policy, Republican miscalculations about the war and mismanagement of it are sufficient reason to vote them out of office. Proponents of responsible theory argue that even if newly installed leadership does nothing at all different from the previous one, by punishing an incumbent party voters send a signal to avoid mistakes in the future. (In 2006 the electorate evidently found the responsible argument more compelling.)

Popular democracy favors more direct forms of democracy—the ideal is the kind of face-to-face small-group democracy still practiced in some New England towns and still advocated by theorists of "strong" democracy and other variants of participatory democracy.[12] Theorists of responsible democracy favor representative democracy and are suspicious of more direct forms even where they are technically feasible. In addition to valuing widespread participation in order to express the popular will, advocates of popular democracy such as Rousseau and J. S. Mill also value participation because they consider it to be an important means to educate and develop citizens. Those in the responsible democracy camp value the development of good citizens, of course, but regard the purpose of politics as principally a means of governing complex societies and settling conflicts amicably.[13]

Every democratic polity embodies elements of both theoretical traditions, to be sure, but polities around the world and through history fall at different points on the continuum between the two. Probably Britain during much of the twentieth century came closest to the responsible pole, with its governments behaving almost as elected dictatorships. And, as noted above, some small New England towns continue to determine policies via lengthy meetings open to all town residents. At its founding, the American polity leaned toward the responsible pole, with the federal Constitution leaving suffrage qualifications to the states (whose constitutions and laws were quite restrictive), electing presidents and senators indirectly, and not electing judges at all.[14] But two centuries of history have seen a movement of the American political order toward greater participation—periodic extensions of the suffrage; direct election of senators; and adoption of progressive reforms, such as direct primaries, the initiative, referendum, and recall, to name a few of the more noteworthy ones. Change need not be linear or gradual, however. The old elite-dominated order of the early Republic gave way to a more participatory order with the rise of the Jacksonian Democratic Party in the late 1820s. Notwithstanding the Progressive Era, that order in turn continued relatively unchanged in many of its fundamentals until the 1960s, when the American political order experienced another sharp shift in the direction of greater participation. For a long generation now, reformers (joined by various others seeking political advantage) have steadily stripped away the insulation around political institutions and processes, leaving them far more open to popular participation and pressures than they were in the mid-twentieth century.[15] The list that follows gives some of the more important changes that have taken place during the past four decades:

- Presidential nominating process
- Candidate-centered politics
- Open meetings
- Recorded votes
- Expanded rules of standing
- Enhanced judicial review
- Open bureaucracy
- Interveners
- "Maximum feasible participation"
- Proliferation of local bodies
- Advocacy explosion
- Propositions
- Proliferation of polls
- New technologies

Some of the changes are widely recognized, but others are less so. Among the former, changes in the presidential nomination process are the best known example; indeed, we can treat this example as iconic. Since the early 1830s presidential nominations have been formally bestowed by national conventions.[16] Until the mid-1960s the stereotypical description of the process held that every four years party leaders—governors, senators, mayors, and state and local "bosses"—and followers designated by them would come together and choose the nominees. During the Progressive Era some states adopted presidential primaries, but these did not significantly alter the process. Too few delegates were chosen in them to determine the nominees. Instead, they functioned as arenas in which candidates could showcase their qualities or demonstrate their electability. Thus, Democratic Party leaders blithely ignored Sen. Estes Kefauver's (D-Tenn.) 1952 primary victories (twelve out of thirteen) and nominated Adlai Stevenson instead. In 1960 Sen. John Kennedy (D-Mass.) won seven primaries, but their importance was not in the delegates he won; rather, it was in the demonstration to party leaders that a Catholic nominee could win, even in Protestant states. As late as 1968 Vice President Hubert Humphrey received the Democratic nomination without entering a single primary.

But Sen. Barry Goldwater's (R-Ariz.) "insurgents" upset the Republican establishment in 1964 by combining primary victories with support from sympathetic party leaders. Then, when the bitterly divided 1968 Democratic convention agreed to establish a commission to study the party's nomination rules, the demise of the old order was at hand.[17] The new rules shifted the power to nominate candidates away from established party leaders and vested it in the hands of rank-and-file party members, who would express their preferences through a system of primaries and caucuses; as a result, the number of presidential primaries doubled between 1968 and 1980. Moreover, delegates chosen in primaries and caucuses now typically were "pledged" to particular candidates, not free agents or the instruments of party leaders as they previously had been. In addition, the new rules set quotas and goals for the representation of young people, racial and ethnic minorities, and, later, other minority categories.

Although such changes generally were greater on the Democratic side, the Republicans experienced similar developments, in part because their grass roots, too, wanted a more open and responsive party, and also because when state laws governing the conduct of primaries were written, they applied to both parties, and Democrats controlled most state legislatures. The rules changes were so successful in eliminating traditional party leaders from the process that from the 1984 convention onward the Democrats reserved about one-sixth of their seats for party leaders and elected officials, fearing that party professionals had become too separated from the grass roots, which were more prone to choose poorer (i.e., electorally weaker) nominees. (These "superdelegates" were the subject of much discussion during the 2008 Democratic nomination contest.)

Meanwhile, the decline of old-style local party organizations, the weakening of citizen party identifications, the advent of television campaigning, and various other factors contributed to a broader change—the development of what came to be called "candidate-centered politics." The most notable (and most studied) example was in the congressional arena, where the personal advantage of incumbency surged in the late 1960s.[18] But more generally, the old order in which a single party organization (or an encompassing interest group, such as labor) within a legal jurisdiction provided political support for a larger set of candidates associated with it was replaced by a new order in which each individual candidate built a personal organization and communicated directly with supporters. Two-step flows of influence, opinion leaders, and related concepts from the voting literature of the 1940s and 1950s largely disappeared from the literature of the 1970s and 1980s, as the influence of intermediaries in the electoral process declined.[19]

Important changes also occurred in arenas other than the electoral arena, although these are less widely recognized. A broad movement toward "government in the sunshine" resulted in widespread changes in the internal processes of governing institutions. In Congress, for example, the early 1970s saw the opening of many committee meetings to the public and a movement away from anonymous voting procedures (voice, standing, and teller voting) in favor of putting everything on the record, a development that accelerated after electronic voting was instituted.[20] Although government reformers believed that greater transparency would make it more difficult for members of Congress to conceal votes cast on behalf of special interests, they seem to have ignored the symmetric possibility that more openness made it much easier for special interests to determine whether members were actually delivering on their end of the deal. Many scholars pondered the consequences of congressional decentralization in the 1970s, but fewer reflected on the consequences of making the activities of its members so much more visible to interest groups.[21] Movement in the direction of greater openness occurred all through American democracy as open meetings, agendas published in advance, and opportunities to comment and otherwise participate increasingly became the norm.

During this same period it also became easier to get one's day in court. The Supreme Court expanded doctrines of standing, enlarging the class of interests entitled to a hearing in the courts.[22] In a similar manner, new Congressional statutes expanded the legal bases of standing. Most policy today is implemented through bureaucratic regulations, and in policy area after policy area Congress and the courts joined to shine more light on bureaucratic decision making. Congress mandated new procedures that enabled interested constituencies to learn about agency proposals and participate in agency decision processes, and the courts reinforced these requirements and became increasingly aggressive about judicial review, questioning the substance of such decisions and no longer deferring to agencies so long as their decisions were not "arbitrary and capricious." Congress even subsidized nongovernmental interveners in some cases by allowing them to collect legal fees for bringing legal challenges of agency actions. The end result of these changes is an administrative process that is far more visible and open to public participation than was the case in 1950.

At the local level, the domestic program of the "Great Society" emphasized "maximum feasible participation."[23] Old structures were bypassed in favor of new ones that empowered new groups. For a variety of reasons, local bodies of various kinds proliferated—the number of governmental jurisdictions grew from about fifty thousand in 1952 to about seventy-five thousand in 2002.[24] And most of these were subject to the kind of open government requirements mentioned above. The days when many smaller cities and towns were run by mayors and councils responsive to a few major local interests are long gone.[25]

Changes such as these occurred on what political economists refer to as the supply side of politics—the people and processes that supply public policy outputs are more exposed to popular influence today than a generation ago. But there have been important changes on the demand side as well. Most obvious and arguably most important is what Jeffrey Berry calls the "advocacy explosion"—the proliferation of interest groups in the 1960s and 1970s documented by Scholzman and Tierney, Walker, and others.[26] In the 1950s a small number of large sectoral interest groups—business, labor, agricultural, professional—worked with party and institutional leaders. Today a plethora of smaller particularistic interest groups lobby everyone—often working indirectly through the grass roots—and help to finance the campaigns that grow ever more expensive. This subject is covered in much greater detail in chapter 6.

Another demand-side change is the increasing information available to politicians. Not only do constituents have more information about what politicians do, politicians have much more information about what constituents think.[27] Younger Americans may not appreciate how recently the widespread use of polling came to American politics. But John Brehm's striking tabulation (see figure 4.1) shows the polling explosion—beginning, of course, in the 1960s.

Polling is just the most prominent example of new technologies that provide more direct links between politicians and voters. From the 1830s to the 1950s, the U.S. mail was the principal means by which the represented communicated with their representatives—when they could not speak face-to-face. Long-distance telephone was an expensive proposition for most

Figure 4.1 Media Coverage of Poll Results

The graph shows the number of stories cited under "public opinion" in the *New York Times*. According to John Brehm, the cited opinion stories "by and large report poll results, and only rarely reflections on public opinion in the broader sense."

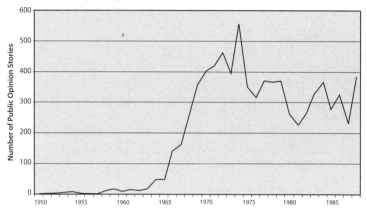

Data and quote from John Brehm, *The Phantom Respondents* (Ann Arbor: University of Michigan Press. 1993), 4.

people. But with the communications revolution came WATS lines (which made long-distance calling more affordable), fax, e-mail, and the Internet. Today citizen can contact their representatives (or at least their offices) in seconds, a far cry from the 1950s, when the time and effort to write a letter or the nontrivial expense of a long-distance phone call were required. Most attention to these developments has focused on the enhanced ability of members to contact constituents, but the new technologies work in both directions: constituents also find it much easier to contact elected officials.

Finally, to a greater extent than in the past, politically active citizens and groups now dispense with leaders and representative institutions altogether. Commentators have noted the growing use of the procedures of direct democracy—the initiative, referendum, and recall.[28] Many decry this trend, but the point here is simply that for better or for worse, it is another example of how popular pressure can increasingly make itself felt in the governmental arena.[29]

Figure 4.2 Voter turnout and trust in government

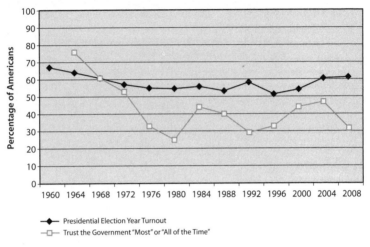

-◆- Presidential Election Year Turnout
-□- Trust the Government "Most" or "All of the Time"

Data from National Election Studies and the Federal Election Commission

The preceding list is not exhaustive, but I think it is sufficient to make the point. During the past generation many of the gatekeepers of the old political order were swept aside. The governmental process became more permeable as political institutions and processes became increasingly open to popular participation and increasingly subject to popular influence. The 1960s protesters demanded "power to the people," and apparently they got it. The great irony, then, is that after this explosion of openness and the transfer of power to the people, turnout in elections fell and trust in government plummeted (see figure 4.2). Against all natural expectations, Americans liked their government better, trusted their leaders more, and voted in higher numbers in the bad old days when party bosses chose nominees in smoke-filled rooms; when several dozen old White men (mostly Southerners) ran Congress; when it was more difficult to get a hearing in court; when legislatures, agencies, city councils, and local boards made decisions behind closed doors; when big business, big labor, and big agriculture dominated the interest group universe; and when politicians didn't have the tools to figure out what their constituents wanted. Why?

A NEW POLITICAL CLASS

No doubt the preceding ironic development has multiple causes, but as I have argued elsewhere, a significant part of the explanation for the unexpected conjunction of more open politics with a less trusting, less satisfied, and less involved citizenry is that the changes that occurred during the past generation had the unanticipated and perverse effect of making American politics less representative. Contrary to the implicit assumptions of most democratic political theorists, the typical American does not wish to devote very much of his or her free time to politics. Political theorists figuratively get tears in their eyes when reading accounts of the popular audience for the 1858 Lincoln—Douglas debates, contrasting the political engagement of the Illinois crowds with the lack of engagement today, apparently overlooking the fact that if there is no Internet, television, or radio and you spend most of your days working in the fields and taking care of animals, a day in town seeing other people and cheering on a political debate is a welcome diversion. The simple fact we must deal with is that for most people political participation is not a natural act.[30] Thus, the institutional changes described earlier that transferred power to the people had a perverse consequence: political power and influence were transferred to political activists who were not like most people. As discussed in the first two chapters of this book, the priorities of the political class are different, their points of view are more extreme, their feelings about issues are more intense, and their operating style is unappealing. When the doors to the political system were opened wider, less representative people walked through them.

Let us immediately dispense with any notion that the old order was perfect. Its imperfections and even pathologies are well known. Legislative redistricting before the 1960's "one person, one vote" Supreme Court decision made a mockery of political equality.[31] And, of course, the *citizens* who were formally represented were a smaller class than the population. In particular, women did not receive formal representation until 1920, although they received some favorable policies nonetheless.[32] And African Americans were not represented until after the old order had largely crumbled. But these glaring failures of representation that existed in the past were due largely to institutional arrangements, such as malapportionment, suffrage restrictions, and Jim Crow laws that removed any "incentive" (read, votes) for elected officials to represent particular classes of Americans. When the institutions were reformed, representation followed. Once African Americans became a significant presence in the North and began to organize and vote, northern politicians of the old order took account of their votes and responded, contrary to the common but naïve view that advances in racial equality stemmed primarily from the actions of noble judges.[33]

Here is also an appropriate place for a brief digression to make an important point. The kinds of moral and cultural issues that receive so much attention today have always been around—they are nothing new in American politics. On the contrary, the New Deal era was unusual in that such issues were largely absent, overwhelmed by broader concerns like the Depression, World War II, and the cold war. Consider that in the 1854 congressional elections, the Know Nothings (an anti-immigrant, anti-Catholic party) won forty-three seats in the U.S. House of Representatives, which corresponds to eighty seats in today's 435-member House. Conflict between the dominant Protestant culture and Catholic communities was commonplace in the nineteenth century and was still virulent as late as the 1928 presidential election (and even as late as the 1960 presidential election in some areas).[34] Nineteenth-century religious conservatives (called "pietists") were outraged by the failure of immigrant Catholics and some liberal Protestants to keep Sunday holy. Not only did they work on Sundays, they played on Sundays, they danced on Sundays, and they even drank on Sundays! Pietists, outraged by such violations of traditional values, agitated for temperance and sumptuary laws.

Or to take another example, most Americans today think of bilingual education as a modern issue. Contemporary debate often presumes that previous generations of European immigrants came to the United States, abandoned their old customs, and enthusiastically learned English. Supporters of monolingualism think that such rapid assimilation was good, supporters of multiculturalism consider it an instance of cultural oppression, but neither recognizes that the process of acculturation was far more difficult and complex than popular commentary suggests. In large sections of the Midwest, school was conducted in German. In some areas of New England, school was conducted in French. Outraged natives demanded mandatory public schooling and mandatory English language instruction.[35]

One of the reasons that facts like these are little known outside of a small fraternity of political historians is that the materially oriented parties of the old order did their best to keep divisive moral and cultural issues off the political agenda; hence, American history books do not give them the space given to issues such as free silver, the tariff, the trusts, and other old favorites. Allowing small groups of intensely committed citizens to place moral and cultural issues on the ballot often resulted in splits in political coalitions and electoral disasters. In Wisconsin, for example, the Republican Party lost only two statewide elections between 1858 and 1890. One loss came after an increase in liquor license fees, and the other came after passage of a measure requiring English language instruction in the schools.[36] In both cases German Lutherans abandoned the Republicans, giving victory to the Democrats. When the pietists finally succeeded in nominating a presidential candidate of their own—William Jennings Bryan in 1896 (and 1900 and 1908)—it led to a generation-long Republican presidential majority.

When such issues reemerged in the 1960s, however, there was little chance of keeping them off the agenda. In the political order that has developed since the 1960s, party leaders do not control the agenda in the manner that their predecessors did. Indeed, leaders of various party constituencies take the lead in placing such issues on the agenda. An important part of the explanation for why their calculations differ is that the political class that engages in politics today does not have the same motivations as the political class in the old order. The distribution of motivations has changed: material motivations are less important today than they were prior to the 1960s, and policy and ideological motivations are more important.

DECLINE OF MATERIAL MOTIVATIONS

American history textbooks associate the presidency of Andrew Jackson with the rise of the spoils system—the practice of rewarding members of the winning political coalition with government positions. Under such a system many people participate actively in politics because of material incentives—their very livelihoods depend on winning elections. Not only was politics a primary source of jobs through much of American history, but it was also a primary means to personal advancement through what was pithily referred to as "honest graft."[37] Whom you knew in politics was the key to a contract, a tip, or some other means of turning a profit. Thus, it paid—quite literally—to participate in politics and government. Despite the well-publicized Washington scandals of the 2000s, politics today is much "cleaner." As some wag once commented, conflict of interest used to be the reason people went into politics; today it is a crime.

Two important clarifications are necessary. First, no one would claim that members of the political class used to be entirely motivated by material incentives or that they now are entirely motivated by policy concerns. The suggestion is only that the balance has shifted. Material concerns are relatively less important today and policy concerns relatively more important. Second, in no way am I claiming that the material rewards allocated by government have diminished. On the contrary, they are larger than ever. Insurance companies, teachers' unions, agribusiness, energy companies, trial lawyers, and myriad other interests stand to gain or lose huge amounts of money from government actions, as suggested by their campaign contributions and their lobbying expenditures. But although the actions of government have enormous material consequences for large classes of people, those consequences are not a reason why any particular individual would individually choose to participate. Following is a list of some reasons for the declining importance of material incentives:

- Civil service
- Public sector unionization
- Universalistic policies/entitlements
- Conflict-of-interest laws
- Media (junkyard dogs)
- Changes in political culture

Civil service, of course, is the oldest and most widely recognized means of removing material incentives for political activity. Accounts of late-nineteenth-century politics attribute staggering patronage resources to the parties—tens of thousands of jobs in large states like Pennsylvania and New York.[38] And not only were patronage recipients themselves subject to political mobilization, the party organizations appropriated portions of their paychecks and expected them to help mobilize others on election day. For more than a century, however, both reformers and elected officials have extended protection from arbitrary control of public employment, for different reasons to be sure, but with predictable consequences for participation. If government clerks, toll-collectors, sanitation workers, and other "nonpolitical" employees today knew they would lose their jobs if the mayor or governor lost the next election, their levels of political participation no doubt would be much higher. Extension of civil service historically may be the largest single contributor to the removal of material incentives for political activity.

During the past generation, the accumulating effects of civil service protection were reinforced by public sector unionization. Although unionization of the total labor force in the United States has declined precipitously since its midcentury peak, public-sector unionization has waxed since the 1970s. The unionized public-sector labor force accounts for about 6 percent of the total nonagricultural labor force and almost half of the unionized labor force. Public employees, of course, participate at higher rates than others, but their activities no longer are subject to the control of party leaders. Indeed, the direction of influence has reversed in some cases: teachers unions, for example, increasingly determine who holds school board office, rather than school boards determining who holds teaching jobs.[39] Several years ago I reviewed tapes of interviews made in the mid-1970s when I conducted research in two congressional districts for an earlier project. In one interview a county chairman in a state then undergoing public employee unionization asserted that this would kill off the patronage system in his state. He said that the political parties had managed to work around civil service, but unionization would be the death knell for the patronage system. In retrospect, we can see that unionization diminished the ability of parties and public officials to mobilize public sector workers and their families. Today the members of the American Federation of State, County, and Municipal Employees, the National Education Association, and other public-sector unions depend primarily on the power of their unions to bargain for economic gains and not on the beneficence of individual public officials in the country's 86,000 jurisdictions. This is a subject that cries out for more systematic study.

Just as jobs are no longer bestowed at the pleasure of party leaders and elected officials, neither are policy outputs. If your neighborhood's garbage collection or snow removal depends on its turnout rate, turnout probably will be higher ceteris paribus than if such services are automatic, a matter of right. Scholars long have recognized the negative impact of government-provided social welfare on the urban machines.[40] This is only a special case of a broader phenomenon. When people feel that tangible public benefits depend directly on their personal actions or those of their close associates, they will be more engaged than when those benefits accrue as a matter of law or right. Whatever its positive aspects, the modern movement toward universalism and entitlements is a movement that encourages free-riding on the political engagement of others.

As various scholars have noted, the decline of old-fashioned parties organized around material rewards also is associated with a change in campaign style. Labor-intensive campaigns staffed by party workers have given way to the modern hi-tech campaign staffed by professionals.[41] The transformation has gone along with a sharp rise in the costs of campaigns, driven in large part by the costs of television. Corporations and other interest groups contribute for instrumental reasons now as they always have, but it is likely that the basis for individual campaign contributions has shifted. In the older party era, patronage workers often were dunned a portion of their salaries, recipients of contracts and other favors were expected to make reasonable kick-backs, and so forth. Such "contributions" were the price of a job or other material government benefit. Today, many fewer people are subject to such material pressures. Instead, individuals voluntarily contribute to political campaigns on the basis of the causes they believe in. And campaign contributors, like those who participate in other ways, are more extreme in their views.[42]

Finally, changes in media values and practices have helped to drive out personal material rewards as a reason for political activity. Scandals of all kinds are a staple topic of the "junkyard dog" media.[43] The media ferret out and publicize instances of conflict of interest, honest graft, and favoritism. Even where old-time temptations still exist, the potential costs of succumbing to temptation may deter potential sinners. Moreover, the media analyze motives and speculate on the presence of ulterior ones ("never assume a good motive if a bad one is available"). It often seems that the only way for a participant in politics to demonstrate credibility is to show that his political stands hurt his personal material interests.

All of the aforementioned changes probably both reflect and contribute to evolutionary change in the American political culture, an admittedly amorphous but undoubtedly significant factor in diminishing the personal, material rewards of political participation. As Mayhew noted, in what he calls "traditional party organization" states the parties rely on material rather than purposive incentives, to use Wilson's typology.[44] In such states the public sector is viewed as a large employment bureau. The cost of government is regarded as a benefit in part, because government spending provides jobs.[45] And part of the exchange is the expectation that those who benefit will participate in politics when the party calls on them. The expectations of a modern, well-educated population that thinks the public sector should provide efficient services at minimum cost conflict with the older party subculture, and this newer culture is historically ascendant. For this reason it is useless for anyone to advocate a return to the spoils system, even if one genuinely believed it to be a good idea.

If the material reasons to participate in politics diminish, why would people participate? Well, there is altruism. Some people desire to serve their fellow human beings by working for public policies that help them. Still, politics would seem to be a particularly inefficient way to satisfy one's altruistic urges. After all, one can feed the poor, adopt an orphan, minister to those suffering from AIDS in third-world countries, and engage in any number of other activities where the benefits of one's efforts are more immediately visible. So, I don't think it's overly cynical to suggest that this is not a major factor in explaining political participation, although for some people it undoubtedly is the explanation.

At the opposite end of the spectrum, a second incentive would be the desire for visibility and acclaim, a "love of fame" as Alexander Hamilton put it in *Federalist No. 72*. But again, there are other arenas of life that provide far more immediate outlets for such motivation than political participation does. In particular the insatiable demands of the entertainment industry offer publicity seekers and exhibitionists far more opportunities for visibility and acclaim. But it is likely that at least some people participate in politics from a desire to be admired by like-minded others or simply to be noticed by someone.

A third reason people participate reflects what Wilson calls "solidary" incentives. People want to belong to a group, to interact with others whom they like, to affirm valued symbols and allegiances, and so forth. Historians argue that such incentives were extremely important stimuli for political participation in the American past, although we have no direct evidence in support of that contention.[46] Clearly such incentives continue to have some importance today—those who belong to various cause groups no doubt take satisfaction in joining with others who share their concerns.

But as the material incentives for political participation declined, it seems likely that ideological and programmatic incentives took up most of the slack. More than in our earlier history, participation today reflects a desire to impose one's view of a better world on the rest of society. As Verba, Brady, and Schlozman reported, most people give policy explanations for their participation—they want to save the whales, outlaw abortion, stop global warming, starve the beast, or achieve some one of a plethora of other ends.[47] And although many people share such goals, the people who participate are those who feel most intensely about them and whose points of view are most one-sided. Again, the reemergence of social issues—racial, ethnic, religious, and cultural—in the 1960s and afterward reinforces these trends. Today the small minorities who feel most strongly about such issues have no difficulty injecting their concerns into politics.

Thus, the political class that has evolved during the past generation has a different composition from the political class that operated American politics for the preceding four generations. Its members have deeper policy commitments and are willing to accept a greater risk of political defeat in pursuit of their goals than was the traditional political class. In 1964 worldly wise political scientists and journalists chuckled at the Goldwater campaign slogan "I'd rather be right than President," but in the ensuing decades such sentiments became widespread—particularly among Democrats in the 1970s and 1980s, then among Republicans in the 1990s. Close observers maintain that in Congress, at least, members coming into the institution in the 1970s were more policy-oriented than those they replaced.[48] The traditional party organizations selected candidates on the basis of party loyalty and service—and electability if the district was competitive. But as I argue in chapter 6, as the traditional parties declined, a newer generation of candidates increasingly was recruited by or at least supported by social movements and interest groups. Thus, even if they are not personally more policy committed, newer members are more dependent on activist constituencies who compose their personal organizations and fund their campaigns.

In sum, the displacement of material incentives by programmatic and ideological ones has transformed political participation in America. People who went to meetings or worked in campaigns because their jobs depended on it were different from people who now do so out of ideological zeal. In particular, people who participated because it paid to do so probably were a reasonable cross-section of the electorate, certainly a more representative sample than self-selected participants activated by various causes. Moreover, with real economic benefits at stake, materially motivated participants naturally would be concerned to keep the benefits flowing, which gave them a strong incentive both to represent the opinions of the electorate whose decisions controlled the flow and to find acceptable compromises rather than gridlock over nonnegotiable principles.

SUMMARY

Former U.S. Representative (D-Ill.) and Federal District Judge Abner Mikva tells an anecdote about the old Chicago machine that illuminates the changes in American politics that have contributed to our present condition.[49] Then a law student at the University of Chicago, Mikva wanted to get involved in the 1948 campaigns of liberal stalwarts Paul Douglas (running for the Senate) and Adlai Stevenson (running for governor): "I was all fired up from the Students for Douglas and Stevenson and passed this storefront, the 8th Ward Regular Democratic Organization. I came in and said I wanted to help. Dead silence. 'Who sent you?' the committeeman said. I said, 'Nobody.' He said, 'We don't want nobody nobody sent.'" Today, of course, one simply goes to a campaign website and signs up. But in those days parties ran campaigns and acted as gatekeepers. Unless someone they knew, or owed, or feared sent you, your participation was not welcome.

Mikva was not easily discouraged, so he persisted: "Then he said, 'We ain't got no jobs.' I said, 'I don't want a job.' He said, 'We

don't want nobody that don't want a job.'" Here we see the notion
that material motivations are essential to the old-style party.
Unless the party controls your livelihood, they do not control you.
"The committeeman went on: "'Where are you from, anyway?'
I said, 'University of Chicago.' He said, 'We don't want nobody
from the University of Chicago in this organization.'" And here
we see the desire of an old-style party to keep out people with
the "wrong" motivations—people who will endanger the electoral prospects of the party and the positions of those in it by
emphasizing policy concerns that might lead to internal strife
and electoral defeat. At the time I read Mikva's anecdote, I had
little sympathy for the committeeman, but I now realize that he
appreciated some deep truths about politics. In most of the
country the old-style parties are gone, and it is precisely the
issue-oriented University-of-Chicago types who are active in
politics, with the consequences described in earlier chapters.[50]

More generally, several noted senior scholars of American politics have previously called attention to the changing political
class in the United States. A generation ago James Q. Wilson discussed the rising importance of the "amateurs," contrasting
them with the "professionals" who had dominated American
politics since the rise of mass parties in the 1830s.[51] A few years
later, Aaron Wildavsky wrote about "purists" who wrested the
Republican Party away from the professionals in 1964 and nominated Barry Goldwater.[52] According to Wilson, the professional
is not motivated by a grand vision of the public good. Rather,
politics is about power—winning and losing elections. Wildavsky characterized the professional similarly as one who has
"The belief in compromise and bargaining; the sense that public
policy is made in small steps rather than big leaps; the concern
with conciliating the opposition and broadening public appeal;
and the willingness to bend a little to capture public support."[53]

In contrast to the professional, the amateur, as described by
Wilson, is more interested in ideas and principles that, if followed,
advance his or her conception of the public interest. Politics is
about the considered choice of policies that reflect deeper principles, not the residue of the compromises and bargains required to

win elections.[54] Wildavsky characterized "purists similarly as rejecting compromise and discounting the importance of electoral victory relative to faithful adherence to principles."[55]

In these prescient writings from a generation ago, Wilson and Wildavsky foresaw the evolution of the political class from the more materially oriented individuals who had conducted American politics since the 1830s to the policy-oriented activists of today. Those whom they called amateurs and purists now dominate the political class. Rather than broad coalitions deeply rooted in the American social structure, today's parties are coalitions of minorities who seek to impose their views on the broader public. We no longer think of the Democrats as a cadre of political professionals leading a broad coalition of working- and middle-class Americans and Republicans as an opposing cadre centered around a smaller but still broad coalition of professionals and managers. Although it is true that unions, especially the public employee unions, continue to play an important role in the Democratic Party, as business does in the Republican Party, today we are more likely to think of the Democrats as the party of environmentalists, government employees, identity groups, pro-choice groups, and gun-control groups, whereas the Republicans are the party of evangelical Christians and of pro-life, traditional-values, anti-tax, and pro-gun groups. Issue activists of various types define the party images today.

But the question now arises: why did such changes occur, and why did they occur when they did? If the conduct of politics was relatively stable for more than a century, why did this apparent equilibrium of social and political factors begin to break down around the middle of the twentieth century? The political sphere operates within a broader social context. Thus, rapid and significant changes in the conduct of politics might well be a reflection of rapid and significant changes in that larger social context.

CHAPTER 5

SOCIAL CHANGE AND PARTY SORTING

"To a child with a hammer, all the world looks like a nail."

THE ACADEMIC ANALOGUE of this old folk-saying is that when confronted with some question or development, academics look first to their disciplinary specialties for an answer or explanation: economists look for economic explanations, sociologists for social and organizational explanations, political scientists for political and institutional explanations, and so on. No doubt reflecting that tendency, for some years I regarded the participatory turn in American politics described in the preceding chapter as, if not a sufficient cause, at least a principal cause of the contemporary disconnect between the ideologically and temperamentally moderate American public and the more extreme political class. Gradually, however, I came to believe that the participatory turn served more as a facilitating factor than a fundamental cause. By itself, replacement of an older, materially motivated political class of party professionals by a newer, more ideologically motivated political class of activists would not generate systemic polarization. Such a transformation in the composition of the political class would push individual politicians toward more extreme positions but would not account for why the political class as a whole polarized along partisan and ideological lines. By itself, the transformation of the political class could have produced the opposite effect, fracturing both parties and preventing either from presenting a coherent face to the public.

To explain, consider abortion, an issue that energizes a significant element of today's political class. Had northern Catholic and southern evangelical pro-life activists decided to pursue their goals through the Democratic Party—their traditional home— then other things being equal, the effect would have been to divide the Democratic Party. In areas where such demographic groups were large, they would pull their representatives farther to the pro-life side. Meanwhile, in districts where post-1960s-lifestyle liberalism was strong, pro-choice activists would have pulled *their* representatives farther toward the pro-choice pole. (As for Republicans, they might have maintained their traditionally moderate stance and enjoyed watching the Democrats come apart over the issue.) But rather than divide the Democrats internally, the pro-life side quickly migrated to the Republican Party and the pro-choice side to the Democrats, increasing the distance between the parties.[1]

Another example is environmentalism, an issue that burst on the national scene in 1970 when 20 million Americans took part in Earth Day activities.[2] The Republican Party had a long-standing claim—dating from the Presidency of Theodore Roosevelt—to be the conservation party. A number of the older conservation groups, such as the Audubon Society and the Sierra Club, traditionally had their roots in the Republican-friendly upper middle class.[3] Meanwhile, industrial unions were a major component of the New Deal Democratic Party, and the livelihoods of their members were threatened by proposals to clean up industries that employed them. Showing the unsettled state of public opinion on the environment, in 1972 Republican president Richard Nixon and Democratic senator (and aspiring presidential nominee) Edmund Muskie engaged in a credit-claiming battle over the Clean Air Act, hoping to capture the support of the emerging environmental movement.[4] Had environmental activists entered both parties in roughly equal numbers, the effect would have been to divide both parties on the issue. Subsequent environmental policymaking would have pitted bipartisan coalitions of supporters versus bipartisan coalitions of opponents. But in little more than a decade environmental activists had become part of the Democratic base, the image of the Republican Party had become one of anti-environmentalism, and elected party representatives are now far more polarized on environmental issues than a generation ago.[5]

One can raise an analogous question even about race, which for a generation has divided the parties so clearly. Although

New Deal and Fair Deal policies peeled off a majority of African Americans from the party of Lincoln, the racial split in presidential voting in the 1950s was about 2 or 3:1 Democratic, not the 8 or 9:1 ratio of today.[6] And despite Republican presidential nominee Barry Goldwater's vote against the 1964 Civil Rights Act in the Senate, it was southern Democrats who had oppressed their African American constituents for three generations after the Civil War, it was Republican chief justice Earl Warren who orchestrated the unanimous Supreme Court decision in *Brown v. Board of Education* in 1954, it was Republican president Dwight D. Eisenhower who sent U.S. Army paratroopers to Little Rock in 1957 to protect Black children enrolling in previously segregated schools, and it was Republican minority leader Everett Dirksen of Illinois who delivered the Republican votes that broke the southern Democratic filibuster in the Senate and allowed passage of the 1964 act.[7] In retrospect, why did some civil rights activists not choose to work through the Republican Party, reinforcing the party's traditionally moderate position and delaying or even preventing adoption of the so-called southern strategy by Richard Nixon?[8]

With the benefit of hindsight, the contemporary line-up between issues and parties often seems natural, indeed inevitable, but in each of the preceding examples the future must have looked more contingent to the participants at the time.[9] Why did the influx of myriad issue activists into politics in the 1960s and afterward not deepen the divisions *within* both parties, rather than increase the distance *between* the parties and make both of them more homogeneous internally? In other words, why did the new political class sort itself along partisan lines so quickly and distinctively?

At least part of the answer is that there were signals emanating from the larger political environment indicating that one party promised a more favorable future for a particular constituency than the other did. And I suggest that these signals were generated by social changes that had predictable political implications. In chapter 3 I discussed party sorting at the micro-level—the tendency for party identification, ideological self-classification, and issue positions to cohere more closely today than a generation ago. I said little about the causes of such a process, however. Naturally, as parties develop clearer and more distinct images, it becomes easier for individuals to notice the differences and to take cues about their own positions. But what set such a process of political clarification in motion in the first place? One obvious answer is candidates trying to win elections, and a major factor underlying their electoral calculations is social change. Macro-level developments caused micro-level changes.[10]

SOCIAL CHANGE IN MID-TWENTIETH-CENTURY AMERICA

Over the years I have come to believe that seven major social changes have significantly affected the course of American politics during the past half century or so.[11] In rough chronological order these changes are as follows:

1. The migration of African Americans from the South to the North
2. The suburbanization of the nation
3. The rise of the Sunbelt
4. The advocacy explosion
5. The revolution in the role of women
6. The resumption of immigration
7. The politicization of evangelicalism

Not all of these are equally relevant to the topic at hand, but of these seven, at least six probably are implicated to some degree in the growing disconnect in American politics that is the concern of this book. As Nelson Polsby and other scholars have previously pointed out, the exodus of African Americans from the South and the rise of the Sunbelt have relatively clear implications for the process of party sorting discussed in chapter 3.[12] In a similar manner, one can see in retrospect that the women's movement and, partly in reaction, the reentry of evangelicals into the political arena also contributed to party sorting. But less direct processes have been at work as well. In particular, I will argue that suburbanization of the country made it more difficult for contemporary politicians to communicate with constituents and build electoral coalitions, forcing them to innovate in order to take advantage of new opportunities for coalition building that social changes had put forward. The advocacy explosion and, somewhat later, the reentry of evangelicals into politics provided such new opportunities.

In the remainder of this chapter, I discuss the contributions of the African American migration, the rise of the Sunbelt, the women's movement, and the resurgence of evangelical participation to party sorting. In the next chapter I take up the more difficult task of considering how politicians adapted to the changing coalitional environment. In both chapters I am fortunate that I can build on the contributions of other scholars, although much work remains to be done.

BLACK MIGRATION AND A MORE LIBERAL DEMOCRATIC PARTY

When the Constitution was adopted African Americans constituted about one-fifth of the U.S. population, a proportion that gradually declined to about one-eighth by the late nineteenth century, where it has remained since. The regional distribution of African Americans shifted dramatically in the mid-twentieth century, however (see figure 5.1). From the birth of the republic through the first decade of the twentieth century, the proportion of African Americans living in the South, broadly defined, ranged between 90 and 93 percent.[13] As late as the 1940s the stereotypical Black American was a sharecropper in the rural South, but in the span of a generation the popular image changed to one of a tenement dweller in a large northern city. Relative to the rest of the country, the South's share of Black Americans began to decline in the early twentieth century, accelerated after World War II, and leveled off in the 1970s, by which time the South contained only a little more than half of the African American population, much of it in burgeoning southern cities rather than on farms. Most of the out-migration went to the big cities of the East and Midwest, with relatively little going to the West. In these northern cities the Black proportion

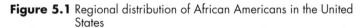

Figure 5.1 Regional distribution of African Americans in the United States

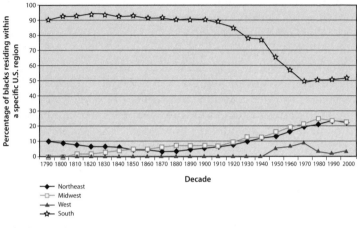

Data from the U.S. Census Bureau

of the population doubled between 1930 and 1950, then doubled again between 1950 and 1970, with cities like Chicago and Detroit showing even greater increases in African American residents (see table 5.1).

As in many migrations, this one had multiple causes, push and pull.[14] Rural poverty worsened to destitution as improvements in agricultural efficiency (especially the invention of the tractor, which could do the work of three to four men with mules) pushed tenant farmers—Whites as well as Blacks—off the land. The agricultural labor force was in long-term decline nationwide, of course, but the South felt the decline more deeply because the agricultural population was so much larger there (more than 60 percent in 1900, almost double the agricultural percentage outside the South). On the pull side, the prospect of good jobs in unionized industries surely played a major role in luring southern Blacks to the north. In addition, the social safety net was far more generous in the more affluent north than in the poorer south. And, less tangibly, while racism was certainly

Table 5.1 Black population in central cities in the 12 largest Standard Metropolitan Statistical Areas

U.S. City	1930 % of Population	1950 % of Population	1970 % of Population	2000 % of Population
New York	5	10	23	27
Los Angeles	5	10	21	38
Chicago	7	14	34	37
Philadelphia	11	18	34	44
Detroit	8	16	44	82
SF Bay Area	5	12	33	36
Boston	3	12	18	25
Pittsburgh	8	18	27	31
St Louis	12	15	41	52
Washington, DC	27	35	72	80
Cleveland	8	16	39	54
Baltimore	18	24	47	65
Total	8	14	31	45

Source: Data calculated from U.S. Census Bureau's Decennial Census data files.

present in the north, it was less virulent than the institutional-ized racism in most of the Jim Crow South.

Although the causes behind the Black migration are interesting, they are not critical for our purposes here; rather, the political consequences are. Those consequences were, in short, a more liberal and more northern Democratic Party. Secondary-school treatments of the civil rights revolution emphasize the courageous actions of Black protesters and the path-breaking decisions of judges who graduated from our elite law schools. But there were less exalted political factors at work as well. In the early New Deal period, attempts to pass civil rights and antilynching bills came to naught in a Congress where southern Democrats held enough seats to block legislative action. Regardless of how sympathetic northern members were to attempts to improve the conditions of Black Americans, they did not have the votes to win, especially in the Senate, where a southern filibuster would kill any bill. And even on a purely symbolic level northerners had little to gain politically by fighting the good fight for racial justice. Most of them had few Black constituents to reward them, and southerners, who controlled many of the committee chairman-ships, were in a position to punish any antagonists. Thus, from an electoral standpoint at least, most northern members had little upside and significant downside to working for civil rights.

By 1948, however, the political landscape was changing. With prospects for reelection looking dim, President Harry Truman recognized the importance of Black voters in compet-itive midwestern states.[15] Although his personal views about race were certainly not enlightened by modern standards, in his State of the Union message Truman called for the abolition of poll taxes, the protection of voting rights, and the establish-ment of a civil rights section in the Justice Department.[16] He issued executive orders abolishing segregation in the military and guaranteeing fair employment practices in the federal civil service. That summer, the Democratic National Convention rejected a states'-rights platform plank and adopted a strong civil rights plank, amid stirring pro-civil-rights speeches by Sen. Hubert Humphrey (D-Minn.) and others. In reaction many southern delegates bolted the party. A rump convention met in Birmingham and nominated Sen. Strom Thurmond of South Carolina for president. Running on a states'-rights ticket, Thurmond carried four deep southern states in the November elections, the beginning of a long Democratic slide in the South (table 5.2)

At the presidential level the solid South clearly passed from the scene in the 1950s as a number of southern states voted for Eisenhower, but at the congressional level the South stayed solid. The next Republican breakthrough came in the mid-1960s, by which time the Democrats had become closely associated with the ongoing civil rights movement. At the presidential level the Democrats became the minority party in the South and have remained so since, while in Congress Democratic seat con-trol slipped to about the three-quarter level. Moreover, among the remaining Democratic seats, some were held by African Americans who resembled northern Democrats far more than their conservative White predecessors, and others were held by Whites who were far more responsive to newly enfranchised

Table 5.2 Declining Strength of the Democratic Party in the South

Year	Number of Democratic Presidential States	Number of Democratic House Seats	Number of Dixiecrats
1944	11	102	–
1948	7	103	–
1952	7	103	–
1956	6	100	–
1960	7*	102	62
1964	6	95	47
1968	1	84	65
1972	0	79	66
1976	10	78	59
1980	1	78	43
1984	0	80	31
1988	0	77	26
1992	4	77	18
1996	4	56	9
2000	0	58	–
2004	0	54	–

Source: Column 1–*Congressional Quarterly Guide to U.S. Elections*; Column 2–*Vital Statistics on Congress*; Column 3–Polsby (2004).
Note: Asterisk indicates the national Democratic nominee, John Kennedy, did not carry the state.

Black constituents than their predecessors had been, a reflection of the reality of growing Black political power even in the South. Polsby calculated that old-time Dixiecrats (conservative southern Democrats) constituted only about a third of the southern Democrats by 1980 and were almost extinct by 2000 (table 5.2). Finally, the 1994 elections reduced the Democrats to congressional minority status in the South (and the country), completing the regional realignment that had begun a generation earlier.

In sum, at the end of World War II the Democratic Party was a heterogeneous party with electoral strength widely distributed geographically—northern and southern states, and urban and rural areas. It was supported by people of different ethnicities with different religious commitments—southern Protestants and northern Catholics and Jews. Its base was in interest groups with relatively little in common—southern planters and northern blue collar workers. And although individual factions of the party had identifiable ideologies, the party as a whole could not be described as an ideological party. Today, of course, much has changed. The electoral strength of the Democrats is geographically concentrated in the cosmopolitan northeast and west coast states. It is an urban party with its strongest support among racial and ethnic minorities. Seculars increasingly define the party's image as Catholics and evangelical Protestants have drifted away from the party. Interest groups popularly associated with the party—unions, environmentalists, identity groups, pro-choice groups, pro-GLBT (gay, lesbian, bisexual, and transgender) groups, and various cause groups—are generally liberal.[17] A look at the congressional leadership of the party provides a before and after picture of its transformation. In 1955 when the Democrats began their forty-year reign in the House of Representatives, the leadership was as follows:

Speaker: Sam Rayburn of Texas
Majority leader: John McCormack of Massachusetts
Majority whip: Carl Albert of Oklahoma

Hence, the House leadership consisted of one southerner, one northerner, and one border-state representative, reflecting the geographic distribution of the party's seats and the range of ideological viewpoints contained within its ranks. In the Senate, a southerner, Lyndon Johnson of Texas, was majority leader, and a border-state senator, Earle Clements of Kentucky, was majority whip. In 1994 when forty years of Democratic congressional hegemony was about to come to an end, the House leadership was as follows:

Speaker: Thomas Foley of Washington
Majority leader: Richard Gephardt of Missouri
Majority whip: David Bonier of Michigan

Thus, the leadership was composed of two northerners and a border-state representative, all liberal. In the Senate, the majority leader was a liberal northerner, George Mitchell of Maine,

and the whip was a moderate border-state senator, Wendell
Ford of Kentucky.

RISE OF THE SUNBELT AND A MORE CONSERVATIVE REPUBLICAN PARTY

In 1950 the southernmost major league baseball franchise was the
St. Louis Cardinals, and the westernmost franchise was the
Kansas City Athletics. Except in spring training no major league
games were played in Florida and Arizona. Georgia, Texas, and
California did not even have spring training games. Seven of the
twelve largest cities in 1950—six of them from the Northeast—
were no longer among the largest in 2000 (table 5.3). Of their
seven replacements, six were from the South and Southwest. In
the 1948 presidential election Kansas and West Virginia each cast
as many electoral votes (eight) as did Florida. In the 2004 elections
Florida cast two and one-half times as many electoral votes
(twenty-seven) as Kansas and West Virginia combined (eleven).

Table 5.3 The Twelve Largest U.S. Cities, Then and Now

1950	2000
New York City	New York City
Chicago	Los Angeles
Philadelphia	Chicago
Los Angeles	Houston
Detroit	Philadelphia
Baltimore	Phoenix
Cleveland	San Antonio
St. Louis	Dallas
Washington, DC	San Jose
Boston	Detroit
San Francisco	Indianapolis
Pittsburgh	Jacksonville

Source: U.S. Census Bureau. City population estimates calculated post 1950 and
        2000 censuses.
Note: City size is a function of city limit population, not the entire metropolitan region.

Such contrasts reflect the late-twentieth-century growth of the "Sunbelt," an imprecise term that some writings have extended as far north as Virginia on the East Coast and as far into the interior as Denver in the Mountain West.[18] Typically, however, the term refers to the coastal belt of states that runs from the Carolinas, through the Gulf states, around Texas, to the desert Southwest and California.

The last half of the twentieth century saw a redistribution of the American population from the older, more settled areas of the Northeast and Midwest—the "Frostbelt"—to the newer and faster-growing areas of the Sunbelt (figure 5.2). Again, a variety of factors was at work. One was federal spending, especially on defense. To some extent this made good sense—naval bases logically should be on the water, and many of the sunbelt states had coastlines. Open space and good weather made sunbelt states—especially in the Southwest—attractive locations for Air Force bases. But good old-fashioned pork barrel politics also played a significant role. At midcentury southerners dominated the committees in Congress and worked diligently to bring bases and other military installations to their districts and states.[19]

In addition to federal fiscal stimulus, the sunbelt states offered a favorable business climate—that is, low taxes and weak or nonexistent unions. (Consider that in the 1950s only about 10 percent of U.S. auto assembly plants were located in the Sunbelt, whereas the figure is approaching 45 percent today.)[20] But as Polsby argued, all of this would have come to naught but for a technological innovation—air conditioning—which made summers in the hot, humid South and hot, arid Southwest bearable; certainly it is difficult to imagine Atlanta, Houston, or Phoenix growing to their present size in the absence of air conditioning.[21] The window unit was introduced in 1951, and air conditioning spread rapidly through the South until by 1980 about three-quarters of southern households had some air conditioning. Affluent northern retirees could now think of moving permanently to the South rather than spending only their winters there. Employers could now set up new plants, and their executives could imagine managing them. Veterans who had passed through the region in World War II now could consider emigrating to take up the new

Figure 5.2 The Changing Regional Distribution of the U.S.
Population

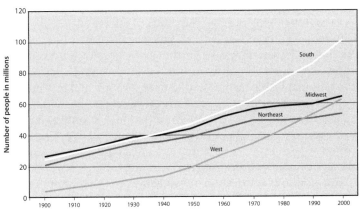

Source: Data from the U.S. Census Bureau.

jobs. The resulting population growth led to a redistribution of
political power in the United States.

In the four decades between the 1950 and 1990 censuses,
northern states lost forty-eight seats in the House of Representatives to the states of old Confederacy (nineteen seats), the
desert Southwest (seven seats), and California (twenty-two
seats). This shift of seats amounted to more than 10 percent of
the total membership of the House. Given the constitutional definition of electoral votes, the shift also resulted in a shift of forty-
eight electoral votes away from the Frostbelt to the Sunbelt.

Such shifts could have been politically neutral, of course, but
they were not. As Polsby has argued, new migrants contributed
significantly to the growth of the Republican Party in the South.
Meanwhile, the increasingly liberal stance of the national Democratic Party drove some White southern Democrats away from
their historical allegiance into the arms of a more congenial
Republican Party—in their voting behavior for the presidency,
if not always in their voting behavior for lower offices or in their
profession of party allegiance.[22] Democratic support among
White southerners, especially men, plummeted between 1960

and 1980 as new cohorts of voters increasingly declined to identify as Democrats.[23] Finally, as noted above, the elections of 1994 made the Republicans the majority party in the South.

Elsewhere in the Sunbelt the political effects were somewhat different. The brand of cultural conservatism that flowered in the South had less appeal in the more libertarian mountain states and desert Southwest, but the increasing association of the national Democratic Party with environmental and antidevelopment constituencies was unpopular in the wide open spaces. The social conservatism of the new Republican party had even less appeal in California, which shifted its political hue from red to blue as the state party increasingly nominated candidates out of the California mainstream.[24]

But all things considered, the net effect of the shift of population from the Frostbelt to the Sunbelt benefited the Republicans and left both parties more homogeneous than they had been at midcentury. As African Americans in the South gained political influence, the surviving congressional Democrats became more liberal—more like their northern colleagues. And majority—minority districting enabled African Americans to win more seats in the South. With a few exceptions these members tended to be liberal. Meanwhile, the drift of conservative White southerners to the Republican Party removed a dissident element from the Democratic Party and reinforced the growing conservatism of the Republicans. Prior to the 1994 elections, the Republicans had last controlled Congress in 1953–54. Their House leadership then was as follows:

Speaker: Joseph Martin of Massachusetts
Majority leader: Charles Halleck of Indiana
Majority whip: Leslie Arends of Illinois

Hence, a northeasterner and two midwesterners comprised the House leadership. In the Senate the majority leader was Robert Taft of Ohio, and the majority whip was Leverett Saltonstall of Massachusetts, a midwesterner and a northeasterner.[25]

After the 1994 elections when the Republicans reemerged from forty years of wandering in the minority wilderness, they elected the following members as House leaders:

Speaker: Newt Gingrich of Georgia
Majority leader: Richard Armey of Texas
Majority whip: Thomas DeLay of Texas

So all three House leaders were southerners. In the Senate, Trent Lott of Mississippi (formerly the legislative assistant to Dixiecrat William Colmer) became majority leader, and a border-state senator, Donald Nickles of Oklahoma, became majority whip.

1960s SOCIAL MOVEMENTS

Soon after the civil rights movement achieved its greatest legislative successes in the form of the 1964 Civil Rights Act and 1965 Voting Rights Act, a variety of other social movements appeared on the scene coincident with the baby boom generation leaving home and going off to congregate in the nation's colleges and universities.[26] The escalation of the war in Vietnam gave birth to the peace movement, which disrupted the 1968 Democratic National Convention and generally convulsed American politics during the late 1960s and early 1970s. In 1961 President John F. Kennedy issued Executive Order 10980, establishing the President's Commission on the Status of Women. Two years later Betty Friedan wrote *The Feminine Mystique*, challenging 1950s notions of a woman's place in the ideal family.[27] Three years later Friedan became the first president of the newly established National Organization for Women (NOW), the spearhead of the new women's movement. Numerous other less politically focused (and less serious) groups, such as the hippies and yippies, also emerged. Members of these movements overlapped somewhat—especially in the minds of those offended by their appearance and behavior—and collectively they came to be known as the "counterculture."

With the end of the war in Vietnam, the peace movement faded from the scene, and most members of the various self-expression groups of the counterculture gradually grew up and took their place in mainstream society (although they clearly left an imprint on societal attitudes toward sexual behavior and drug use). The women's movement persisted, however. Congress passed an Equal Rights Amendment (ERA) in 1972 and

submitted it to the states for ratification. Twenty-two states ratified it quickly, but in the end the campaign failed as only thirty-
five states ratified it—three short of the thirty-eight states
needed to constitute a three-fourths majority.[28]

The U.S. Supreme Court meanwhile administered what
social scientists call an "exogenous shock" to the system in the
form of the *Roe v. Wade* decision in 1973. It was not truly exogenous, of course, in that the new women's movement must
surely have entered the consciousness of the justices who constituted the majority in the decision, but few anticipated such a
sweeping judicial pronouncement, especially one that short-
circuited an ongoing political process in many state legislatures. Within a few years a backlash in the form of the pro-life
movement had emerged, and the now familiar battle between
the two sides was joined.[29]

By the mid-1960s the Democratic Party was closely associated
with the civil rights movement, and although the peace movement mobilized against a Democratic administration, politicians who offered themselves as leaders of the peace movement,
such as Eugene McCarthy and George McGovern, emerged
from the Democratic Party rather than the Republican Party. The
behavior of the various parts of the counterculture badly split
the Democrats but clearly was more acceptable in some Democratic circles than in most Republican circles. In a similar manner, although the Republican Party had traditionally supported
an ERA, the women's movement quickly became a close associate of the Democratic Party.

EVANGELICAL REACTION—RELIGIOUS REPUBLICANS AND SECULAR DEMOCRATS

When born-again Christian and Sunday school teacher Jimmy
Carter defeated mainline Protestant Gerald Ford in the 1976
presidential election, surveys showed only a weak relationship
between the votes Americans cast and their church-going practices. According to the NES, Carter received 41 percent of the
vote among Whites who said they went to church weekly or
more often compared with 48 percent of those who reported

Figure 5.3 Relationship between church attendance and presidential vote

Numbers represent the difference in percentage of votes for the Democratic candidate (in two-party vote) between regular church attenders and nonattenders (for white voters only)

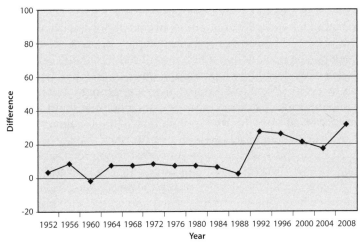

Data from National Election Studies.

attending services rarely or never, a difference of only 7 percent. In contrast, twenty years later when mainline Protestant Robert Dole lost to born-again Christian Bill Clinton, there was a much stronger relationship between voters' church-going behavior and their presidential vote. According to the 1996 NES, Clinton received the votes of only 38 percent of Whites who reported going to church weekly or more often compared with 63 percent among those who reported going to church rarely or never, a difference of 25 percent. The oft-noted contemporary relationship between church-going habits and presidential vote actually emerged quite suddenly between the 1988 and 1992 elections (figure 5.3), but the reemergence of a religious dimension in national politics was building over a longer period.[30]

In 1966 the cover of *Time* magazine posed the question "Is God Dead?[31] The provocative cover article reflected the secularization hypothesis that was then widely accepted among academics and intellectuals, which held that as societies modernized, traditional religion inevitably would fade away. Geographic and social mobility would break down the primary group attachments that reinforced traditional religion, and education—especially science education—would provide superior explanations of worldly phenomena. As belief in a traditional God disappeared and modern societies became more secular, people would construct their own personal, more humanistic moral codes to guide behavior.

The next decade was not kind to the secularization hypothesis, except in Western Europe, where it appears to describe the contemporary condition where great cathedrals stand largely empty except for elderly worshippers.[32] In the United States, however, the 1980 elections seemed to indicate that not only was God alive and well, but even more disturbing for Democrats, she apparently favored Republicans. In 1979 the Reverend Jerry Falwell founded the Moral Majority, the first of the so-called religious right or Christian right organizations, and such evangelical groups made their entry into modern politics in the 1980 elections.[33] When Ronald Reagan defeated Jimmy Carter, he carried ten of the eleven states of the old Confederacy, plus Kentucky and Missouri—Carter's 1976 performance in the mirror. In addition, the Republicans captured the Senate with a twelve-seat gain and achieved a conservative majority in the House with a thirty-seat gain. Religious right groups were quick to claim credit for this sharp turnabout in the political balance.[34] And although disagreement about their precise impact on election outcomes periodically flares, there can be no doubt that the religious right has been an important element of American politics for nearly three decades, with most observers considering it to be one the most important components of the Republican base. Informal estimates are that the religious right is moderately to highly influential in well over half the Republican state party organizations.[35]

Between the zenith of the "God is dead" movement and the present, traditional religion obviously has staged something of a comeback in the United States, although the data suggest something more complicated than a simple decline and resurgence of religion. The mainline Protestant denominations have continued to show the decline that may have stimulated some of the "God is dead" discussion a generation ago. The growth rate of Catholics, partly attributable to the influx of Latino immigrants (another of the social changes listed at the beginning of this chapter), has been sufficient to keep that denomination steady at about a quarter of the population. The big gainers have been the various evangelical churches and sects as well as Mormons. Popular accounts, especially those penned by unsympathetic secular writers, often conflate evangelicals and fundamentalists, but a belief in Biblical inerrancy is not a principal component of evangelicalism. Rather, a personal experience with Jesus Christ (the experience of being born again) is the critical component. So defined, surveys typically report that the proportion of evangelicals falls in the 30–40 percent range (figure 5.4), although for a number of reasons, those figures are overestimates.[36] Interestingly, Gallup data show a relatively constant level of "born again" Christians during the past three decades. Apparently, God was never as close to death as the intellectuals claimed.[37]

Standard treatments recount that evangelicals generally eschewed political activity after suffering major defeats on the issues of evolution and prohibition in the early twentieth century. For a half century evangelical leaders focused on individual salvation and the life of the spirit rather than on saving the temporal world.[38] But developments in that world provoked their reengagement in politics. In 1962 the U.S. Supreme Court banned school prayer in *Engel v. Vitale*, a decision that was unpopular, to say the least. The coming of age of the baby boom generation in the 1960s produced cultural ferment that challenged traditional notions of sexual morality and led to greater acceptance of drug use and, still later, of homosexuality. The year 1973 brought *Roe v. Wade* and the right-to-life movement. The feminist movement in general and the battle over the ERA in particular threatened traditional notions of the family. Militant seculars and the courts fueled a growing perception that religion was being banished from public life. And the popular culture increasingly explored territory heretofore reserved for adult bookstores and movie

Figure 5.4 Evangelical Americans

"Evangelical" defined by a "yes" answer to the question, "Would you say that you have been born-again or had a born-again experience—that is a turning point in your life when you committed yourself to Jesus Christ?"

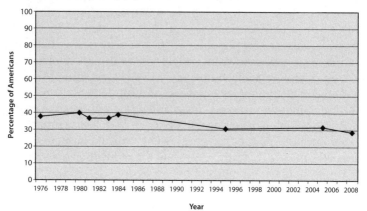

Data from the Gallup Organization

theaters. In reaction to such developments, evangelical leaders called on their followers to reengage in secular life and fight back against its threats to their beliefs and, ultimately, their salvation.

At midcentury most evangelicals were Democrats—a by-product of the historic allegiance of the South, where most evangelicals happened to live. With a base that included northern Catholics and southern evangelicals, the Democratic Party could be described as liberal economically but not culturally. This situation persisted for some decades even though educated, upper-middle-class Democratic activists from the civil rights and anti-war movements were the avant-garde of the American cultural revolution. Indeed, when the abortion issue first became prominent, rank-and-file Democrats were as likely as Republicans to express more conservative positions—as pointed out in chapter 2, it was not until the early 1990s that Democrats consistently began to look more pro-choice than Republicans. Some of this sorting out undoubtedly reflected the movement of evangelicals from Democratic to Republican

Figure 5.5 Party Sorting of Americans on Religiosity

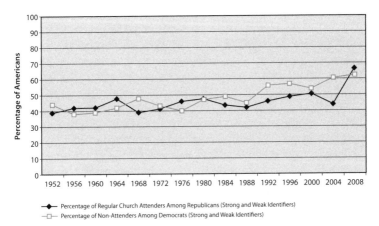

— ◆ — Percentage of Regular Church Attenders Among Republicans (Strong and Weak Identifiers)
— □ — Percentage of Non-Attenders Among Democrats (Strong and Weak Identifiers)

Data from National Election Studies and are for white voters only. Definition of "church attender" and "nonattender" are from Fiorina, Abrams and Pope, 2006.

allegiance, leaving Catholics as a culturally conservative minority in the Democratic Party.

Political actions often stimulate opposite, if not equal, reactions. And as figure 5.5 shows, the increasing representation of religious Americans in the Republican Party was mirrored by an increasing representation of less religious Americans in the Democratic Party, with the divergence becoming apparent between 1988 and 1992. As is usual, sorting within the political class was underway some years before sorting within the larger population began—there is evidence of divergence after 1980 for some high-level members of the political class (compare figure 5.6 on national convention delegates with figure 5.5 on ordinary Americans).

Throughout the 1980s the religious cleavage was developing, but when Democratic candidates were the children of Methodist ministers (Walter Mondale in 1984) or personally conservative Greek Orthodox worshippers (Michael Dukakis in 1988), the religious divide was muted. When Bill Clinton appeared on the

Figure 5.6 Religiosity of national convention delegates: Percentage of Republican delegates who identify as evangerlicals and Democratic delegates who identify as secular

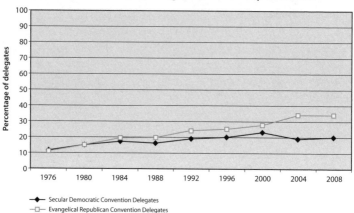

— ◆ — Secular Democratic Convention Delegates
— ☐ — Evangelical Republican Convention Delegates

Data from the Voter News Services and Convention Delegate Polls.

national scene in 1992 the cleavage opened wide, and when the Republicans in 2000 nominated a former sinner who had seen the light and found God, the divide became a major element of contemporary politics.

SUMMARY

In chapter 3 I discussed party sorting at the microlevel, using individual-level data from surveys to describe the increasing internal homogeneity of the two parties. In this chapter I have discussed party sorting at the macrolevel. A natural question is how much of the sorting among individuals reflects the social changes discussed here: the population movements of African Americans from the South to the North, the movement of White Americans from the North to the South, and the reorientation of the two parties along a morality/religious axis? There is some research indicating that these macromovements account for a significant portion of the microsorting. For example, the North—South geographical realignment accounts for roughly one-third of the observed polarization of the congressional parties.[39] Still, within a census region or within a particular state or other jurisdiction, increasing polarization cannot be explained by population movements from south to north and vice-versa.[40] Migration among smaller jurisdictions occurs of course, but we can think of no persuasive reason why they would all result in increased sorting rather than partly offset.[41] Religious sorting has more potential to explain political sorting within smaller jurisdictions, but there are broad areas of the country where the religious right is weak and polarization still reigns. Thus, I think other factors are at work as well, factors whose operation is more difficult to trace than the effects of the Black migration, the growth of the Sunbelt, the American cultural revolution, and the resurgence of evangelical religion.

As for the larger question of how the disconnect between the political class and the larger electorate has developed, clearly party sorting plays a major role. Although issue and ideological sorting among ordinary voters remains far from complete, as shown in chapter 3, the most knowledgeable members of the electorate are far better sorted than the average voter, and more knowledgeable, more interested people are most active in politics.[42] In particular, the primary constituencies of representatives have become increasingly homogeneous—more liberal for Democrats everywhere, more conservative for Republicans everywhere. And in the era of candidate-centered politics that prevailed in the late twentieth century, elected officials became increasingly dependent on those homogeneous bases.

CHAPTER 6

SUBURBS, NEW INTEREST GROUPS, AND POLITICAL ADAPTATION

IN 1962 THE U.S. SUPREME COURT decided *Baker v. Carr*, the first of a series of cases that came to be known as the "one person, one vote" decisions.[1] The case came from Tennessee where the legislature had not redistricted since 1901, despite significant population shifts in the intervening half-century. Ignoring Justice Frankfurter's long-standing injunction to stay out of the "political thicket," the Court held in *Baker* that the malapportionment of state legislatures was a justiciable question, not (as previously held) a "political" question beyond the reach of the courts. In 1964 the Supreme Court decided *Reynolds v. Sims*, holding that the equal protection clause of the 14th Amendment required districts of equal population in both houses of state legislatures (at the time many state constitutions mimicked the federal constitution by allotting equal numbers of senators to counties, or otherwise basing upper chamber representation on government units rather than population.)[2] Earlier in 1964 the Court had extended the one person, one vote requirement to the U.S. House of Representatives in *Wesberry v. Sanders,* although that decision was based on Article 1 of the Constitution rather than the 14th Amendment.[3] In the ensuing years legislative districts of precisely equal population became the Holy Grail of redistricters, trumping traditional criteria such as contiguity, compactness, and preservation of natural communities.[4]

The intervention by the Supreme Court was a classic "shock" to the existing system of representation. Within the span of a very few years in the mid-1960s, most states were forced to redistrict one or more times. Many academics and political observers expected a significant partisan consequence from what often was described as the "orgy of redistricting." After all, conventional wisdom held that rural areas (read "Republican" outside the South) had been vastly overrepresented under existing districting plans; now, urban areas (read "Democratic") would get their due. The expected influx of urban Democratic state legislators, in turn, would produce higher spending in general and more liberal social welfare policies in particular. However plausible such expectations seemed at the time, in the years following the reapportionment revolution an accumulation of academic research found that both the partisan and policy consequences of the revolution were minimal.[5]

A few scholars reached the discouraging conclusion that "politics doesn't matter" for determining public policies—the negative results for redistricting were consistent with earlier studies that concluded that state socioeconomic, not political, characteristics determined their public policies.[6] Methodological problems in such studies, however, led most scholars to discount them. A more plausible explanation for the surprising failure of the reapportionment revolution to work a major transformation of American politics was a previously underappreciated social change—the rapid increase in suburbanization of the country. The urban era already had peaked, the argument went, so the suburbs had been the major beneficiaries of the shift to fairer representation.[7] As figure 6.1 shows, at the time of the reapportionment cases the American population was roughly evenly divided into central city, suburban, and nonmetropolitan (i.e., small-town and rural) areas, and suburban areas were growing the fastest. Thus, much of the representation lost to rural Republican areas had gone to suburban Republican areas rather than to Democratic central cities as anticipated, so the partisan and policy consequences largely offset one another.[8]

The shift of representation to the suburbs is clearly apparent in the changing composition of congressional districts (table 6.1). At the time of *Wesberry v. Sanders*, about 40 percent of the districts created in 1962 under the old rules contained a preponderance of people who lived in nonmetropolitan areas.[9] A decade later the first national redistricting under the new rules found nonmetropolitan areas with about fifty fewer districts

Figure 6.1 The Growth of Suburbia as a Percentage of the U.S.
Population

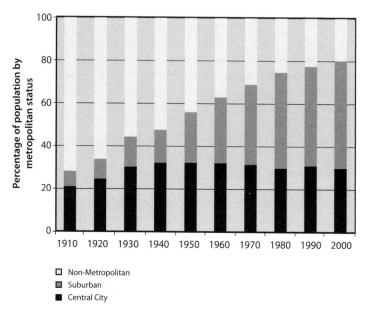

□ Non-Metropolitan
▨ Suburban
■ Central City

Data from U.S. Census Bureau Decennial Census of Population

than ten years earlier, but more than three-quarters of those districts had migrated to suburban areas and only a few to urban
areas. In the ensuing decades the number of rural and small-
town districts plummeted; the number of urban districts
declined, although not as much; and freed of traditional requirements that districts be compact, composed of natural communities, or respectful of jurisdictional boundaries, redistricters
created many more districts that contained mixtures of urban,
suburban, and nonmetropolitan populations.

Suburbanization is a long-running process in the United
States but one that accelerated after World War II. Suburbanization and the rise of the Sunbelt are related, of course. Sunbelt
cities often are referred to as suburban cities (the most rapidly

Table 6.1 Growing Political Power in the Suburbs: Number of U.S. House Districts from 1962 to 1992

Metropolitan status	1962	1972	1992	% Change from 1962 to 1992
Metropolitan districts	254	305	378	49
Central City	106	109	67	-37
Suburban	92	132	160	74
Mixed Metropolitan	56	64	151	170
Rural Districts	181	130	57	-69

Source: Richard Lehne, "The Suburban Seventies," *Annals of the American Academy of Political and Social Science* 422 (1975): 141–51; *Congressional Quarterly*; U.S. Census Bureau, and the Congressional Research Service.

growing ones—especially in the Southwest—have been characterized as "boomburbs").[10] But suburbanization began outside the Sunbelt, although it has flourished there. As with the social changes discussed in the preceding chapter, a variety of factors encouraged suburbanization, and public policies were among the most important. One factor that facilitated suburban development was improvements in transportation. Historically, the limits to how far non-farm families could live from their places of work were set by the time it took to walk, ride a trolley or train, or drive from home to workplace. Although technological advances undoubtedly would have facilitated longer commutes in any case, the National Interstate and Defense Highways Act of 1956 made possible the building of the interstate highway system and the beltways and bypasses taken for granted by American commuters today.

But bedroom communities would not have proliferated so quickly were it not for an earlier set of public policies. The Federal Housing Act of 1934 led to the adoption of uniform building standards and the provision of mortgage insurance, reducing the risk facing lenders. Lower risk, in turn, led to lower down payments, lower mortgage rates, and lower monthly payments, making homeownership more affordable to a higher proportion of Americans. Federal programs under the act emphasized construction of single-family homes and were less generous in subsidizing rehabilitation of existing housing, thus encouraging new suburban development at the expense of existing urban housing.[11]

In 1944 Congress anticipated a severe postwar housing shortage. Despite the FHA, there had been little home construction during the Depression and World War II, and the return of hundreds of thousands of veterans was imminent. The response was the Veterans Administration Housing Program as part of the GI Bill, which extended loan guarantees to mortgages taken out by veterans. The cumulative product of these federal housing programs was rapid expansion of new home construction. Levittown, on Long Island, was a planned community of 17,000 homes. "Cheaper than renting," buyers could purchase a house for $7,000—$10,000 and no money down, with the whole process of home-buying taking about one hour.[12] Other instant suburbs soon followed.

The onrush of suburbanization certainly did not go unnoticed, and in the 1950s popular commentators warned of a variety of negative consequences: suburbanization would weaken the extended family as children moved away from parents and each other; suburbs were unfriendly to stay-at-home wives cut off from the denser social networks of urban neighborhoods; homogeneous middle-class suburbs produced stifling pressure for conformity; suburban development diverted badly needed human and economic resources from the problems of the cities; and, later, suburban sprawl contributed to a variety of environmental problems. But in the 1960s, academic research debunked much of the earlier popular commentary.[13] Of course, despite the laments of academics and intellectuals Americans continued to vote with their wallets and move to the 'burbs. By the 1990s an absolute majority of the American population was suburban, and commentators could proclaim the beginning of the "suburban century."[14]

Politicians, pundits, and political scientists all hypothesized political impacts of suburbanization. In particular, as upwardly mobile young workers migrated from the older, Democratic cities to the newer, Republican suburbs, would their partisan allegiances and voting behavior follow their social and residential moves? Such arguments were in vogue during the 1960s, and the election of Republican Dwight Eisenhower after five consecutive Democratic presidential victories provided circumstantial evidence that suburbanization was strengthening the Republican Party; however, a major election study of the time found scant support for suburban political conversions.[15] Indeed, until quite recently, studies have concluded that after controlling for the standard social and economic characteristics, Americans who live in suburbs do not differ from those with similar characteristics who live in cities or rural areas.[16]

SUBURBANIZATION AND REPRESENTATIONAL CHALLENGES

Even if suburbanization did not directly produce large-scale partisan and policy consequences, suburbanization may have had less-noticed, indirect, but consequential impacts on American politics. In particular, politicians representing suburban areas had to cope with rapid population change and learn how to represent constituencies that were not self-contained natural communities like the small towns and bounded cities that had formed the cores of legislative districts throughout most of American history. Views from the trenches are suggestive.

In his 1993 Rothbaum lectures, Richard F. Fenno, Jr., discussed his travels with U.S. senators in the late 1970s through the 1980s as they campaigned in their states.[17] Earlier Fenno had conducted a less campaign-centered study of U.S. representatives, observing their activities and studying their constituency relations while accompanying eighteen of them as they traveled about their districts between 1970 and 1977.[18] Rereading his account today, one finds suggestive observations by members whose districts were undergoing suburbanization or who were redistricted into new suburban areas. Following is Fenno's description of Congressman M.:

> Congressman M had established a person-to-person home style in his rural, small-town district when he was redistricted into unknown territory—suburbia. For three and a half hours, we drove around, "exploring" the new suburban segment. A primary

opponent had emerged from the area; and we set out first to find his home. We drove up and down his street several times. . . . For a man who campaigned comfortably along the main streets of little towns, the amorphous suburban area was puzzling.

"How would you campaign in this kind of district? It's going to be an entirely different kind of campaign for me. It's going to be hard to reach. You can't do it by TV, because you reach such a small part of the market you pay for. So economics rules that out. And there's no focal point of interest, no incorporated areas."

Reference points were hard to find. As we wandered about the busy area, he grew frustrated. "We've been exploring the new district for one hour and we haven't seen one person yet." We had "seen" thousands of people. But he had no idea how to make contact with them. He had not stopped to shake hands and chat with them as he would have done in "the old part of the district."

We drove into the parking lot of a large, modern shopping mall and rode up and down along the store fronts, sizing up this strange terrain. Again, Congressman M was baffled by its stylistic implications.

To my way of thinking, campaigning in shopping centers is a complete and total waste of time. I may be wrong, but I believe that when people are shopping, they don't want to be interrupted by someone handing out political literature.[19]

Unlike Congressman M., Congressman C. had not been redistricted into suburbia—he had lived in the district all his life and experienced the changes. However,

"There is about a 30 percent turnover in bodies every two years—even though the type of bodies remains the same . . . [It's] a game of musical houses." Furthermore within each household, there is constant motion. "My district is a typical suburban district in a frenzy. Suzie has to be taken to her piano lesson, mom has to sing in the choir, dad's on a business trip." This hypermobility renders even the census bureau statistics suspect. Besides the one-third turnover, "there's a lot of double job holding. And they go bowling at night, fishing on the weekends. So, nobody's home most of the time." . . . Congressman C's greatest strategic problem is not how to present himself. It is how to find people to present himself to.[20]

Another member "representing a fast growing area of suburban sprawl" faced a similar problem: "It's a mystery to me. I go there and all I see are row after row of mobile homes and apartment houses. It's just a collection of shopping centers. . . . It's not a community. They have no rotary clubs or groups like that. It's just a bunch of houses. . . . I don't know how you would campaign there."[21]

Fenno's Congressman L. identified another problem with suburbs. Previously he had "an urban district whose city had lost population," and he had received "compensating suburban territory" in the recent redistricting.

And that change, after many years, had made him uneasy about constituency relationship. He did not feel at home in the suburbs. "My old district was easier to run in. I don't feel comfortable in suburbia. They have so many local jealousies and rivalries. I wasn't prepared for their pettiness and petulance, for the dozen different city councils and all those government districts of one kind or another. I'm used to dealing with a city. It has problems, but if you have reasonable solution to those problems, people listen to you and you can accomplish something. Not in suburbia."[22]

Here is an interesting reference to the representational problems created by the proliferation of governmental jurisdictions discussed in chapter 4. Overlapping and competing jurisdictions created problems for a representative that he did not have when representing one urban jurisdiction.

Generalizing from these suggestive examples, it is likely that many elected officials in the United States faced new challenges in the 1960s and 1970s. Whereas they had once represented relatively stable districts centered around a single city or composed of a number of small towns, they now represented districts that were changing more rapidly, districts that cut across natural communities, and districts whose population centers were not communities in the sense they understood. Given changes like these, the old ways of representing constituents were increasingly outmoded. Representatives had to adapt, and those who did not adapt successfully were replaced by others who were better suited to the new conditions.

What sort of adaptation did representatives make? Fenno's Congressman O. (not a suburban representative) provides a hint: "The people in the peace movement are probably my very strongest supporters. Don't forget, I was one of the first congressmen to come out against the war. To the peace people, I'm a semihero. We went through hard times together when being against the war wasn't popular, and they worked very hard for me. . . . There probably aren't more than 100 of them in all, scattered around the district. But 100 activists can do a lot."[23]

TRANSFORMATION OF ASSOCIATIONAL LIFE

Two decades after one of Fenno's suburban congressmen complained about the absence of Rotary clubs where he could make contact with constituents, Robert Putnam observed that not only were Rotary clubs disappearing but so were the Kiwanis, Knights of Columbus, Masons, Odd Fellows, Shriners, Elks, Lions, parent teacher associations, Granges, 4-H clubs, and numerous other organizations that were prominent in the mid-twentieth-century landscape.[24] Moreover, although the declines were most pronounced in the larger urban concentrations and suburbs, small-town and rural areas showed declines as well. Putnam's findings indicated that it wasn't only suburban representatives who faced new challenges in representing their constituents—representatives all over America faced similar challenges, even if to a lesser degree.

Some observers responded critically to Putnam's findings, noting that he focused on groups that existed at midcentury and declined thereafter but ignored myriad other groups that formed after midcentury.[25] After all, as noted in chapter 4, there was an advocacy explosion during the 1960s and 1970s, when in Jeffrey Berry's words, "interest group activity skyrocketed."[26] Recent research by Schlozman and Burch shows that the skyrocketing did not cease in 1980. On the contrary, in the past two decades the number of explicitly political groups—those listed in the *Washington Representatives* directory—increased by 75 percent (table 6.2).[27] At first glance such data support the assertions of some of Putnam's critics: in sheer numbers new associations have more than replaced the declining ones that Putnam identified. But Putnam has countered that

Table 6.2 The Advocacy Explosion: 1981–2001

Type of Group	Number in 2001	Increase from 1981 to 2001
Corporations	4075	1004
Trade and Other Business	1548	506
Occupational Associations	786	249
Unions	113	6
Education	486	383
Health	409	349
Public Interest	537	279
Racial/Ethnic/Religious	369	230
Youth	67	43
Elderly	28	17
Women	45	15
Sexual Orientation-GLBT	7	6
Social Welfare or Poor	93	61
State and Local Government	1211	877
Foreign	901	314
Farm	125	55
Veterans	36	16
Disabled and Health Advocacy	159	136
Party, PAC and Candidate	70	59
Cooperatives	42	29
Men	1	1
Recreational	37	12
Arts/Cultural	128	103
Charity/Philanthropy	45	34
Think Tanks/Non-Profit Research	152	103
Other/Don't Know	196	100

Source: Kay Lehman Schlozman and Traci Burch, "Political Voice in an Age of Equality," in Robert Faulkner and Susan Shell, eds., *America at Risk: The Great Dangers* (Ann Arbor: University of Michigan Press, 2008).

many if not most of the new organizations are not membership groups in the traditional sense; rather, they are "checkbook groups," whose members are no more than a mailing list of people who receive communications from central headquarters and respond by sending checks. They do not interact face to face and participate in group activities like the members of the organizations that have declined. Indeed, Putnam has suggested that the "members" of such groups are more accurately called "donors" or "supporters."[28]

Theda Skocpol made this distinction between the older declining groups and associations and the newer ascendant ones a central element of the argument in her 1999 Rothbaum lectures, contending that the United States has experienced a transformation of associational life, "a reorganization of national civic life."[29] Skocpol has asserted that "U.S. civic life has been extraordinarily transformed. Where once cross-class voluntary federations held sway, national public life is now dominated by professionally managed advocacy groups without chapters or members. And at the state and local levels 'voluntary groups' are, more often than not, non-profit institutions through which paid employees deliver services and coordinate occasional volunteer projects."[30] Significantly, Skocpol's dating of the era of mass membership, chapter-based national federations roughly parallels the four-generation span of the old political order discussed in chapter 4—the 1830s through the 1950s, with a rapid decline after the 1960s.[31] This dating is probably more than coincidental, because, as she argues, civic organizers and politicians of the period had a similar goal: "Both party builders and association builders sought to mobilize a democratic citizenry."[32] When this goal changed in the late 1960s, so did both the political and associational orders.

The new associations and organizations that made up the advocacy explosion have three general characteristics that differ from many of the associations they supplanted. First, as noted above, Putnam and Skocpol have emphasized that in many cases the new associations are memberless.[33] They do not have local chapters where members pay dues, attend meetings, elect officers, and participate in organizational activities. Rather, they are often "letterhead groups," with a visible leadership cadre that relies on mass appeals to pay their salaries and support their activities.

Second, the associations established in recent decades are in most cases narrower in their foci than the associations that have declined. "Because . . . [pre-1960s membership federations] aimed for massive dues-paying memberships as a route to national influence, classic associations had an incentive to espouse broad values and speak to encompassing constituencies."[34] But old-line associations like the American Farm Bureau were joined by the National Corn Growers Association, the Rocky Mountain Llama and Alpaca Association, the National Cricket Growers' Association, and numerous others. The U.S. Chamber of Commerce was joined by the National Tank Truck Conference, the Frozen Food Institute, the Greyhound Track Operators, the Council of Korean Travel Agents, and numerous others. Narrowly focused nonprofit and public-sector groups proliferated: the U.S. Police Canine Association, the Association of State Drinking Water Administrators, the National Association of State Alcohol and Drug Abuse Directors, the National Association of Student Financial Aid Administrators, and numerous others. New interests were discovered: the Children's Defense Fund, the American Association of Retired Persons, and the National Alliance to End Homelessness. And, perhaps most important for our concerns, the social movements of the 1960s spun off numerous cause groups—peace, racial, environmental, feminist, consumer—all manner of groups focused on particular, mostly liberal, causes, which in turn provoked conservative cause groups to form to oppose them. In sum, after the advocacy explosion what had previously been called special or particularistic interests became even more special and particularistic. Indeed, the term "single-issue group" came into widespread use during this period, in recognition of the narrow focus of many of the new groups.

A third characteristic of many of the associations that have organized in the past generation is that they do not cut across social and economic strata to the same extent that the declining organizations did. Rather, they are more upscale, directing their appeals to the relatively affluent upper middle class. If all the leaders of a group want from their members are checks, then it makes sense to go hunting where the ducks are—to direct your appeals to where the money is. Skocpol has paid particular attention to the consequences for political and social equality in America. Lower income Americans are now less well-represented by the associational universe than they were in the past and are less well-represented relative to more affluent Americans.

In retrospect, the cumulative effect of these changes in the interest group universe probably has contributed a great deal to the present disconnect between elected representatives and the American public. Skocpol's summary description of the associational transformation bears quoting at length:

Reconfigured by the advocacy explosion, the new universe of national American associations that emerged after the 1960s not only features proportionally more nonbusiness groups and thousands more groups overall than the federation-heavy civic universe of the 1950s. It also has many more small groups and many more memberless entities and groups with constituents attracted through the mail and the media. Specializing in this or that constituency, cause, or activity, civic entrepreneurs by the thousands have founded advocacy organizations without individual members, groups that represent other organizations, and groups that speak for modest numbers of individual adherents who respond to mass mailings or canvasses by giving money. . . . And the reconfigured civic universe is much more focused on specialized, instrumental activities than on broad expressions of community or fellow citizenship.[35]

How would we expect American representatives to respond to such changes in the social environment? Fenno noted that the U.S. representatives he followed in the 1970s were operating under conditions of increasing uncertainty: "These years were characterized by the steady decline of strong national party attachments and strong local party organizations."[36] Political scientists have traced the rise of candidate-centered politics to such uncertainty. With voters no longer voting as much along party lines, the electorate became more responsive to the members' personal characteristics, positions, and performance. And with the old-style local party organizations in disrepair, members had to construct personal organizations to replace them.

Groups and associations are obvious building blocks for such candidate-constructed organizations. But the groups and associations that representatives had long been familiar with were in decline (e.g., "They have no Rotary clubs"). With electoral survival at stake, representatives had compelling incentives to search for new building blocks, and like the peace activists in Congressman O.'s district, the groups and associations that constituted the advocacy explosion were the obvious candidates. Occupational groups, environmental groups, business groups, civil rights groups, consumer groups, pro-choice and pro-life groups, pro-gun and anti-gun groups, and innumerable others gradually took the place of Rotaries, Kiwanis, Elks, Chamber of Commerce, AFL-CIO, and other older groups as conduits through which representatives could communicate to constituents and appeal for their support. Most of the new associations did not have local chapters like the old groups where the representative could give a speech, but they did have mailing lists that could be used to communicate with constituents and raise funds.

Now consider the implications of these new groups' characteristics for the behavior of the politicians who sought to incorporate them into their electoral coalitions. Because these groups were generally narrower in focus, they had more specific policy concerns and thus expected a more specific policy response than just the assurance that the representative was broadly sympathetic to the values and concerns of their members.[37] In consequence, representatives devoted increased attention to the narrow agendas of such groups, detracting attention from the more general concerns of the larger public and distorting the priorities of American politics. Because the people most likely to support various causes were those who felt more strongly and had more extreme views about their causes, their money and activism pulled representatives away from the broader public on those issues, exaggerating the polarization of American politics. And because the new associations were operating in a hypercompetitive environment where numerous other groups were attempting to catch the attention and capture the resources of the same narrow constituencies, the groups were motivated to emphasize threats and dangers from their enemies, thus encouraging the uncivil, exaggerated, "politics as total war" style of contemporary American politics. All of these considerations apply to individual candidates, of course, but when combined with the party sorting described in the preceding chapter, the combined effect was to pull the parties as aggregates away from the political center and away from the priorities of the larger public.

Moreover, given that local party organizations had withered, one would expect that as time passed the new associations and organizations increasingly produced candidates for public office. And candidates with such backgrounds probably had more intense and more extreme policy commitments—genuine or feigned. Writing in 1981, a long-time observer of Congress contrasted "old-style" members with "new-style" members who had come to dominate the institution in the 1970s:

> The typical member produced by an old-style pre-Progressive party organization—whether Republican or Democratic, liberal or conservative, urban or rural—had been trained to be deferential. Coming from a political apprenticeship in which leadership and hierarchy were normal and accepted, he accepted them in the Congress, too. His views on political issues were compatible with those of his organization. . . . Since the nomination was, in some measure, a reward for past services, he might look on the job as largely honorary, and he might or might not work hard at it. Except for one aspect of his job: getting material rewards for his constituents—judgeships, postmasterships, jobs in Washington, pork in many forms for his state or district. . . . His career did not depend on any showing of brilliance in the conception or advocacy of legislative measures, and he was not likely to mount a challenge to the way the Congress was organized or run.
>
> The new-style member contrasts with the old in political manners, political vocabulary, interests, and conception of the proper nature of the institution in which he serves. As a congressional candidate, he was self-chosen. Nobody handed him the nomination; he won it in open competition, usually by the vote of the party rank and file in a direct primary. He won it by identifying and articulating the issues better than his competitors. . . . His background is likely to be less in party service than in intellectual and advocacy organizations, of all kinds. . . . His absorbing interest is governmental policy. He came to the Congress with a sense of mission, even a mandate, to have an impact on the legislative process. He is impatient, for those who backed him expect legislative results. An upstart as a candidate—self-selected, self-organized, self-propelled, self-reliant—he will be an upstart in the House or Senate, too.[38]

According to Sundquist, the "new-style" members of Congress reached critical mass in the Democratic caucus after the Democratic landslide of 1958, the vanguard of a new political order that would supplant the old order in little more than a decade.

SUMMARY

In all likelihood the transformation of associational life that Putnam and Skocpol described is an important part of the explanation of the disconnect that developed between the American public and its representatives in the last third of the twentieth century. For four generations American politicians communicated with and mobilized constituents through relatively representative, broad-based associations that were not primarily organized for political purposes. But as living patterns and other sociodemographic changes occurred, those associations declined (at the same time as traditional party organizations were declining), and American politicians turned to newer organizations that were more narrowly based and less representative, many of which were organized precisely for political purposes. I will not attempt to specify the causal and temporal links more exactly, other than to suggest as in chapter 5 that social changes produced political pressures and demands that produced procedural and institutional changes. Once set in motion, however, the process very likely became one of mutual reinforcement.

If such a developmental sequence is an important part of the explanation for the disconnect between representatives and represented, then any attempt to alleviate the disconnect faces the difficult task of somehow overriding the dependence of today's politicians on the new associations and groups that now populate the American social landscape. For most of American history, the political parties were broad coalitions that appealed to the common interests of their members. But as John Aldrich has argued, American parties reinvent themselves to deal with the electoral and governmental problems they face during different political eras.[39] Today, the parties have reinvented themselves as holding companies for a host of identity, affinity, and special interest groups. Controlling neither nominations nor patronage as their forerunners did, the parties today must work through allied or associated groups that are both incomplete and inaccurate representations of the broader public.

In the first half of the twentieth century, pluralist political scientists argued that the interest group universe in the United States represented the interests and values of the American people to an acceptable degree. Moreover, interest group competition was inherently moderating—group competition took the form of bargaining and compromise among political leaders, and countervailing power would prevent one coalition from becoming dominant.[40] Whatever the empirical accuracy of the pluralist vision at that time, it has a poor fit with American politics today. The transformation of associational life has produced a less representative politics, one whose characteristics are anything but moderating.

CHAPTER 7

THE DISCONNECT:
HOW UNUSUAL? HOW BAD?

IN CHAPTERS 1–3 I DESCRIBED a multifaceted disconnect between the contemporary political class and the electorate—a disconnect in public policy positions, public policy priorities, and preferences over how public policy debates should be conducted. In chapters 4–6 I suggested that institutional changes and background sociological changes are likely contributors to this disconnect. In the current chapter I reconsider two assumptions that underlie the arguments in these preceding chapters: first, that the contemporary disconnect is a new development in American politics; and second, that this disconnect is normatively undesirable. Although the earlier discussion obviously makes both these assumptions, there is certainly enough evidence and argument in the historical and political science literatures that skeptical scholars could make reasonable cases to the contrary. In this chapter I consider these contrary arguments.

DISCONNECT: NEW OR NORMAL?

In chapter 1 I contrasted the highly polarized U.S. House of Representatives of our time with the far less polarized House of a generation ago (see figure 1.1 or left panel of figure 7.1). To scholars of my generation, this seems like a natural starting point—our lives span these two eras of significant change. But what if scholars of a generation ago had started with the middle panel of figure 7.1, contrasting the more polarized Congress of the late-nineteenth century with the less polarized Congress of their time?[1] Such a starting point would likely have led them to ask, why has American politics become so much *less* polarized today than it was a generation ago? And returning to our contemporary vantage point, if a scholar today compared the

Figure 7.1 Congressional Polarization

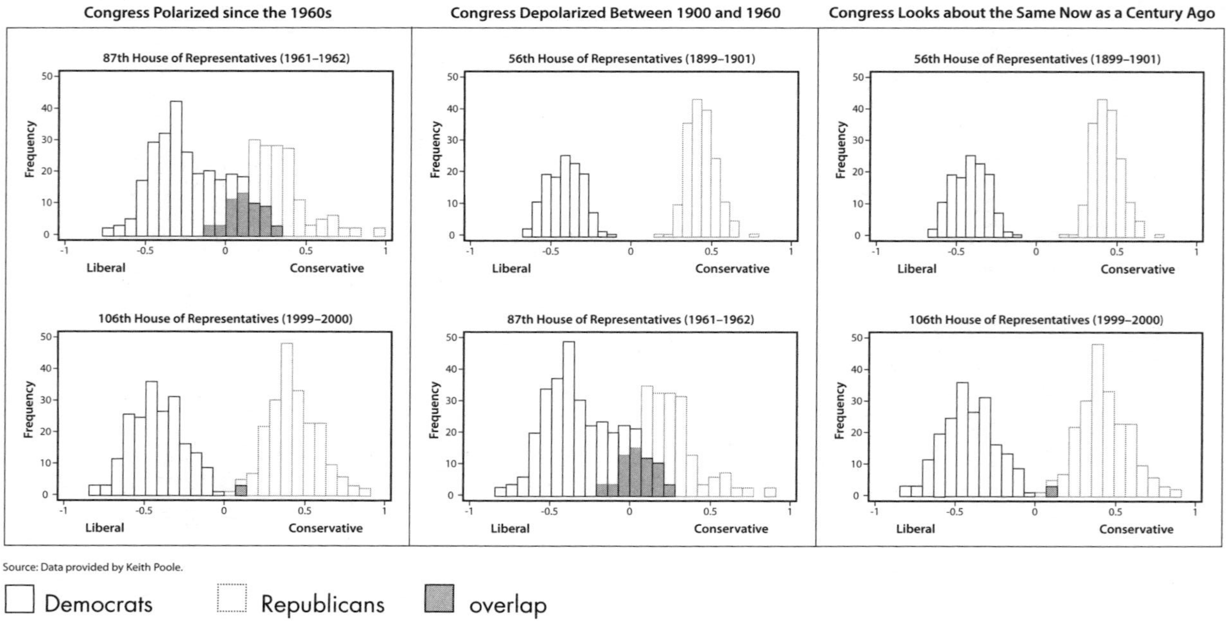
Congress Polarized since the 1960s
Congress Depolarized Between 1900 and 1960
Congress Looks about the Same Now as a Century Ago
87th House of Representatives (1961–1962)
56th House of Representatives (1899–1901)
56th House of Representatives (1899–1901)
106th House of Representatives (1999–2000)
87th House of Representatives (1961–1962)
106th House of Representatives (1999–2000)
Frequency
50
40
30
20
10
0
-1
-0.5
0
0.5
1
Liberal
Conservative
Democrats
Republicans
overlap

Source: Data provided by Keith Poole.

end of the nineteenth century with the end of the twentieth century (see the right panel of figure 7.1), the likely question would be, what factors led to the unusually *low* polarization of the mid-twentieth century as compared with the more "normal" state of high polarization?

These are valid questions that deserve consideration. Of course, the first question one should ask is whether congressional polarization in the past was accompanied by polarization in other electoral arenas of the time. That is, were the polarized Congresses of the late-nineteenth century typical of state legislatures, city and county boards, and other government bodies of that time, and were other members of the political class as polarized as members of Congress? In a similar manner, were the less polarized Congresses of the mid-twentieth century typical of state and local government bodies of that time, and were mid-century members of the political class similarly unpolarized? Unless the answers are yes, we would be dealing with a congressional phenomenon, not a systemic phenomenon as seems to be the case today.

So, assume positive answers to these questions. Then the second question one would raise is whether the representative institutions of earlier times were disconnected from the American public in the same way as they are today. If the public itself was polarized, there would be no disconnect—the political class would have been faithfully representing the people. Unfortunately, the latter question is a difficult one, and perhaps unanswerable. The most ambitious effort to date has been reported by Brady and Han, who provided an in-depth examination of congressional polarization over a broad sweep of American history—the Civil War era, the late-nineteenth-century period of industrial strife, and the New Deal era.[2] Unfortunately, generalizations are hard to come by. Their findings suggest the tentative conclusion that the current era differs from several other periods of polarization, although it resembles the late-nineteenth-century era in some respects and differs in others.

The huge obstacle researchers face is that although we can compare levels of roll call voting polarization of legislators today with those in the past (assuming we make the heroic assumption that agenda strategies have not changed or that they do not matter), we cannot determine whether past polarized eras were characterized by the same sort of disconnect that is evident today.[3] The reason is the lack of public opinion data on the voters' positions.

Any attempt to compare the contemporary era with past periods of elite polarization faces the problem that for those earlier eras we have only election returns—data on the *choices* of ordinary voters but not on their *positions*. And as emphasized in chapter 3, voter choices reflect both their positions and the positions of the candidates and parties. As shown in figure 3.1, moderate voters can elect polarized or moderate candidates depending on the choices they are offered, and the same is true for polarized voters. Today public opinion data enable us to know that a relatively moderate electorate is often choosing between relatively extreme candidates, but we have no way of directly measuring the shape of the electorate in earlier eras.

Of course, political historians tell us that levels of popular political involvement were exceedingly high in the late-nineteenth century.[4] Thus, given the argument advanced in earlier chapters, I am tempted to conclude on the basis of such accounts that there was no disconnect: a polarized political class represented a similarly polarized electorate. But however much anecdotal evidence about torchlight parades one amasses, we do not know how large a proportion of the electorate marched or how closely intense issue differences accompanied participation. Maybe it was mostly sound and fury. Considering how badly data-unencumbered political observers have mischaracterized the level of polarization among contemporary Americans, it is certainly possible that historical accounts significantly exaggerate the extent of grass roots involvement and concern. If public opinion polling had not yet been invented, imagine the distorted account of popular polarization circa 2000 that historians might write a century from now based on examination of election returns alone.

Thus, whether today's disconnect between the political class and ordinary Americans is something new and different or the reemergence of something older and more familiar cannot be answered unless future generations of scholars can figure out ways to estimate the positions of voters from their observed choices, something that is beyond the reach of current scholarship. And although mainly of importance to academic political scientists, whether today's disconnect between electors and elected is common or uncommon as an empirical matter still leaves the question of how and why the actual practice of American politics today violates decades of generally held theoretical and observational accounts of that practice—recall Rossiter's "unwritten laws" that require American politics to be centrist politics.[5]

DISCONNECT: IS IT BAD?

Rarely have I given a talk on the matters discussed in this book when someone in the audience does not ask a question of the following sort: "Isn't the polarization of the political class that you are concerned about exactly what some political scientists of the mid-twentieth century fervently wished for?" With some qualifications to be noted below, yes. In fact, not only does the perspective underlying this book clash with that of earlier generations of political scientists, it clashes with my own earlier views as well.[6]

Some twenty-five years ago I wrote an article entitled "The Decline of Collective Responsibility in American Politics."[7] In that article I updated the classic arguments for party responsibility in light of which the politics of the 1970s looked seriously deficient. A subsequent article with a similar theme appeared in a 1984 collection, with revised versions in 1988 and 1990.[8] In these essays I noted that in the 1970s party cohesion had dropped to a level not seen since before the Civil War. As a result, national politics had degenerated into a free-for-all of unprincipled bargaining in which participants blithely sacrificed general interests in their advocacy of particularistic constituency interests.[9] The unified Democratic government of President Jimmy Carter that failed to deal effectively with national problems such as "stagflation" (high inflation accompanied by high unemployment) and successive energy crises exemplified the sorry state of national politics.

Moreover, not only had policy failure become more likely, but because voting for members of Congress increasingly reflected the particularistic activities and personal records of incumbents, members had little fear of being held accountable for their contributions to the failures of national politics. In that light I sympathetically reasserted the arguments of earlier generations of political scientists who advocated more responsible parties.[10] Not all problems are amenable to government solution, of course, but unified political parties led by strong presidents were more likely to act decisively to meet the challenges facing the country, and when the politicians took their collective performance records to the electorate for ratification or rejection, the voters at least had a good idea of whom to reward or blame.

As I noted in a 1990 epilogue to one of these essays, however, the prevalence of divided government in the late-twentieth century had raised doubts in my mind about the arguments articulated a decade earlier.[11] These doubts cumulated into a change of position explicated at length in *Divided Government* and later writings.[12] Briefly, as the parties became more distinct and cohesive during the 1980s, voters seemed to show little appreciation for the changes. Rather than entrust control of government to one unified party, Americans were increasingly voting to split control of government—at the state as well as the national level. And whether split control was voters' actual goal or not—a matter of continuing debate—polls showed that most voters were happy enough with the situation, whatever political scientists thought of the supposed programmatic inefficiency and electoral irresponsibility of divided government.[13] By the early 1990s I had reversed myself and come to appreciate the electorate's point of view.

Moving from one side of an argument to the other in a decade suggests that the protagonist either was wrong earlier or (even worse!) wrong later. But there is another possibility; namely, that the shift in stance did not reflect error in the earlier argument so much as changes in one or more unrecognized but important empirical premises that vitiate the larger argument. I think that at least to some degree, that is the case here. To quote from the 1990 epilogue "I am now less optimistic than when I first wrote this essay that a stronger role for the parties *as presently constituted* would bring about better government" (italics in original).[14] For, as discussed in chapter 4, by 1990 I had come to believe that in important respects the parties we were observing in the contemporary era were different in composition and behavior from the ones described in the political science literature I had studied in graduate school. Parties organized to solve the governance problems of one era do not necessarily operate in the same way as parties organized to solve the problems of later eras.[15]

In the remainder of this chapter, I focus more specifically on the normative questions raised by a polarized political class. What was it about the centrist politics of the early- to mid-twentieth-century United States that some political scientists of that time saw as something that needed to be reformed in the direction that American politics has since traveled? And what is it about the more polarized politics of today that makes many of us sorry that we got what we once wished for? I begin by briefly contrasting American politics in the 1970s and the 2000s.

POLITICS THEN AND NOW

The decade of the 1970s began with divided government (then still regarded as something of an anomaly), proceeded through the resignations of a vice president and president followed by the brief administration of an unelected president, then saw the restoration of the "normal order"—unified Democratic government—in 1976, only to see it collapse at the end of the decade in the landslide rejection of a presidency mortally wounded by international humiliation, stagflation, and energy crises. Contemporary critics placed much of the responsibility for the "failed" Carter presidency at the feet of Carter himself—his obsession with detail, his inability to delegate, his political tin ear, and so forth, but I felt then that the critics were giving insufficient attention to larger developments and more general conditions that would have posed serious obstacles for presidents who possessed much stronger executive and political skills than Carter.[16]

POLITICAL CONDITIONS IN THE 1970S

Not only did Jimmy Carter's 1976 victory restore the presidency to the Democrats, but large Democratic majorities controlled both the House and Senate.[17] Seemingly, the great era of government activism that had been derailed by the war in Vietnam would resume. Such was not to be. After four years of political frustration, Carter was soundly defeated by Ronald Reagan, the Republicans captured the Senate with a remarkable gain of twelve seats, and the Democrats lost thirty-three seats in the House. What happened?

Basically, the country faced a series of new problems, and the Democratic Party failed to deal with them in a manner satisfactory to electoral majorities in the nation as a whole and in many states and districts. Gas lines, in particular, and the energy crisis, in general, were something new in modern American experience, as were double-digit inflation and interest rates near 20 percent. Middle-class tax revolts were a startling development that frightened Democratic politicians and energized Republicans, and a succession of foreign policy setbacks led many to fear that the United States was ill-prepared to deal with new challenges around the world. Facing such developments, Democratic majorities in Congress failed to adapt. In the aftermath of Vietnam, the party had come to be viewed as soft on defense, and it appeared increasingly outmoded in domestic affairs where Democrats seemed fixated on old, particularistic policies like public works spending and protectionist trade policies. The honeymoon between Carter and congressional Democrats ended fairly quickly, and the partnership was under strain for most of Carter's administration. Members worked to protect their constituencies from the negative effects of the new developments and worried much less about the fate of Carter or the Democratic Party as a whole. As figure 7.2 shows, this was a period of low party cohesion, and although cross-party majori-

Figure 7.2 Political party conflict in Congress

Plotted points show the percentage of congressional votes that were along party lines.

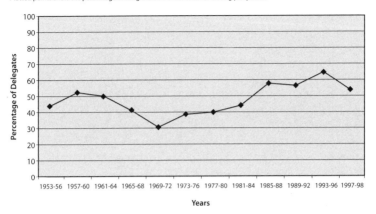

Data from *Vital Statistics on Congress.*

ties were not as common as in the late 1960s, figure 7.3 shows that they still were common.

For the most part the generation of congressional scholars who contributed to the literature of the 1950s and 1960s had defended the decentralized Congresses of the period against the centralizing impulses of presidential scholars and policy wonks. True, Congress was slow and inefficient, and often it did not defer to presidential leadership, but most congressional scholars would have characterized this more as pragmatic incrementalism than as the "deadlock of democracy."[18] More than the presidency did, the Congress reflected the heterogeneity of interests in the country and was responsive to them. In all likelihood, most of the community of established congressional scholars sympathized with Julius Turner's critique of the 1950 American Political Science Association (APSA) report that called for more distinct and more responsible parties.[19]

To a younger generation of scholars, however, the failings of the increasingly decentralized Congresses and the increasingly disorganized parties were cause for concern. The country faced serious problems. Presidents were held responsible for solving

Figure 7.3 Political Party Unity in Congress

Plotted points show that party unity has resurged since the 1960s.

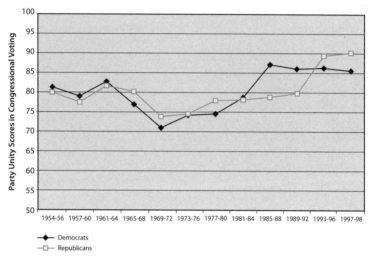

Data from *Vital Statistics on Congress.*

these problems, but incumbent members of Congress seemingly could win reelection by abandoning their presidents and parties in favor of protecting parochial constituency interests. By emphasizing their individual records, members of Congress had adapted to an era of candidate-centered politics. From a historical perspective they had less to gain or lose from the effects of presidential coattails, and they did not have to be very concerned about midterm electoral swings against their president's party.[20] Collective responsibility traditionally provided by the political parties was at low ebb. "Pluribus" was running rampant, leaving "unum" in the electoral dust. Strengthening the two parties seemed like the obvious first step to reverse the decline in governmental effectiveness.

POLITICAL CONDITIONS NOW

In retrospect, the trends decried by political observers in the 1970s had already bottomed out by the Carter presidency. The cross-party majorities that passed President Reagan's budget and tax cuts may have obscured the fact, but party unity and party differences already were on the rise and continued rising in succeeding years (see figures 7.2 and 7.3). In a related development, the electoral advantages accruing to incumbency already were receding as national influences in voting reasserted themselves.[21] And a new breed of congressional leaders emerged to focus the efforts of their parties in support of or opposition to presidential proposals. In 1993 President Bill Clinton's initial budget passed without a single Republican vote in the House or Senate, and in 1994 unified Republican opposition contributed greatly to the demise of the administration's signature health care plan.[22]

And then came 1994 when the Republicans finally succeeded in an undertaking they had sporadically attempted for a generation—nationalizing the congressional elections. In the 1994 elections personal opposition to gun control or various other liberal policies no longer sufficed to save Democrats in conservative districts whose party label overwhelmed their personal positions. The new Republican majorities in Congress seized the initiative from President Clinton to such an extent that he was asked at a press conference whether he was "still relevant?" But when congressional Republicans overreached, Clinton answered questions about his continued relevance, beating back Republican attempts to cut entitlement programs and saddling them with the blame for the government shutdowns of 1995–1996.

At the time, the Republican attempt to govern as a responsible party struck many political scientists as unprecedented in the modern era. But as Baer and Bositis pointed out, politics had been moving in that direction for several decades; indeed, a great deal of what the 1950 APSA report called for already had come to pass (table 7.1).[23] Now, a decade later it is apparent that the Congress elected in 1994 was the leading edge of a new period in national politics. Party unity and presidential support among Republicans hit fifty-year highs during the first term of President George W. Bush, and in 2002 the president pulled off the rare feat of leading his party to seat gains in a midterm election. After his reelection in 2004, President Bush spoke in terms clearly reminiscent of those used by responsible-party theorists. On the basis

Table 7.1 American Political Science Association Report After 40 Years

Fate of proposal	Democrats	Republicans	System
Full implementation	13	6	5
Partial implementation	7	5	5
De facto movement	8	9	5
No change	3	10	3
Negative movement	2	3	2

Source: Adapted from Denise Baer and David Bositis, *Politics and Linkage in a Democratic Society* (Englewood Cliffs, NJ: Prentice-Hall, 1993), Appendix.

of a 51 percent popular majority, he claimed a mandate to make his tax cuts permanent and to transform Social Security. Moreover, early in 2005 when the president was asked why no one in his administration had been held accountable for mistakes and miscalculations about Iraq, he replied in words that should have warmed the hearts of responsible-party theorists: "We had an accountability moment, and that's called the 2004 election. And the American people listened to different assessments made about what was taking place in Iraq, and they looked at the two candidates, and chose me, for which I'm grateful."[24] No president in living memory had articulated such clear statements of collective responsibility legitimized by electoral victory.

In sum, the collective responsibility that some political scientists found wanting in the 1970s seems clearly present in the 2000s. Why, then, would we be troubled by the arrival of something we wished for?

PROBLEMS WITH TODAY'S RESPONSIBLE PARTIES

In 2002 a Republican administration ostensibly committed to free enterprise endorsed tariffs to protect the U.S. steel industry, a policy condemned by economists across the ideological spectrum. Also in 2002 Congress passed and President Bush signed an agricultural subsidy bill that the left-leaning *New York Times* decried as an "orgy of pandering to special interest groups," the centrist *USA Today* called "a congressional atrocity," and the right-leaning *Economist* characterized as "monstrous."[25] In 2003 Congress passed and the president signed a special-interest-riddled prescription drug plan that was the largest entitlement program adopted since Medicare itself in 1965, a fiscal commitment that immediately put the larger Medicare program on a steeper slide toward bankruptcy. In 2004 congressional Republicans proposed and President Bush supported a constitutional amendment to ban gay marriage, a divisive proposal that had no chance of passing. After his reelection, President Bush declared his highest priority was to avert a crisis in a Social Security system he insisted was bankrupt, by establishing a system of personal accounts, while disinterested observers generally pronounced the situation far from crisis and in need of relatively moderate reform—especially compared with Medicare.[26] In 2005 the Republican Congress passed and President Bush signed a pork-filled transportation bill that contained 6,371 congressional earmarks, forty times as many as contained in a bill vetoed by an earlier Republican president in 1987. Meanwhile, at the time of this writing Americans continue to die in a war of choice launched on the basis of ambiguous intelligence that appears to have been systematically interpreted to support a previously adopted position.

The preceding are only some of the more noteworthy lowlights of public policies adopted or proposed under the responsible-party government of 2001–2006. All things considered, if someone wished to argue that politics and policymaking in the 1970s was better than in the 2000s, I would find it hard to rebut them. Why? Are today's problems and challenges so much more difficult than those of the 1970s that the decentralized, irresponsible parties of that time would have done an even poorer job of meeting them than the more responsible parties of today? Or are today's responsible parties operating in a manner that was not anticipated by those of us who wished for more responsible parties?

WHAT DIDN'T RESPONSIBLE-PARTY SCHOLARS ANTICIPATE?

With the benefit of hindsight, it is now rather clear that political competition between cohesive, differentiated parties raises the stakes of politics.[27] Certainly, majority status in institutions always is valuable; committee chairs, agenda control, staff budgets, and numerous other benefits go to the majority. But if majority control of a legislative chamber means relatively little for policymaking because moderate Republicans and Democrats hold the balance of power, which party formally holds control means less than when policy is decided within the majority party caucus and the minority is shut out.[28] In a similar manner, the knowledge that the president's program either will be rubber-stamped by a supportive congressional majority or killed by an opposition majority makes unified control of all three institutions that much more valuable. And as the Bush administration learned in 2007–2008, the power to squelch hostile congressional investigations may not be fully appreciated until it is gone.

With the political stakes ratcheted upward, politics naturally becomes more conflictual. The benefits of winning and the costs of losing both rise. Informal norms and even formal rules come under pressure as the legislative majority strives to eliminate obstacles to its agenda.[29] Meanwhile, the minority is first ignored, then abused. House Democrats under Jim Wright marginalized House Republicans in the 1980s, and the Republicans enthusiastically returned the favor after taking control in 1994.[30] Even in the far less rule-bound Senate, in 2005 then-majority leader Bill Frist threatened the minority Democrats with the "nuclear option"—a rules change that effectively eliminated the filibuster on presidential appointments. Examples like these indicate that the increasing disparity between majority and minority status raises the electoral stakes and makes politics more conflictual.

The fact that the parties have been so closely matched in the past decade further heightens the electoral stakes. Not only are the benefits of winning and the costs of losing higher, but the likelihood of winning or losing is more in doubt. In retrospect, it is probable that the development of more responsible parties was a factor—certainly not the only one—that contributed to the rise of the permanent campaign.[31] With majority status that much more valuable and minority status that much more intolerable, politicians are less willing to observe a hiatus between elections in which governing takes precedence over electioneering. All else now is subordinated to party positioning for the next election. Free trade principles? Forget about them if Pennsylvania and Ohio steel workers are needed to win the next election. Budget deficits? Ignore them if a budget-busting prescription drug plan is needed to keep the opposition from scoring points with senior citizens. Politics always has affected policy, of course, but as both participants and academic observers have noted, today the linkage is closer and stronger than ever before.[32] Rather than make the governmental process more efficient, the development of responsible parties may have further subjected the governmental process to electoral considerations.

A second feature of American politics today that was not foreseen by the responsible-party theorists is that it is more complex than in the 1950s. At the time that the APSA report was written, race was not on the agenda.[33] And as noted in chapter 4, social and cultural issues were largely dormant in the midcentury decades, their importance diminished by the end of immigration in the 1920s, the Great Depression, and World War II. A bipartisan consensus surrounded the goals of foreign and defense policy. (To be sure, there was the McCarthy episode, but note that McCarthy was censured by a Senate controlled by his party, indicating that his behavior was the exception, not the norm.) Under such conditions it is understandable that a midcentury political scientist could have felt that all the country needed was two parties that advocated alternative economic programs.[34] For example, in 1962 political historian James McGregor Burns wrote the following: "It is curious that majoritarian politics has won such a reputation for radicalism in this country. Actually it is moderate politics; it looks radical only in relation to the snail-like progress of Madisonian politics. The Jeffersonian strategy is essentially moderate because it is essentially competitive; in a homogeneous society it must appeal to the moderate, middle-class independent voters who hold the balance of power."[35] To most contemporary observers the

United States looks rather less homogeneous than it apparently did to observers of Burns's era. Compared with 1950 our present situation is more complex with a more elaborate political issue space.

Burns's contention that majoritarian politics is moderate politics is particularly striking in light of the contemporary concern about the polarization of American politics. That party polarization would accompany party responsibility is a third development that Burns and other scholars of his era evidently did not foresee. On the contrary, the APSA report asserted that "Needed clarification of party policy in itself will not cause the parties to differ more fundamentally or more sharply than they have in the past."[36] But as I argued in chapter 4, today's parties are not the same as the parties described in midcentury textbooks. The old distinction between "professionals" and "purists" no longer has the same conceptual value because in many cases the professionals now are purists. At the time the responsible-party theorists wrote, parties nominated candidates on the basis of their service to the party and their connections to party leaders or, in more competitive areas, their electability. Aside from times when a party was bitterly divided, policy positions were seldom a litmus test of a candidate's suitability.[37] Material motivations— control of offices, patronage—were dominant. But as discussed in chapter 4, various developments have lessened the personal, material rewards that once motivated many of those active in politics. Today, ideological motivations are relatively more important than previously. Candidates today must have the right set of issue stances to attract support, and many of the potential supporters would prefer to lose with a pure ideological candidate than to win with a mushy moderate. Some candidates themselves no doubt feel the same.

The preceding developments contributed to the shift in party electoral strategy in the late-twentieth-century United States. In the quotation above, Burns was expressing the political science conventional wisdom of midcentury—that two-party competition induces parties to move toward the center in order to capture the median voter.[38] But in the last decades of the century we saw the shift to the strategy of concentrating on the party base—doing whatever is necessary to maximize loyalty and turnout by core party constituencies. Thus, the aforementioned forcing of a Senate vote on gay marriage was an entirely symbolic gesture toward elements in the evangelical Christian base of the Republican Party. It had nothing to do with governing; it was a costly signal that the Bush administration was on their side.

Concentrating on the base indicates that today's parties no longer strive to maximize their vote, only to "satisfice"—to get more votes than the other party.[39] At one time a maximal victory was desirable because it would add credibility to the victors' claim that the voters had given them a mandate for bold action—Roosevelt's 100 Days, Lyndon Johnson's 89th Congress, and the Reagan Revolution are familiar examples. But as the previously quoted remarks of President Bush indicate, at least some of today's politicians consider any victory, however narrow, as a mandate.[40]

A fourth problem with cohesive parties that offer voters a clear choice is that voters may not like clear choices. The APSA report asserted that responsible parties would offer voters "a proper range of choice."[41] But what is "proper?" Voters may not want a clear choice between a constitutional prohibition of abortion and abortion on demand, between privatizing Social Security and ignoring unsustainable fiscal imbalances, between launching wars of choice and ignoring developing threats. Given that the issue positions of the electorate as a whole are not polarized, it is likely that many voters today would prefer a fuzzier choice than typically provided by the candidates on their ballots.

Even if voters *were* polarized on issues and wished the parties to offer clear choices on those issues, they would still be dissatisfied if there were more than one issue and the opinion divisions across issues were not highly correlated. For example, contemporary Republicans are basically an alliance between economic and social conservatives, and Democrats are an alliance between economic and social liberals. So, in which party does someone who is an economic conservative and a social liberal belong?

What about an economic liberal and a social conservative? Such people might well prefer moderate positions on both dimensions to issue packages consisting of one position they like a great deal and another they dislike a great deal.[42] The simple fact is that the majoritarianism that accompanies responsible parties may be ill-suited for a heterogeneous society, as Turner argued a half century ago.[43] With only one dimension of conflict, a victory by one party can reasonably be interpreted to mean that a majority prefers its program to that of the other party. But with more than one dimension, a victory by one party by no means guarantees majority support for its program(s). Indeed, as Anthony Downs pointed out a half-century ago, given variations in voter intensity on different issues, a party can win by constructing a coalition of minorities—taking the minority position on each issue.[44]

At one time political scientists saw strong political parties as a means of controlling interest groups.[45] Parties and groups were viewed as competing ways of organizing political life. If parties were weak, groups would fill the vacuum; if parties were strong, they would harness group efforts in support of more general party goals. Two decades ago I was persuaded by this argument, but time has proved it suspect. Modern parties and their associated groups now overlap so closely that it is often hard to make the distinction between a party activist and an issue activist. Here is a fifth respect in which midcentury thinking proved wrong.

Parties composed of issue activists and ideologues behave differently from the parties described in the political science literature of the mid-twentieth century. At that time each party appealed to a different swath of the American public, Democrats primarily to blue-collar workers and Republicans to middle-class professionals and managers. Because such large social groupings were far from homogeneous internally, the party platform had to tolerate internal heterogeneity in order to maintain itself and to compete across a reasonably broad portion of the country. Although both parties continue to have support in broad social groupings like blue-collar workers and white-collar professionals, their bases now consist of much more specifically defined groups. Democrats rely on public-sector unions, environmentalists, and pro-choice and other liberal cause groups. Republicans rely on evangelicals, small business organizations, and pro-life and other conservative cause groups. Rather than compromise on a single major issue, such as economics, a process that midcentury political scientists correctly saw as inherently moderating, parties can now compromise across issues by adding up constituency groups' most preferred positions on a series of independent issues. Why should conservative today mean pro-life, low taxes, pro-capital punishment, and pre-emptive war and liberal mean just the opposite? What is the underlying principle that ties such disparate issues together? The underlying principle is political, of course, not logical or moral. Collections of positions like these happen to be the preferred positions of groups that now constitute important parts of the party bases.

Although it is more speculative, I believe that unbiased information and policy effectiveness are additional casualties of the preceding developments. The APSA report asserts that "As a means of achieving responsibility, the clarification of party policy also tends to keep public debate on a more realistic level, restraining the inclination of party spokesmen to make unsubstantiated statements and charges."[46] Recent experience shows just the opposite. Policies are proposed and opposed relatively more on the basis of ideology and the demands of base groups and relatively less on the basis of their likelihood of solving problems. Disinformation and even outright lies become common as dissenting voices in each party leave or are silenced. A disturbing example came out of Congressional passage of the 2003 Medicare prescription drug add-on bill. Political superiors threatened to fire Medicare's chief actuary if he informed Congress that the estimated cost of the add-on would be far more costly than the administration publicly claimed. The administration apparently was willing to lie to members of its own party to assure passage of a bill whose basis was mostly political.[47] Justice Department lawyers concluded that Rep. Tom DeLay's

(R-Tex.) mid-decade redistricting of Texas violated the Voting Right Act, but political superiors approved the plan anyway.[48] On a more mundane level, President Bush introduced his campaign to add personal accounts to Social Security by claiming that Social Security was bankrupt and that personal accounts were a means of restoring the system to fiscal solvency. Although many experts see merit in the idea of personal accounts, most agreed that implementing them would increase Social Security's fiscal deficits in the coming decades. Even greater agreement surrounded rejection of the claim that Social Security was bankrupt. Although politically difficult, straightforward programmatic changes in the retirement age, the tax base, or the method of indexing future benefits would make Social Security solvent for as long as actuaries can reasonably predict.[49]

Moreover, because parties today focus on their ability to mobilize the already committed, the importance of actual performance for voting declines in importance relative to ideology and political identity. It was telling that in 2004 Democratic presidential candidate John Kerry frequently was criticized for not having a plan to end the war in Iraq that was appreciably different from President Bush's. This seems like a new requirement. In 1952 did Dwight Eisenhower have a specific plan to end the war in Korea that differed from President Truman's? "I will go to Korea" is not exactly a plan. In 1968 did Richard Nixon have a specific plan to end the war in Vietnam that differed from President Johnson's? A "secret plan" to end the war is not exactly a precise blueprint that voters could compare with the Johnson policy. Some decades ago voters apparently felt that an unpopular war was sufficient reason to punish an incumbent whether or not the challenger offered a persuasive "exit strategy."

A final consideration relates to the preceding ones. Because today's parties are composed relatively more of issue activists than of broad demographic groupings, they are not as deeply rooted in the mass of the population as was the case for much of our history. The United States pioneered the mass party, but as Steven Schier has argued, in recent decades the parties have practiced a kind of exclusive politics.[50] The mass mobilization campaigns that historically characterized American elections gave way to the high-tech media campaigns of the late-twentieth century. Voter mobilization by the political parties correspondingly fell.[51] Late-century campaigns increasingly relied on TV ads, and there is some evidence that such ads demobilize the electorate.[52] In a kind of "back to the future" development, the three most recent presidential elections have seen renewed party effort to get out the vote, with a significant impact.[53] But modern computing capabilities and rich databases enable the parties to practice a kind of targeted mobilization based on specific issues that was more difficult to do in earlier periods. It is not clear that such activities make the parties more like those of yesteryear, or whether they only reinforce the trends I have previously discussed. One-third of the voting-age population continues to eschew a party identification, a figure that has not appreciably changed in three decades.[54] And party registration figures in states that tabulate them show the parties losing ground relative to independent and "decline to state" voters.[55]

SUMMARY: IS TODAY'S SORTED, POLARIZED POLITICAL CLASS BAD?

The parties today are far closer to the responsible-party model than those of the 1970s, a development that some political scientists wished for some decades ago. But many scholars today are not happy with this development. In truth, most of the unhappiness probably reflects disapproval with the *process* of politics today—more contentious and less civil. In recent years retiring politicians have complained about the deterioration in the quality of political life, and long-time observers of our politics agree with them.[56] Skeptics retort that we should not be greatly concerned about whether our elected officials find their lives satisfying. The important question is whether they are meeting the challenges of our times with the appropriate public policies. Process is mere window-dressing.

I am reluctant to dismiss the importance of process. For one thing the uncivil style of modern politics may affect the electorate in a variety of negative ways, making many voters even less willing to take a more active role in politics, for example. There is also some evidence that the polarization of the political class makes voters less likely to trust government.[57] Research on these matters is ongoing, and we will probably know considerably more about such questions in the not-too-distant future. But does the polarization of the political class have a significant negative impact on the policies that our governments adopt? A definitive answer to that question lies in the more distant future. In the 1990s scholars carried on a lengthy debate about whether divided government resulted in poorer legislative outcomes than unified government.[58] More than a decade later there is still considerable disagreement on the effects of unified versus divided control on the amount of important legislation, let alone its quality and effectiveness. Some scholars suspect the same will be true of polarized versus centrist politics.[59] If so, judgments about the consequences of polarized politics will remain matters of judgment and impression for some time.

While conceding the lack of conclusive evidence that the party system of today is any worse at solving societal problems than the system of a generation ago,[60] I think it would be very hard to argue that today's party system is *better* at solving problems than the disorganized decentralized party system that it replaced. Rather than seek power on the basis of coherent programs, the parties at times throw fundamental principles to the wind when electoral considerations dictate, just as the decentralized parties of the mid-twentieth century did. At other times they hold fast to divisive positions that have only symbolic importance—President Bush reiterated his support for a constitutional amendment to ban gay marriage in his 2005 State of the Union Address while evidently not intending to do anything to achieve it. On issues like Social Security and the war in Iraq, facts are distorted and subordinated to ideology, and party members hesitate to raise a dissenting voice. Mandates for major policy changes are claimed on the basis of narrow electoral victories. And problems continue to fester even when there is general agreement on the outlines of the legislation needed to address them. Again and again immigration reform dies in Congress.

To be sure, I have painted with broad brush, and my interpretations of recent political history may prove as partial and inaccurate as some of those advanced in the 1970s. Furthermore, I recognize the possibility that unified Democratic government under present conditions might be significantly different from the unified Republican government we have experienced—Gilman argued that the features of responsible parties discussed above are really Republican features.[61] But even if true, this implies that an earlier generation of political scientists failed to appreciate that Republican and Democratic responsible-party government would be significantly different, let alone identify the empirical bases for such differences.

In sum, my belief is that the political process today not only is less representative than it was a generation ago and less supported by the citizenry, but the outcomes of that process are at a minimum no better. The present disconnect is cause for concern and not something that can be discounted as either normal or unimportant.

CHAPTER 8

RECONNECTING THE PEOPLE
AND THEIR GOVERNMENT

BEFORE CONCLUDING BOOKS like this the author is expected to lay out solutions for the problem(s) the book describes. In *Culture War?* I followed that custom, albeit with appropriate caution about the likely efficacy of the solutions offered.[1] To be quite candid, I cannot repeat the exercise here. I do not believe that there are any off-the-shelf solutions that would have a major impact on the disconnect described in the preceding chapters. If the African American internal migration, the growth of the Sunbelt, and the reentry of evangelicals into politics largely account for the party sorting described in chapters 3 and 5, then the increased ideological homogeneity of today's parties has its roots in large-scale demographic changes operating over decades. The consequences of such changes are unlikely to be countered or even significantly mitigated by institutional and procedural reforms. Demography is destiny, the old saying goes, and demographic and social changes appear to be major parts of the explanation for the present condition of our politics.

In a similar manner, if the post–World War II decline of traditional, locally based, general-interest organizations increasingly led candidates to build their electoral coalitions out of new, nationally organized, narrowly focused groups that demand attention to narrow agendas and fealty to unrepresentative points of view, there is little or nothing we can do to affect that development. The single-issue groups spawned by the advocacy explosion show no signs of disappearing, and there is no obvious reason to expect a major resurgence of Elks, Grange, Kiwanis, Odd Fellows, Rotaries, and other such groups that once organized American social life and connected it to the political order.

Thus, any institutional or procedural reforms that we can imagine are likely to operate on the margins of the problem, which is not to say that they should be ignored, of course. In the first part of this chapter, I will briefly consider some of the usual suspects—redistricting reform, primary reform, and public financing of elections. Then I will attempt to think outside the box about the possibilities of change; for if such change were to come, almost certainly it would come from factors that are not currently prominent in our thinking.

INSTITUTIONAL AND PROCEDURAL REFORMS

Gerrymandering and Polarization

If one systematically surveyed editorial and op-ed writing about polarization, I suspect that partisan gerrymandering would emerge as the single most commonly identified cause. The logic is straightforward: a redistricting plan that maximizes the number of districts safe for one party or the other results in general elections where the result is a foregone conclusion. The usual incentives for candidates to move to the center are absent because the *district* center is actually well over to the left in safe Democratic districts and well over to the right in safe Republican districts. Candidates need only keep the support of their primary electorates, and because primary electorates are generally noncentrist, the result is elections won by candidates who are mostly liberals and conservatives rather than moderates.

Gerrymandering is generally a plausible card to play in any argument about what's wrong with American politics. A generation ago when analysts noted a sharp decline in the number of competitive House districts and an associated rise in the electoral value of incumbency, some immediately suspected the flurry of 1960s court-ordered redistricting.[2] Subsequent research showed, however, that incumbent-protection gerrymandering had little to do with the increased advantage of incumbency.[3] In the late 1980s when analysts pondered the continuing juxtaposition of Republican presidents and Democratic Congresses, many observers (especially on the Republican side) postulated a Democratic gerrymander as the basis of the seemingly permanent Democratic House majority. But again research concluded that gerrymandering had little to do with it.[4]

Proponents of the gerrymandering explanation of polarization point out that gerrymandering has become far more sophisticated in recent years. Databases that were once closely guarded are now widely available and more detailed than ever; sophisticated software is cheap and easy to use; and aside from equal population, the courts do not constrain the line drawers to respect values like compactness and contiguity, especially where minority representation is an issue.[5] Thus, gerrymanderers have a freer hand and an easier task than a generation ago.

Yet once again, recent research provides little basis for the common belief that gerrymandering is a significant cause of contemporary political polarization.[6] There is, of course, the obvious counterexample of the U.S. Senate. States are not subject to redistricting, but roll-call voting has polarized in the Senate as much as in the House, and it began at about the same time, so it is unlikely to be a product of the gradual movement of members of the House into the Senate.[7] In a similar manner, there is anecdotal evidence that even bodies elected at-large—various local councils and boards—have experienced the same polarization that is evident on the national level.

Some research does show that representatives from competitive districts are slightly more moderate than members from safe districts, but the effect is tiny—even in the most competitive districts, Democrats and Republicans move only slightly toward the center from the heart of their respective bases.[8] The upshot is that even if the vast majority of legislative districts could be redrawn to be competitive in terms of party registration, the impact on observed levels of polarization would be slight. Some observers believe that if the entire country could move to an Iowa-type system of redistricting by independent commission, bigger effects would be observed, but there is little in the way of actual data in support of that view.

Despite the lack of evidence that reform of the redistricting process would do much to alleviate political polarization, I would still favor comprehensive reform on the grounds that some reforms are good in and of themselves, regardless of their impact. There is something outrageous about allowing incumbent representatives to choose their voters when the essence of representative democracy is the opposite. Moreover, the courts' obsession with exactly equal district populations to the exclusion of everything else (except race and ethnicity) makes it easier than ever to draw lines on grounds of pure partisan and incumbent self-interest. Those who draw the lines now are largely free to ignore traditional criteria such as compactness, contiguity, and the preservation of communities of interest (other than racial and ethnic). The irony is that even if it were possible to count people with the accuracy court decisions presume, which it is not, there would still be significant interdistrict differences in the number of *eligible voters*, not to mention vast differences in the number of *actual voters*, subjects that are highly relevant for any evaluation of a representational scheme.[9]

Primaries and Polarization

Perhaps the common presumption that gerrymandering produces polarization reflects a confusion of the effects of primaries with the effects of gerrymandering. Primary turnout is normally very low. Recall from chapter 3 that in the hotly contested 2006 Connecticut Democratic Primary where challenger Ned Lamont defeated incumbent Joe Lieberman, the turnout among registered Democrats was only 40 percent. (Connecticut is a closed primary state.) Nationally in 2006, turnout in the thirty-eight states that held *statewide* primaries (governor, U.S. senator) was less than 16 percent of the eligible electorate.[10] Turnout in local primaries often falls in the single-digit range.

If primary voters were a representative sample of the American electorate, low turnout would pose no great problem (except to political theorists enamored of popular participation). Some studies of presidential primary voters have concluded that the primary voters are not as unrepresentative as popular commentary assumes, but when we are talking about a sixth to a tenth of the electorate voting in a subpresidential primary—

often split between two parties—the likelihood is that we are talking about a primary electorate composed disproportionately of the hard-core wing-nuts in the two parties.[11]

A generation ago, the presumption was that candidates would be pulled toward their party bases in the primaries but would then move back toward the center in the general election. Richard Nixon, that avowed practitioner of centrist politics, repeatedly offered such advice to his party comrades (and in the view of some followed it to the extent that he overshot the center to the left side when he instituted the first significant federal affirmative action program, imposed wage and price controls, and established the Environmental Protection Agency, among other centrist to liberal policy initiatives). But it may be that developments in the past generation have made it more difficult for candidates to follow Nixon's advice. If today's party foot soldiers and contributors are primarily motivated by ideological or programmatic commitments, they may be less willing to abide a candidate's centrist moves after the primary. And the media revolution has made it more difficult for candidates to stake out a position at one time and modify it at another time. Indeed, in today's YouTube world the negative fall-out from such midcourse corrections ("flip flops") may make them impossible.[12]

Logically, such a primary effect should be strongest in closed primaries and weakest in open primaries. Thus, one avenue of reform would be to open up the primary process. An extreme example is the blanket primary adopted by California voters in 1996. In this system, all eligible voters, regardless of party registration, received the same ballot. For each office they were free to vote for one candidate of whichever party they wished, Democratic for one office, Republican for another, Libertarian for a third, and so forth. The top vote-getter of each party then advanced to the general election. Notably, Prop 198 establishing this primary received nearly 60 percent of the vote in a *primary* election, and it was supported by majorities of both Democratic and Republican primary voters—even the hard-core primary voters favored opening up the candidate selection process!

The proposition was opposed by the formal leadership of all the California parties, however, who had no wish to share the nominating power with independents or members of other parties. After Prop 198 passed, the parties sued on the grounds that the blanket primary violated their associational rights. Overruling the federal district and appellate courts, the U.S. Supreme Court held for the parties seven to two in an opinion that shows the continuing hold of outmoded patterns of thinking.[13] In essence, the Court placed the associational rights of the parties above the revealed preferences of the people those parties purport to represent—the people whose taxes pay for the electoral process operated by their state and local officials. The opinion clearly reflected mid-twentieth-century political science thinking about the value of parties for democratic government. In 1942 Professor E. E. Schattschneider wrote "This volume is devoted to the thesis that the political parties created democracy and that modern democracy is unthinkable save in terms of the parties."[14] A half century later Justice Scalia wrote for the majority, "Representative democracy in any populous unit of governance is unimaginable without the ability of citizens to band together in promoting among the electorate candidates who espouse their political views."[15]

But as discussed in the preceding chapter, the parties of the 1990s are not the same entities as the parties of the 1940s. The party theorists of that era failed to anticipate many of the developments that have since come to pass. This is not to claim that we can operate a modern democracy without parties but, rather, to suggest that today's party leaders should not be accorded the exalted status that the court majority granted them in protecting their right to operate an electoral oligopoly contrary to the wishes of the voters whose choices that oligopoly restricts.

The Court did expressly separate the nonpartisan run-off primary used in Louisiana from its determination that the blanket primary was unconstitutional, so although it is messier in its operation the so-called "jungle primary" is still an option worth considering. But again, when all is said and done, I am dubious that primary reform would have a major impact on polarization.

The 1998 California blanket primary saw about a 2.4 percent increase in turnout over the average of the previous three midterm-year primaries, although one could argue that it might take some time for the electorate to realize the opportunities afforded by the blanket primary.[16] Still, it is doubtful that primary reform would produce an explosion in voter turnout that would bring a flood of moderates to the polls. After all, the midterm general election turnout is rarely more than 40 percent. Americans already are called on to vote more often than the citizens of other democracies, and it is unlikely that changing the primary rules would have more than a marginal effect. Still, it's better than nothing in my opinion. Moreover, nonpartisan primaries could operate as the proverbial "club behind the door," serving as a kind of background threat that voters might use if both parties became too much the prisoner of unrepresentative base groups.

Campaign Finance and Polarization

Another common explanation for heightened political polarization is the need to raise money. Those content with the status quo on any given issue are not as likely to contribute money as those who desperately wish to change it. People with ambivalent or uncertain beliefs are not as likely to contribute as those who hold black-and-white beliefs with certitude. Thus, the natural place to look for campaign money is in the ranks of the single-issue groups, and a natural strategy to motivate their members is to exaggerate the threats their enemies pose. Political folklore, for example, holds that interest group membership is countercyclical to electoral success—groups gain membership and contributions rise when the party hostile to their interests does better, environmental groups when Republicans win, gun groups when Democrats do.

Campaign finance is not high on the reform agenda at the time of this writing. Perhaps all parties to the debate are still tired from the battle over McCain—Feingold (the Bipartisan Campaign Finance Reform Act of 2002). Or perhaps reformers have become more cautious after seeing that the attempt to outlaw soft money contributions to the parties spawned an explosion in the number of so-called 527 groups, which are even more unrepresentative than the two parties.[17] Or perhaps the partisan incentive for campaign finance reform has diminished because Democrats are raising more money than Republicans of late.

Some commentators believe that public financing of elections would reduce the dependence of candidates on special interest groups. The first-order effect might run in this direction, but how big would it be? Campaign spending without reference to target groups is a very inefficient way to campaign. Interest groups would still have the membership lists that identify who might respond to particular sorts of appeals, and group members and supporters would continue to be a primary source of campaign workers. Moreover, there is at least a possibility that the reform could be counterproductive. Many incumbents never face well-funded challengers. Doing so might make them more dependent on interest groups than they currently are, not less.

There are a number of practical difficulties with this argument as well. A public financing scheme could apply to all federal elections, but each individual state would have to adopt its own, as a few already have. And public finance for candidates still leaves the question of initiatives: should proponents and opponents receive public finance to conduct their campaigns?

But in the end, surveys show that the electorate has so little enthusiasm for public financing that it is not productive to spend any more time contemplating it. Whatever its theoretical effect on polarization, we are extremely unlikely ever to observe it in the real world.

ELECTORAL STRATEGY AND CLOSING THE DISCONNECT

Although I do not believe that we can intentionally do much to close the disconnect between the American people and the political order, I am coming to believe that the current divisiveness in our politics has peaked. The divisions evident in the political class are in part tactical and in part genuine, and one can identify considerations working to lessen both.

By tactical divisiveness I mean the deliberate attempt by important political actors to open or deepen cleavages where they might otherwise not exist or where they appear in milder form. Of course, such a strategy only works if your party is on the correct (majority) side of the resulting divide. The use of "wedge" issues like gun control, partial birth abortion, bilingual education, and gay marriage has been a significant component of Republican electoral strategy in recent decades.[18] Arguably, Democrats have not engaged as often in such tactics, but probably because they have not been able to find wedge issues on which they are on the right (majority) side. Several times they have assessed the political situation incorrectly and their attempt to use wedges backfired, as with gun control in the early 1990s and again in the 2000 presidential campaign. (A party rooted in the cosmopolitan cities of the two coasts and in university towns is not well-situated to hear the voice of America.) At the time of this writing, it looks like there is some promise for Democrats in the issues of stem cell research and perhaps end-of-life decisions. The more that Republican candidates are pulled to the absolutist "culture of life" position on such issues, the more likely are they to fall on the wrong (minority) side of the wedge.

By genuine divisiveness I mean the actual beliefs of members of the political class about the issues that ostensibly motivate them. Although candidates may be tactically divisive and interest group leaders may view divisiveness primarily as a tactic for maximizing contributions, many of the rank-and-file who support the causes and candidates are sincere in their beliefs. Thus, any lessening of genuine divisiveness presumes a change in beliefs and values on the part of members of the political class.

Although I may be looking at the future through rose-tinted glasses, I believe that both kinds of divisiveness may have peaked, opening the way for a more problem-solving politics to play a larger role in the years to come.

Passing of the Base Strategy?

Both print and broadcast journalists have dissected and evaluated Karl Rove's electoral strategy of relying predominantly—if not exclusively—on the party base. The Republican congressional seat gain in 2002 and the reelection of President Bush in 2004 were widely viewed as a vindication of Rove's bold and risky departure from the centrist strategy that traditionally dominated political thinking in the United States. My view has always been different. The 2002 midterm gain should be viewed as a special case in the changed circumstances of the post-9/11 world.[19] And George Bush won reelection in 2004 *in spite of* following a suboptimal strategy. Indeed, only a superior get-out-the-vote operation and the ability of the Republican campaign to maintain the conflation of the war on terror with the war in Iraq through the election saved the president from defeat.

The base strategy only makes sense when two conditions are simultaneously met: (1) your base is bigger than the base of the other party, and (2) your base is near a majority in size—even if your base is 30 percent of the electorate and theirs is 25 percent, a base strategy has little to recommend it. The belief that the first condition was met in the 1990s probably owes a lot to surveys that consistently report that self-identified conservatives outnumber self-identified liberals in the country by a considerable margin: 35–40 percent compared with 20–25 percent (recall the bottom panel of figure 1.5). That still leaves a 40–45 percent plurality of moderates, so the second condition appears problematic.

But as I noted in chapter 3, journalist Thomas Edsall reported that Karl Rove was happy enough with the "compassionate conservative" strategy that the Bush campaign used in 2000 until analyses by campaign pollster Matthew Dowd showed that swing voters had largely disappeared.[20] That is, even if a large number of Americans professed ideological moderation and political independence, their actual behavior in the voting booth contradicted their verbal claims. The Republican base was nearly big enough to constitute a majority in itself.

Many political scientists would be dubious about both the underlying conditions of the base strategy. Although far more Americans consider themselves conservatives than liberals, that datum does not mean as much as members of the political class presume. As discussed in chapter 2, ordinary Americans are not nearly as consistently liberal or conservative in their actual policy views as members of the political class. Moreover, as the research cited in chapter 2 shows, many people who adopt the conservative label do not actually have conservative policy views—recall the serious deficit of popular support for President Bush's initiative to add personal accounts to Social Security. Many relatively uninformed Americans apparently hear or see the latest liberal silliness and figure, "If that's liberal, I must be a conservative." In sum, it is likely that Republican campaign strategists consistently overestimate the size and homogeneity of the conservative base on which they can rely.

I am not privy to the analyses that Dowd used to convince Rove, but one could raise at least two serious questions—or, two versions of the same question—even if these analyses appeared to support Dowd's argument. First, how confident was the Republican high command that the findings for 2000 would continue to hold in 2004 and beyond? After all, in 1984 the number of swing voters was in the same low range as in 2000, but a scant eight years later nearly one in five American voters abandoned the two-party system altogether and voted for Ross Perot. Perhaps Republicans assumed that nearly all the Perot voters were not really swing voters but only temporarily disaffected members of the Republican base, but that would be a truly heroic assumption that is contrary to fact.[21] Political participants and journalists tend to think in the here and now, albeit for different reasons, but political scientists (especially old ones) appreciate how much things can change over time. Like French generals in the 1930s who were well-prepared to re-fight World War I, political strategists focus too heavily on the most recent election.

Second, how much were the Republican analyses dependent on particular candidates? That is, how contingent were the findings? Would they change when new candidates with different positions were on the ballot? As I noted in chapter 3, the number of swing voters is endogenous; swing voters are a function of domestic and international conditions, the candidates on the ballot, and the issues in the campaign.[22] Such contingency is the reason that election results change. In the aftermath of 9/11 and with the war in Iraq raging, it is difficult to remember the conditions under which the 2000 election took place. To recall Pietro Nivola's phrase, it was a period of "petty politics."[23] The Cold War had ended and the budget was balanced—presidential candidates actually talked about school uniforms and V-chips. And despite the change in Democratic candidates from Clinton to Gore, the 2000 election was still largely about Clinton.[24] What would happen when Clinton was no longer the opposition?

Had Republican strategists stepped back and taken a broader look, they would have seen Republican governors in blue states like Connecticut, Massachusetts, Michigan, and New York and Democratic governors in red states like Georgia, Kentucky, Mississippi, and Missouri. In all, after the 2000 elections, nineteen states had governors whose political party affiliation was the opposite of the presidential candidate who carried the state. After the Republicans faithfully followed the base strategy in 2004, the number increased to twenty-one states, and after swing voters suddenly reappeared in 2006, the number rose to twenty-six. In contrast to the red—blue presidential map, a map of gubernatorial control is much more complex (figure 8.1), and if we go further down the ballot, the map of unified party control of states is more complex still (figure 8.2). Voters who look set in their ways when choosing between a typical contemporary liberal and a typical contemporary conservative are quite prepared to change their votes when faced with candidates who run on different issues and take different positions. The Republicans mistook voters who "had not changed" in an election (or two) for voters who "would not change" ever (or at least in the next election).

What If?

President Bush has governed as a divider not a uniter, but maybe he had no choice.[25] Political scientist James Campbell has argued that President Bush's governing style was necessitated by the conditions surrounding his election. To a historically unusual degree Bush owed his election to voters whom Campbell

Figure 8.1 Republican versus Democratic Gubernational Control after the 2006 Elections

Shaded states represent a Republican governor, and white states represent a Democratic governor.

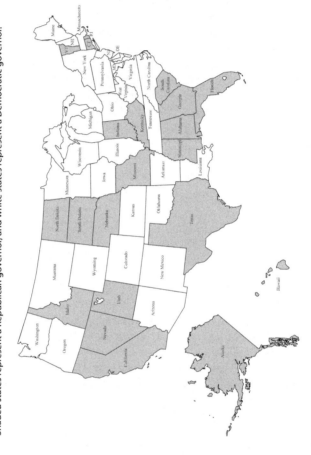

Figure 8.1 Unified Party Control of States after the 2006 Elections

Dark shaded states represent unified Democratic control of state government, light shaded states represent unified Republican control, and white states represent divided party control. Nebraska's legislative is nonpartisan.

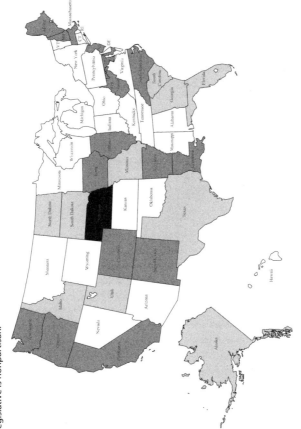

Note: Washington, DC, indicates the Office of the Mayor.

classifies as belonging to the Republican base, rather then to moderate "swing" voters. And, with little possibility of any payoff from reaching out, President Bush made the reasonable choice to "dance with the ones that brung him." Campbell's position is coherent, although his definition of the base is overly broad.[26] But more important, his dismissal of the upside of reaching out seems too pessimistic to me. Consider an alternative account of what might have been.

The later years of the Clinton administration indeed were marked by severe partisan conflict. Both strong Republicans and Democrats were embittered by the impeachment imbroglio, the Republicans because they failed (and lost seats in the 1998 elections, which added injury to insult) and the Democrats because Republicans had tried to impeach the president in the first place. (Characteristically, the American people were somewhere in the middle, with two-thirds supporting censure to show their disapproval of Clinton's behavior but opposing impeachment.) That Bush lost the popular vote and nevertheless became president only further antagonized those not inclined to support him. Under such conditions it seems reasonable to conclude that there was little to be gained by fishing for voters in the middle.

Reasonable or not, maybe that conclusion was too quick. Might the president's political advisers have drawn the wrong lessons from the 2000 election? After all, most political science forecasting models predicted that Bush should have decisively *lost* the 2000 election—seven forecasting models predicted a Gore victory by anywhere between 53 and 60 percent of the popular vote.[27] That Bush came so close to winning the popular vote running as the head of a party recently punished by the electorate and against an incumbent vice president in a time of peace and prosperity perhaps should have been viewed as evidence consistent with the appeal of compassionate conservatism. Why did the outcome necessarily mean that there was little hope of expanding the Bush coalition?

Even if that possibility was rejected, the aftermath of 9/11 offered another opportunity for Bush to follow a more inclusive governing strategy. Of course, no president could have sustained the record high approval ratings recorded in the fall of 2001, but after the widely supported and generally successful invasion of Afghanistan, suppose the president had followed a different course. Rather than adopt the role of "war president," what if he had positioned himself instead as a national unity president? Suppose he had announced that the campaign to destroy Islamic terrorism would be a difficult, lengthy, and costly task that would require sacrifice from the American people. Further tax cuts would be impossible because the money was needed to fund the war on terror. Suppose he had said that the United States could no longer allow its economic health and security to be dependent on unstable and/or dictatorial Middle Eastern regimes and proposed a major initiative to develop greater energy independence by supporting alternative fuels.[28] Suppose he had said that despite his strong personal views Americans could no longer afford to fight each other over moral questions about which people of good faith strenuously disagreed; the states and civil society would have to deal with these. And above all, suppose he had recognized that the main reasons the American public would support a war against Iraq—Saddam's complicity in 9/11 and his possession of weapons of mass destruction—rested on untrustworthy evidence and had chosen instead to continue diplomatic efforts. Given these counterfactual suppositions, I think that President Bush could have been reelected in 2004 with a margin comparable to Bill Clinton's in 1996, and Karl Rove's dream of playing Mark Hanna to Bush's McKinley and creating a generation-long Republican majority would not look as unlikely as it does in 2008. McKinley, after all, did not follow a base strategy—he expanded the Republican Party into the industrial working class.[29]

Of course, had George Bush followed such an alternative path, he would most certainly have lost some support in his base. But given the state of public opinion, I believe he could have drawn support from more moderate voters in numbers closer to those drawn by earlier Republican presidents and sufficient to guarantee an easy reelection. Perhaps he himself was unwilling to act in this fashion, but I do not believe that he was the prisoner of conditions and events and incapable of acting in any way other than the way that he did.

Ironically, after reportedly convincing Karl Rove and President Bush to follow the base strategy, Matthew Dowd went on to become the chief campaign strategist for California governor Arnold Schwarzenegger in 2006. The "governator," of course, is nothing if not a creation of swing voters. In the 2003 recall election the exit polls indicated that one in five 2002 Gray Davis (Democratic) voters switched to Schwarzenegger. And in the 2006 election, more than three-quarters of a million Californians who voted for Schwarzenegger could not bring themselves to support an intelligent, knowledgeable conservative for lieutenant governor one office lower on the ballot. California voters not only swung between elections, they swung within the 2006 election. In early 2007 Dowd made national news by criticizing President Bush for among other things "failing to reach across the political divide to build consensus."[30] Indeed.

SOCIAL CHANGE AND CLOSING THE DISCONNECT

After the collapse of the Soviet Union, political scientist Sidney Verba commented to me that "before it happened no one predicted it; after it happened everyone could explain why it had been inevitable." Verba's quip captures an important truism about social science: we are reasonably able to identify factors that contribute to social and political stability but much less able to specify when other factors are going to produce political and social change. Sometimes analysts are aware of change-inducing factors, but our understanding of the strength of destabilizing factors relative to stabilizing factors is underdeveloped. After the fact, we can say that the former overwhelmed the latter, but before the fact is anyone's guess.

Just as the social and demographic changes discussed in chapters 5 and 6 contributed to the present disconnect in American politics, so there are social and demographic factors at work that are undermining it. Whether and when these sociodemographic factors will change the disconnect situation is a more difficult question, but we can at least identify some destabilizing forces now at work.

Generational Change

In chapter 5 I suggested that seven major sociodemographic changes had significantly affected the course of American politics in the past half century. An eighth is about to: the aging of the population. The first year of the huge baby boom cohort turned sixty-two years of age in 2008. Much has been written about the fiscal challenges to Medicare and Social Security posed by this demographic bulge, but less has been written about the political consequences (except for the political dangers and difficulties of restraining the costs of Medicare and Social Security benefits).

Various commentators have suggested that the culture wars of the past several decades are the continuation of the dormitory debates of the 1960s between those who supported the war in Vietnam and those who opposed it, between those who applauded the activities of the new social movements and those who found them threatening and destabilizing, and between those who embraced the values of the counterculture and those who condemned them. Although such observations obviously are oversimplifications, the kernel of truth is that many of today's political debates have their genesis in the social changes of the 1960s and 1970s—drug usage, sexual morality, abortion, secularism, gay rights, family breakdown, as well as the echoes of Vietnam now reverberating around the Iraq war. Some Americans loathed such changes and mobilized against them, whereas others applauded the changes and treated those not fully comfortable with them as ignorant yahoos.

In 1979 the Reverend Jerry Falwell organized various strands of the evangelical reaction against the *Roe v. Wade* decision and other social changes into the Moral Majority, the first of the so-called religious right organizations that have played a prominent role in our politics for the past generation. Falwell died at age seventy-three as this chapter was being written. Pat

Robertson, founder of the Christian Coalition and one-time presidential candidate, is seventy-nine. Louis Sheldon of the Traditional Values Coalition is seventy-five. James Dobson of Focus on the Family, currently considered to be the most important religious right organization, is seventy-three. Richard Land of the Southern Baptist Convention is a virtual youth at sixty-three.

Close observers of the evangelical movement report that a process of generational change is underway. The influence of the prominent leaders and their organizations listed in the preceding paragraph already has peaked.[31] Although Dobson's Focus on the Family boasts a mailing list of 6 million names (a little less than 3 percent of the eligible voting-age population), the average age of those on the list is fifty-two.[32] The new generation of evangelical leaders is not as well known outside the evangelical community as the giants of the religious right (although Rick Warren, pastor of the Saddleback megachurch, whose book *The Purpose Driven Life* has sold 30 million copies, is getting there), but influence is clearly passing to a new generation. Although conservative on social issues, the younger generation of evangelical leaders is not as focused on abortion and sex. They have expanded the agenda to include third-world poverty and AIDs, the environment, and even global warming. This broader focus is reflected in their congregations, whose political views do not differ from those of nonevangelicals nearly as much as mainstream commentators often assume.[33] In May of 2008 a group of evangelical leaders even issued a manifesto urging that evangelicals pull back from party politics.[34]

While baby boomers age, younger cohorts of Americans have entered the electorate. To a large proportion of them, the social changes of the 1960s and 1970s are not changes—life has always been that way. They must find it curious that American political debate seems dominated much of the time by geezers talking about things that happened before they were born. Eventually, they will say "enough" and look to candidates who talk about the issues and problems they and their children will face and not those that dominated the lives of their grandparents.

Revolution in Women's Roles

Another of the demographic changes noted in chapter 5 reinforces the preceding remarks about the likelihood that many of today's most divisive social issues are on the wane. Older feminist leaders sometimes complain that today's young women take for granted many of the changes that their elders fought for.[35] Certainly when I occasionally relate some (true) anecdote, such as Ivy League graduate programs refusing to consider the applications of women as late as the 1950s, today's students—men as well as women—find it difficult to conceive of such a world, even though it existed little more than a generation ago.

Social changes like abortion, sexual liberation, and workplace equality threatened the traditional family and provoked a reaction by evangelicals, among others.[36] But younger generations of women know no other world. Imagine the reaction if hard-core social conservatives in the Republican Party actually succeeded in prohibiting abortion and birth control. It would probably be the end of the Republican Party as we now know it. To be sure, greater gender equality has brought additional stresses from balancing family and work, and more women today appear to be prioritizing family over career, but it is their choice. Either out of economic necessity or personal desire, most women will continue to work. It is unlikely in the extreme that many in the younger generations of women would support attempts to roll back the clock to a time when they were expected to preserve their virginity until marriage and then stay home with the kids. Again, younger generations more likely will be concerned with how to deal with changes that have already occurred, not how to return to a world now gone.

Immigration

Finally, still another social change that will affect politics in the years to come is immigration, although it is unclear whether this will decrease or increase divisiveness or have no effect. About half the growth in population of the United States since the 1960s, with its changes in the immigration laws, is due to immigration—about 50 million new Americans who would not otherwise be here. This is not the place to enter into a long debate about immigration—reams have already been written about it. Suffice it to say that the issue badly splits the Republican Party.[37] Business interests and philosophical libertarians favor liberal laws and allowing a path to citizenship for those already here illegally. Law-and-order Republicans oppose illegal immigration, and nativists oppose any further influx of Spanish speakers. Pragmatists point to the cultural conservatism of immigrants and their entrepreneurial tendencies and suggest that the party should court them.

Judis and Teixeira have argued that the Democrats will benefit as immigrants become citizens and register to vote.[38] Based on past history and given the location of anti-immigrant sentiment in the Republican Party, that seems like the most likely bet, but much will depend on the future strategies followed by both parties. Despite dire warnings of cultural suicide by writers like Samuel Huntington, the demographic evidence shows that the current wave of immigrants, including those from Mexico, are assimilating at least as fast as earlier waves of immigrants did.[39] And contrary to the fears of English-only advocates as well as the hopes of some Latino ethnic advocates, Spanish is essentially a dead language by the third generation.[40] Presumably, enough Republicans eventually will take note of such developments to prevent their party from committing electoral suicide. But such developments also mean that the Democrats' past reliance on identity politics will likely decline in effectiveness in the years to come as immigrants climb into the middle class. In sum, immigration is a wild card. In the short-term the issue may increase divisiveness, but the longer term is more difficult to predict.

SUMMARY

The usual institutional reforms are unlikely to do much to lessen the polarization of contemporary American politics. That polarization has deep roots in a variety of social changes that have increased the homogeneity of each party, widened the differences between the two parties, and encouraged politicians to construct electoral coalitions out of group building blocks that are less encompassing and less representative of the broader public than was the case for most of American history.

But reality continually changes, and there are some signs that the current period of polarization may have run its course. Social changes now at work are undermining the bases of the current polarization. That does not mean that a return to a more centrist problem-solving politics is inevitable, but it at least provides conditions under which that becomes a possibility.

EPILOGUE

Culture War? first appeared four months prior to the 2004 elections, with a second edition eleven months after the elections. Back then the data presented and discussed in the book seemed at odds with casual impressions of the state of American politics. Although President Bush's proposal for Social Security personal accounts had died a quiet death in the summer of 2005 and Hurricane Katrina had struck soon after, the Republican administration still seemed to be on the offensive and the Democrats in retreat. In 2006 and 2007 while this book was being written, however, the political situation was changing. Today the message of *Culture War?* seems far more plausible, indeed, some might say, almost conventional wisdom.

Once again campaign operatives have learned that they are only as good as their last victory. For most of the period between the 2002 elections and the 2006 meltdown of the Bush administration, Karl Rove was by all accounts a political genius who had engineered two notable victories. His plan for a permanent Republican majority seemed on track to confident Republicans, all too terrifyingly so to Democrats.

But Republican fortunes began to decline near the end of 2005, and a year later the president's approval ratings were flirting with historical lows. In the 2006 elections the Republicans suffered a stunning defeat, losing both Houses of Congress. The election post-mortems declared that the election was "the revenge of the center," "the revenge of the independents," "a move back to the political center," the result of "a rising radical center," and an indication that both parties had better "heed voters' call for moderation."[1] The new consensus held that the elections had "buried the notion that swing voters are a dying breed and that elections are won by mobilizing the base."[2]

Surveying the electoral carnage post-2006, the media collectively decided that the once-brilliant Bush election machine was not so brilliant after all. Even members of the Republican general staff had second thoughts. Former Republican national chair Ken Mehlman cautioned that "we have to win back the confidence we lost in '06 from swing voters and ticket-splitters."[3] And as noted earlier, pollster Matthew Dowd criticized President Bush for following the advice he, himself, had given the president in 2004. As for Karl Rove, his dream of a generation-long Republican majority "is dying."[4] In fact, in May of 2007 a delegation of moderate House Republicans met with President Bush and reportedly warned him that continuation of current policy in Iraq could destroy the Republican Party electorally, making observers think more of Herbert Hoover than of William McKinley. Later that month Newt Gingrich, the architect of the 1994 Republican revolution, pronounced Rove's 2004 campaign to be "maniacally dumb."[5]

Immediate election post-mortems invariably are oversimplifications that later analyses—interested and disinterested—qualify and correct. The faith-based wing of each party proclaims that the election vindicated their ideological position. Thus, in 2006 triumphant liberal Democrats saw Congressional victory as a demonstration that the party finally had shown some backbone, forthrightly running as the liberal opposition to the failed policies of the Bush administration. Despondent conservative Republicans, in turn, argued bitterly that the electorate had punished the administration for straying from the central tenets of conservatism. Meanwhile, those who draw conclusions on the basis of evidence rather than ideology pointed to the war in Iraq, the tarnished image of the Republican Congress, and a succession of policy missteps and reverses that cumulatively brought down the GOP majorities.

Still, there is little question that the 2006 elections showed the vote divisions apparent in the 2000–2002–2004 election period were less fixed than Republican operatives and many political commentators had assumed. The exit polls indicated that Democrats and Republicans voted much the same in 2006 as in

2004—self-identified Democrats were about 4 percent more Democratic in their voting, and self-identified Republicans were about 2 percent less Republican, but independents were 17 percent less Republican. As I argued in the preceding chapter, the decisions of independents and some weak partisans were more contingent than many political operatives and commentators believed. In the 2008 elections, that contingency was all the more important. Turnout typically rises about 50 percent from the midterm to the presidential election, and the lion's share of that increase comes from the ranks of the independents and weaker partisans, who are less motivated to vote in the midterm elections. That held true in the 2008 elections as turnout rose to about 62 percent and political independents and ideological moderates continued to move to the Democrats, resulting in Republican defeats even in states and districts not thought vulnerable a year before the election.

What does all this mean? Were the 2006 and 2008 elections simply rebukes of an administration that many Americans believed had made too many mistakes to tolerate? Or were deeper forces at work? There are some indications that the latter may be the case. Numerous signs of electoral ferment were in the air by early 2007. Procedurally, the 2008 presidential campaign got underway unusually early—by the spring of 2007 most candidates had officially declared, and fund-raising contests, debates, and other early trials were in progress. States leapfrogged each other in an attempt to schedule their primaries as early as possible, increasing the possibility that the 2008 primary season would be too compressed to winnow the field. Rather than allowing a single candidate to develop momentum, gradually build strength, and claim the nomination, the explosion of early contests in large states might leave, a few pundits speculated, a fragmented situation in which one or both parties with several strong candidates split the early primaries with few delegates remaining to be chosen. Before the voting began the Republicans looked like the party more likely to have a protracted nomination fight, but in a year of surprises, the Democrats took until summer to choose their nominee. Most observers agreed that the post-1968 nominating system was broken, and although it could not be fixed for 2008, something would have to change by 2012.

More important, some of the leading contenders in each party did not look like the more recent candidates of their parties. In the summer of 2006, a fairly common expectation was that in the 2008 presidential election Sen. Hillary Clinton (D-N.Y.) would oppose Sen. George Allen (R-Va.). Such a contest would likely have reproduced the voting patterns of 2000 and 2004 fairly closely. In preparation for such an eventuality, an Internet third-party movement, Unity08, made preparations to nominate a bipartisan centrist ticket, and many in the media speculated that billionaire Michael Bloomberg, the Republican/ Democratic mayor of New York, was thinking along those lines himself. But with Allen's defeat in his 2006 senatorial race, the Republican contest became wide open, and the emergence of Barack Obama on the Democratic side further roiled the waters. As I wrote earlier, a Rudy Guiliani or John McCain versus Barack Obama contest very likely would not reproduce the 2000 and 2004 voting patterns.[6]

In short, by late 2007 various indicators of political change were in the air, a condition remarked on by more than a few of our national political commentators. As noted in the preceding chapter, over the years there have been occasional casual observations to the effect that in the past few decades political conflict in the country has been the continuation of the debates of the 1960s. Such sentiments began to appear with increased frequency in 2007. Michael Barone wrote of the "civil war between two halves of the baby-boom generation."[7] Ellen Goodman mused about baby-boomers "dividing into pro- and anti-Vietnam War nursing homes."[8] Daniel Henninger wished that the country would say "bye-bye baby to the children of 1968."[9] *The Economist* wrote of "The 40-Year Itch."[10] Barack Obama charged that Hillary Clinton has "been fighting some of the same fights since the '60s" and offered himself as a way to transcend the past.[11] And in a widely noted essay conservative commentator Andrew Sullivan seconded Obama's offer: "Obama's candidacy . . . is a potentially transformative one. Unlike any of the other candidates, he could take America—finally—past the debilitating, self-perpetuating family quarrel of the Baby Boom generation that has long engulfed all of us."[12] Although such remarks obviously oversimplify, the kernel of truth underlying them is the reaction of some Americans to the social changes described in chapters 5 and 6. Beginning in the 1950s with the civil rights movement; exploding in the 1960s with the addition of the anti-war movement, the counter-culture, and the women's movement; and continuing in the 1970s with the environmental movement, social change occurred with dizzying speed. Most Americans went with the flow, coming to terms with these changes and continuing on with their lives, but a minority who loathed such changes eventually found a home in the Republican Party and the single-issue groups allied with it, and a minority who applauded such changes eventually found a home in the Democratic Party and its allied interest groups. Empowered by the participatory turn discussed in chapter 4, these ideologues and activists have significantly shaped American politics for three decades.

But their time may be coming to an end. The electoral ferment bubbling in 2008 undoubtedly reflects some of the demographic change discussed in the preceding chapter, in particular the inexorable advance of time. Phyllis Schafly, who led the fight against the ERA, is eighty-five years old. Howard Phillips, conservative activist and chair of the Conservative Caucus, a policy advocacy group, is sixty-eight. Richard Viguerie, the conservative pioneer of direct mail, is seventy-six. Longtime conservative activist Paul Weyrich was sixty-seven when he died in late 2007. At fifty-three, anti-tax crusader Grover Norquist is a mere stripling. They and other movement conservatives were unable to prevent the nomination of John McCain for president in 2008. And as noted in the preceding chapter, just as the religious right leaders are getting very long in the tooth, the leaders of the feminist movement they battled are aging with them: Kate Michelman, outspoken former leader of NARAL, is sixty-seven; Eleanor Smeal, twice president of NOW, is seventy; and Gloria

Steinem, cofounder of the National Women's Political Caucus and other feminist organizations, is seventy-five. One of the intellectual mothers of the feminist movement, Betty Friedan, died in 2006 at seventy-nine. During the 2008 Democratic primaries elder-generation feminists complained about the failure of many young women today to appreciate the feminist struggle and to close ranks behind Hillary Clinton. A similar age divide was apparent in another major identity group of our time, African Americans. Consider some of the civil rights icons: Jesse Jackson is sixty-eight, John Lewis is sixty-nine, and Andrew Young is seventy-seven. At a mere fifty-five, Al Sharpton is a kid. African American professor William Jelani Cobb referred to them collectively as the "civil rights gerontocracy" when writing about their ambivalence toward a younger Obama.[13]

A generation ago political scientists elaborated a complex theory of electoral change under the rubric of critical realignment theory.[14] Very briefly, the theory divided the historical series of American national elections into a small number of periods or eras, separated by one or more critical or realigning elections. Within each period, elections were more similar to each other than they were to elections on opposite sides of the period boundaries, where similarity was judged principally by two measures—the similarity of the issues contested in the elections and the similarity of the electoral coalitions supporting each party. The general consensus was that realignments accompanied the victory of Andrew Jackson in 1828; the demise of the Whigs, the rise of the Republicans, and the break-up of the Jacksonian Democrats in the 1850s; the ascendance of the industrial Republican Party in the 1890s; their defeat at the hands of the Roosevelt Democrats in the 1930s; and the break-up of the New Deal coalition in the 1960s. Evidently, these electoral changes tended to occur every generation or so, sometimes precipitated by a critical event that was not foreseen—the Depressions of the 1890s and 1930s, or the Kansas–Nebraska Act in 1854.

The theory has been the target of much criticism in recent years.[15] Clearly, the theory was too stylized—an overgeneralization of the New Deal scenario. In particular, research showed that the voting changes that precipitated the realignments of the 1850s and the 1890s were not tidal waves like that of the 1930s. Rather, relatively small electoral shifts had large consequences for control of national institutions and the policy agenda.[16] In addition, the thirty- to thirty-five-year periodicity included in some versions of the theory was something of a straight-jacket given the less neat sequence of electoral history.

Still, it is clear that roughly every generation or so, there does appear to be a fairly significant shake-up of the American political system. From 1828 through 1856 the Democrats lost only two presidential elections, both to Whig war heroes. Then the party splintered and lost most of the presidential elections for a generation. Between 1896 and 1928 the Republicans won seven of nine presidential elections, losing only to Woodrow Wilson, who was first elected after a split that saw a former Republican president challenging a sitting Republican president for the party's nomination. The New Deal Democratic coalition put an end to this era of Republican dominance and won seven of the next nine presidential elections, falling short only in the losses to Eisenhower, a Republican war hero. The 1964 election seemed to indicate that the Roosevelt coalition was still dominant, but in retrospect, the election was the last hurrah of the New Deal coalition.[17] What followed was a confusing generation of mostly divided control of government, with brief eruptions of unified party control during Clinton's first two years and George Bush's first six.[18]

Now a generation away from the 1960s, the existing order seems fragile—more fragile than I had realized, or I would have tried to finish this book sooner. The Rothbaum lectures were delivered in October 2005 and I began writing in 2006, well before the emergence of Barack Obama as a serious contender for the Democratic nomination and before the extent of the Bush administration's meltdown was fully apparent. But the frailty of the old political order began to show more clearly as the 2008 campaign began. In early 2008 the various factions of the Republican Party—business conservatives, libertarian conservatives, social conservatives, national greatness conservatives, and national security conservatives—all seemed to have their own presidential candidate, although none attracted general enthusiasm, and McCain, the eventual nominee, was strongly opposed by some factions. At the same time, the Democrats turned away from a heavy favorite, the spouse of the first Boomer president, and chose a candidate from Generation X. To one who was in graduate school during the mid-1960s, there is a somewhat familiar feel to our present time. The intensity and violence does not compare, thankfully, but the decline of old coalitions generates a similar uncertainty about the future. That uncertainty may persist for quite a while. After the Democratic Party splintered in 1968, it was another twelve years before the new order took shape (and even longer before political scientists and political commentators consensually recognized it). Electoral triumphs give victors the opportunity to have a lasting impact but provide no guarantees. The victors must exploit the opportunities they are given. Richard Nixon squandered his opportunity to be a transformational president by engaging in personal malfeasance, and Bill Clinton squandered his by his inability to control his personal appetites. Barack Obama now has an opportunity. But he takes office during a time of immense challenges—two wars, the continuing threat of international terrorism, and a global recession with no end in sight. If he succeeds in meeting these challenges while a new generation gradually replaces the old, we may look back someday and conclude that the Obama era was the time when Culture Wars ceased being a topic of political conversation. That is my hope at least.

PROBLEMS IN MEASURING
LEGISLATIVE POLARIZATION

ALTHOUGH THERE IS CONSIDERABLE EVIDENCE—systematic and impressionistic—that the political class today is more polarized than in the past, as in most areas of research there are difficulties in accurately measuring the increase. In particular, as James Snyder pointed out in an important 1992 article, measured polarization among legislators depends not only on their personal positions, but also on the policy status quo and the alternatives that are proposed.[1]

Consider the following simple example. There are two legislative parties, each with five members. There is an economic redistribution policy dimension with complete government control of the economy located on the left and complete private control located on the right. All five Democrats (D_1–D_5)have positions to the left of all five Republicans (R_1–R_5), although some Democrats (Republicans) are more liberal (conservative) than others, and the public policy status quo (SQ) lies squarely between the most conservative Democrat and the most liberal Republican:

Assume each legislator votes for a proposal if it moves government policy closer to his or her position and votes against it if it moves policy away from his or her position. If one of the Democrats were to propose a bill to move policy leftward to the position of D_1, all five Democrats vote yes and all five Republicans vote no. The opposite voting pattern occurs on a bill to move policy rightward to the position of R_1. On such votes party polarization is complete.

But suppose there is another policy dimension—moral or cultural issues with complete personal autonomy on the left and strict government enforcement of traditional values on the right. On this dimension, the parties are divided, with two Democrats to the right of two Republicans and the public policy status quo squarely in between. Now a proposal to move policy leftward to the position of R_1 is supported by three Democrats and two Republicans. A proposal to move policy rightward to D_1 is favored by three Republicans and two Democrats. Both parties are badly split on the issue.

Snyder's important observation is that in addition to the positions of the members, measured polarization depends on the issues voted on and the public policy status quos. This means that from an empirical standpoint, measured polarization will depend on the selection of bills that come to a vote. The conditions sufficient to avoid selection bias are quite restrictive. First, a very specific sample of bills is required.[2] Then, there is a further question of the relative weights to assign to bills—there can be more or less polarization on issues that are more or less important to the voters.

More intuitively, assume in the preceding example that economic and moral issues are of equal concern to legislators but that economic issues are systematically kept off the agenda. In this case, we would underestimate the extent of partisan disagreement. Conversely, if moral issues are kept off the agenda, then we would systematically exaggerate the extent of partisan disagreement. In the real world, of course, bills, amendments, and other proposals are not generated mechanically, let alone in accordance with particular statistical requirements. Just the opposite is true—control of the agenda is considered an important political weapon.[3] Because of this fact, there is no doubt slippage between the positions of legislators as measured statistically and their positions if a full sampling of potential votes were taken.[4]

Do we know if that slippage is likely to be consistent, or at least in one direction, over time—overestimation or underestimation of polarization? Unfortunately, research suggests that it will be very difficult to determine the net effect of changing agendas on measured positions. Roberts and Smith have suggested that party agenda strategies change, and they have shown that although geographic party realignment and the replacement of older, more moderate members by younger, more ideological members both contributed to congressional polarization, moderate members of both parties who continued in office showed increased polarization in their roll call voting as the 1980s and 1990s progressed.[5] This finding is consistent with arguments in the literature that party leaders (principally Democrats in the 1980s and principally Republicans in the 1990s) changed their agenda strategies in ways that highlighted party differences rather than obscured them. The implication of Roberts and Smith's findings is that measured change in roll call voting behavior has been exaggerated by changes in party agenda strategies—either members are less extreme today or were less moderate in the 1970s than standard measures suggest.

On the other hand, Van Houweling provided a rationale for why legislators might be more extreme than their measured positions would suggest.[6] A difficult question for scholars who argue that party leaders have asserted much stronger control over the agenda in recent years than previously is why moderates would permit it?[7] That is, why would party moderates allow their leadership to keep moderate alternatives that they would prefer off the floor and make them choose between more extreme alternatives than they would like? Van Houweling's answer is that party moderates are typically less moderate in their personal views than their public stances suggest. That is, some liberal Democrats and some conservative Republicans publicly moderate their true positions as a matter of electoral necessity. By allowing party leaders to control the agenda, such ersatz moderates get "cover" for votes that reflect their true, but disguised, positions. They can explain to constituents that they would have preferred more moderate courses of action but could only choose between more extreme Republican and Democratic alternatives.

Rodriquez and Weingast introduced yet another complication.[8] Lawmaking is not the province of Congress alone. Any law passed will be administered by the executive and usually reviewed by the courts. Rodriguez and Weingast have observed that a bill's sponsors and supporters have disproportionate influence in compiling the legislative record relied on by the courts that will interpret the law. But passage of a bill inevitably involves compromises with undecided legislators or opponents that result in weaker (i.e., more moderate) legislation than the supporters wanted. Rodriguez and Weingast have argued that courts tend to interpret the legislation in light of the legislative history compiled by supporters of the original version of the legislation rather than the weaker version of the legislation that passes. Foreseeing such an outcome, moderates will insist that liberal legislation be amended in a more conservative direction than they truly prefer and conservative legislation be amended in a more liberal direction than they truly prefer so that the final court interpretations are closer to their true positions. The argument seems a bit esoteric, but it calls our attention to the fact that party leaders are not the only strategic actors in Congress—rank-and-file members also may strategize.

In summary, as in most research areas, there are measurement problems in this one. The implication is that more measurements are better than fewer, and further research should continue. But whatever inaccuracies characterize our current state of knowledge, the weight of the evidence—quantitative and qualitative—leaves little doubt among members of the research community and the large class of political observers that whether as a matter of genuine belief or political tactics, members of the political class in America today are significantly more polarized in their political positions than they were a generation ago.

NOTES

PREFACE AND ACKNOWLEDGMENTS

1. Roger H. Marz, "A Democratic Dissent: The Republican Party Has No Future," *The New Republic* 151, no. 25 (December 19, 1964): 10–11.

2. Richard Nixon said, "The strong conservative wing of the Republican Party . . . deserves a major voice in party councils, and the liberal wing deserves a party voice, but neither can dominate or dictate—the center must lead." Quoted in John H. Kessel, *The Goldwater Coalition* (New York: Bobbs–Merrill, 1968), 310.

3. Pendleton Herring, "Political Parties and the Public Interest," in *Essays in Political Science in Honor of W.W. Willoughby* (Baltimore: Johns Hopkins University Press, 1937), 100—24; and V. O. Key, Jr., *Politics, Parties, and Pressure Groups*, 5th ed. (New York: Crowell, 1964), esp. 214–27.

4. American Political Science Association's (ASPA's) Committee on Political Parties, "Toward a More Responsible Two-Party System," Suppl., *American Political Science Review* 44 (1950).

5. Julius Turner, "Responsible Parties: A Dissent from the Floor," *American Political Science Review* 45 (1951): 143–52, quote at 151.

6. Clinton Rossiter, *Parties and Politics in America* (Ithaca, N.Y.: Cornell University Press, 1960), 108.

7. James Bryce, *The American Commonwealth* (London: Macmillan, 1888).

8. Maurice Duverger, *Political Parties* (New York: Wiley, 1954), esp. 216—28, 245–55, passim.

9. Anthony Downs, *An Economic Theory of Democracy* (New York: Wiley, 1957), esp. chap. 8.

10. For a survey of the theory as it existed three decades after Downs, see James Enelow and Melvin Hinich, eds., *Advances in the Spatial Theory of Voting* (New York: Cambridge, 1990).

11. Perceptions are the point here, not the reality. Some evidence indicates that the Democrats were more moderate than they were popularly viewed, probably because of their association with some

very visible liberal constituencies, such as feminists and civil rights groups. See Henry E. Brady and Paul M. Sniderman, "Floors, Ceilings, Guessing, and Other Pitfalls in Survey Research—The Case of Left Shift" (unpublished paper, August 27, 1984).

12. Morris Fiorina, *Divided Government* (New York: Macmillan, 1992; 2nd ed., Allyn & Bacon, 1996). I considered giving chap. 5 of that book the title, "The Median Voter Fights Back."

13. David Broder, "Vicious Cycle in Governing," *Times-Picayune (La.)*, sec. B, November 13, 1997.

14. Cokie Roberts and Steven Roberts, "GOP Strategy: Make Clinton a Bad Poster Boy," *San Jose Mercury News (Calif.)*, sec. B, September 28, 1998.

15. Morris Fiorina, "Whatever Happened to the Median Voter?" *www.stanford.edu/~mfiorina/*

16. Morris Fiorina, Samuel Abrams, and Jeremy Pope, "The 2000 US Presidential Election: Can Retrospective Voting Be Saved?" *British Journal of Political Science* 33 (2003): 163–87. One wag described Gore's 2000 strategy as, "You've never had it so good, and I'm mad as hell about it." Michael Kinsley, as quoted by Howard Kurtz, "The Premature Post-Mortems Are Starting," *Washington Post*, online extras, October 31, 2000.

17. Morris P. Fiorina, with Samuel Abrams and Jeremy Pope, *Culture War? The Myth of a Polarized America* (New York: Pearson Longman, 2005). Despite its 2005 copyright date, the book actually appeared in late June of 2004—textbook publishers advance copyright dates in order to seem more current to prospective users.

18. On "crafted talk," see Lawrence Jacobs and Robert Shapiro, *Politicians Don't Pander* (Chicago: University of Chicago Press, 2000). On mobilization and demobilization, see Steven Schier, *By Invitation Only* (Pittsburgh, Pa.: University of Pittsburgh Press, 2000).

CHAPTER 1

1. Clem Miller, *Member of the House*, ed. John Baker (New York: Scribner's, 1962), 82–83.

2. Whether this is necessarily a bad thing is a question I confront directly in chapter 7.

3. Although the Speaker, himself or herself, rarely votes.

4. McCormack reputedly had dinner with his wife every night of the fifty years he served in Congress. Reported in former Speaker Tip O'Neill's memoirs, quoted in Nelson Polsby, *How Congress Evolves* (New York: Oxford, 2004), 37.

5. Keith T. Poole and Howard Rosenthal, *Ideology and Congress* (Piscataway, N.J.: Transaction Publishers, 2006). More traditional methods, such as principal-components, yield quite similar estimates as do more recent Bayesian methods. See James Heckman and James Snyder, "Linear Probability Models of the Demand for Attributes, with an Empirical Application to Estimating the Preferences of Legislators," *Rand Journal of Economics* 28:S142–89; and Joshua D. Clinton, Simon Jackman, and R. Douglas Rivers, "The Statistical Analysis of Roll Call Data," *American Political Science Review* 98 (2004): 355–70.

6. More than 10,000 representatives, nearly 2,000 senators, and about 46,000 contested roll calls in each chamber between 1789 and 2004.

7. Poole and Rosenthal, *Ideology and Congress*, chap. 3. At some times in American history, a second dimension emerges. Poole and Rosenthal interpret this dimension as a reflection of racial issues.

8. See, e.g., Sarah Binder, "The Disappearing Political Center: Congress and the Incredible Shrinking Middle," *The Brookings Review* 14 (Fall 1996): 36–39.

9. From unpublished analyses by Sean Theriault, Michael McDonald, and Bernard Grofman, cited in Barbara Sinclair, *Party Wars* (Norman: University of Oklahoma Press, 2006), 16.

10. Keith Poole, e-mail message to author, June 30, 2006. See also Nolan McCarty, Keith T. Poole, and Howard Rosenthal, *Polarized America: The Dance of Ideology and Unequal Riches* (Cambridge, Mass.: MIT Press, 2006), 49–50.

11. McCarty, Poole, and Rosenthal have reported fragmentary evidence that "state legislatures are at least as polarized as the U.S. Congress" (*Polarized America*, 185). Much more systematic evidence will become available as a result of the large state legislative project now in progress under the leadership of Gerald Wright of Indiana University, www.indiana.edu/~ral/.

12. Poole and Rosenthal have shown that at least among the interest groups that rate legislators, the groups are generally more extreme than legislators. See their *Ideology and Congress,* chap. 8.

13. On state and local activists, see Walter J. Stone, Ronald B. Rapoport, and Alan I Abramowitz, "Party Polarization: The Reagan Revolution and Beyond," in *The Parties Respond*, ed. L. Sandy Maisel, 2nd ed. (Boulder, Colo.: Westview Press, 1994), 69–99. McCarty, Poole, and Rosenthal (*Polarized America*, 153–61) have reported that the major soft money and 527 contributors are ideological extremists.

14. Interestingly, the proportion of Republican delegates calling themselves moderates has not declined, and the number of Democratic moderates has actually increased. The most liberal and conservative wings of the parties have grown at the expense of the less extreme left- and right-of-center categories. There is somewhat greater *intraparty* heterogeneity among convention delegates today than in the past.

15. The measures are "thermometer scores." Survey respondents are asked to rate individuals and groups on a 100-point thermometer that indicates how warmly they feel about the person or group they are rating, with 50 degrees being neutral, 100 maximally positive, and 0 maximally negative.

16. A technical note: throughout this book I use a narrow definition of "partisan" (strong and weak identifiers) and a broad definition of "independent" (combining leaners with pure independents). I agree with the argument Warren Miller made late in his career that in general it is misleading to use the full seven-point party identification scale and, in particular, to combine leaning independents with partisans. Briefly, some people call themselves strong or weak partisans depending on how well or poorly their party is doing at any given time; moreover, independents may say they lean toward a particular party because they like that party's candidate or issues better in one election. To say they are closet partisans is an unwarranted inference. See Warren Miller, "Party Identification, Realignment, and Party Voting: Back to Basics," *American Political Science Review* 85 (1991): 557–68.

17. Gallup did not ask this question in the 1980s, instead asking people to place themselves on an 8-position scale that did *not* include "moderate" as a possible position. The result of trying to force Americans into liberal or conservative categories in this way was that about 10 percent of respondents volunteered a "middle-of-the-road" response, and 21 percent said "don't know," in contrast to the 3–5 percent "don't know" with the survey item reported in the top panel of figure 1.5. Even this strange item shows no trend in the number of liberals and conservatives, however.

18. Although both survey organizations use seven-point scales with identical labels, NES includes a qualifying clause "or haven't you thought much about it?" Apparently GSS respondents who do not have this easy out tend to head for the middle category, which supports the common practice of classifying them as moderates. Thanks to Martin Wattenberg for pointing out that the GSS ideological data showed some differences from the NES.

19. Most analysts code those who do not place themselves as moderates.

20. Christopher Ellis and James Stimson, "Operational and Symbolic Ideology in the American Electorate: The 'Paradox' Revisited" (paper presented at the 2005 annual meeting of the Midwest Political Science Association, Chicago, April 7–10, 2005).

21. Together the social conservatives and nonconservatives (Ellis and Stimson call the latter "conflicted conservatives") comprise a clear majority of self-identified "conservatives." In this light, it is easy to understand why President Bush's Social Security privatization proposal went nowhere.

22. Edward Carmines (remarks at the 2006 annual meetings of the Midwest Political Science Association, Chicago, summarizing ongoing research project with Michael Ensley).

23. The locus classicus is Philip Converse, "The Nature of Belief Systems in Mass Publics," in *Ideology and Discontent*, ed. David Apter (New York: Free Press, 1964), 206–61.

24. For a recent survey of how ordinary Americans reason about political affairs, see Arthur Lupia, Mathew McCubbins, and Samuel Popkin, eds., *Elements of Reason* (New York: Cambridge University Press, 2000).

25. Michael Delli Carpini and Scott Keeter, *What Americans Know About Politics and Why It Matters* (New Haven, Conn.: Yale University Press, 1996).

26. Markus Prior, *Post-Broadcast Democracy* (New York: Cambridge University Press, 2007).

27. Text of the questions can be found at *http://electionstudies.org/nesguide/gd-index.htm\#4.*

28. For a classic political theory treatment, see Hannah F. Pitkin, *The Concept of Representation* (Berkeley: University of California Press, 1967). For a survey of applied treatments, see Heinz Eulau and John C. Wahlke, eds., *The Politics of Representation* (Beverly Hills, Calif.: Sage, 1978).

29. Robert Weissberg, "Collective v. Dyadic Representation in Congress," *American Political Science Review* 72 (1978): 535–47.

30. Gary C. Jacobson, "Party Polarization in National Politics: The Electoral Connection," in *Polarized Politics*, ed. Jon R. Bond and Richard Fleisher (Washington, D.C.: CQ Press, 2000), 9–30.

31. Thomas Brunell, *Redistricting and Representation: Why Competitive Elections Are Bad for America* (New York: Routledge, 2008).

32. Andrew Kohut and Carroll Doherty, "A Year Ahead, Republicans Face Tough Political Terrain," Pew Research Center for the

People & the Press, December 19, 2007, http://people-press.org/
report/366/a-year-ahead-republicans-face-tough-political-terrain.
By no means is the 42 percent figure a reflection of a single unrepresentative survey—it is based on more than 19,000 interviews from
eleven 2007 surveys.

33. Jacobson, "Party Polarization."

34. Lydia Saad, "Support Up for Divided Government and Major
Third Party," Gallup News Service Release, September 14, 2006,
www.gallup.com/poll/24502/Support-Divided-Government-
Major-Third-Party.aspx.

35. Jacobson, "Party Polarization." See also Sinclair, *Party Wars*,
chap. 1; and Herbert F. Weisberg, "The Party in the Electorate as a
Basis for More Responsible Parties," in *Responsible Partisanship*, ed.
John Green and Paul Herrnson (Lawrence: University of Kansas
Press, 2002), 161–179.

CHAPTER 2

1. Social scientists have long known that people are not very
good at explaining their motives and decisions. See, e.g., Richard
Nisbett and Timothy Wilson, "Telling More Than We Can Know:
Verbal Reports on Mental Processes," *Psychological Review* 84 (1977):
231–59.

2. Sidney Verba, Kay Lehman Schlozman, and Henry E. Brady,
Voice and Equality (Cambridge, Mass.: Harvard University Press,
1995), 391.

3. John McCarthy, quoted in Carla Marinucci, "GOP to Play
Musical Chairs over Abortion," *San Francisco Chronicle*, May 15,
2000.

4. Peggy Noonan, "In Love with Death," March 24, 2005,
www.wsj.com, italics in the original

5. Ingrid Newkirk, *Washington Post* (1983), quoted in Iain Murray
and Ivan Osorio, "PETA: Cruel and Unusual," *Human Events*, January 16, 2006, quote at p. 15.

6. Steve Crampton, quoted in "'Gay' Marriage Ruling's Consequences 'Dire,'" November 19, 2003, *www.worldnetdaily.com/news/
article.asp?ARTICLE_ID=35687* (accessed September 14, 2006).

7. J. Grant Swank, Jr., "Embryonic Stem Cell Research: It All
Comes Down to Murder," August 1, 2005, *http://mensnewsdaily.com/
blog/swank/2005/08/embryonic-stem-cell-research-it-all.html*.

8. Rep. Tom Tancredo, interview by Sean Hannity, *Hannity &
Colmes*, Fox, June 26, 2006.

9. Michael Gartner, *"Glut of Guns: What Can We Do About Them?"*
USA Today, January 16, 1992.

10. Sen. Orrin Hatch, speech before the American Legion Legislative Rally, Washington, D.C., March 23, 1999, emphasis in the original.

11. Sometimes only the "very" or "extremely" important responses are reported; sometimes the "extremely" plus "somewhat" or "moderately important" responses are reported. Some analysts weight the responses (e.g., 4, 3, 2, 1) and report the weighted sum.

12. D. Sunshine Hillygus and Todd Shields, "Moral Issues and Voter Decision Making in the 2004 Presidential Election," *PS: Political Science & Politics* 38 (2005): 2001–2008.

13. Philip E. Converse, "The Nature of Belief Systems in Mass Publics," in *Ideology and Discontent*, ed. David Apter (New York: Free Press, 1964), 206–61.

14. An interpretation Converse vigorously rejected in "Democratic Theory and Electoral Reality," *Critical Review* 18 (2006): 300–303.

15. For example, James Stimson, *Tides of Consent* (New York: Cambridge University Press, 2004).

16. The leading interpretation is attributable to John Zaller, *The Nature and Origins of Mass Opinion* (New York: Cambridge, 1992).

17. From a September 2004 YouGov Internet survey on which I consulted. The survey included the GSS abortion battery plus one additional circumstance: gender selection. Along similar lines, Bartels reported that in the 1996 NES study about 40 percent reported that they believed a woman should "always be able" to obtain a legal abortion, but when re-interviewed the next year, about 40 percent of those same unconditionally pro-choice respondents favored a ban on partial birth abortions and another 12 percent of them were undecided. See Larry Bartels, "Is 'Popular Rule' Possible?" *Brookings Review* 21 (2003): 14.

18. Stephen C. Craig, James G. Kane, and Michael D. Martinez, "Sometimes You Feel Like a Nut, Sometimes You Don't: Citizens' Ambivalence about Abortion," *Political Psychology* 23 (2002): 285–301.

19. R. Michael Alvarez and John Brehm, "American Ambivalence Towards Abortion Policy," *American Journal of Political Science* 39 (1995): 1055–82; and Paul Goren, "Core Principles and Policy Reasoning in Mass Publics: A Test of Two Theories," *British Journal of Political Science* 31 (2001): 159–77.

20. Stanley Feldman, "Structure and Consistency in Public Opinion: The Role of Core Beliefs and Values," *American Journal of Public Opinion* 32 (1988): 416–40.

21. Stephen C. Craig, Michael D. Martinez, James G. Kane, and Jason Gainous, "Core Values, Value Conflict, and Citizen's Ambivalence about Gay Rights," *Political Research Quarterly*, 58 (2005): 5–17.

22. Wayne Baker, *America's Crisis of Values* (Princeton, N.J.: Princeton University Press, 2005), chap. 2. Compare Simon Schama, "Onward Christian Soldiers," *The Guardian Unlimited*, November 5, 2004.

23. Donald R. Kinder and Lynn M. Sanders, *Divided by Color* (Chicago: University of Chicago Press, 1996), chap. 7. Jacoby recently has shown that at least in the economic domain, most Americans can order their core values in order of importance. This does not mean that they give all weight to one value and none to others, however. So survey questions that implicate different values still can produce different opinions. William G. Jacoby, "Value Choices and American Public Opinion," *American Journal of Political Science* 50 (2006): 706–23.

24. These items were written by Jon Krosnick of Stanford and Morris P. Fiorina and were based on a critique of existing items and a proposal for revisions by David Barker, Lawrence J. Zigerell, Jr., and Heather M. Rice, "New Abortion Items," ftp://ftp.electionstudies.org/ftp/anes/OC/2006pilot/dbarker_ljz201_hmr9_abortion.pdf.

25. This study was a conducted by a consortium of 37 colleges and universities under the leadership of Steven M. Ansolabehere, R. Douglas Rivers, and Lynn Vavreck. The abortion battery was asked of 2,000 respondents in the Stanford and University of California, Los Angeles, modules.

26. Lydia Saad, "Public Divided on 'Pro-Choice' vs. 'Pro-Life' Abortion Labels," Gallup News Service, May 21, 2007.

27. Diana C. Mutz, *Hearing the Other Side* (New York: Cambridge University Press, 2006).

28. These interpretations are mine. Mutz is, herself, more ambivalent in her conclusions.

29. Ann Coulter, "This Is War," *National Review Online*, September 13, 2001, www.nationalreview.com/coulter/coulter.shtml.

30. Michael Moore, "You Say Deserter, I Say More Dessert," January 27, 2004, *www.michaelmoore.com*.

31. Rev. Jerry Falwell, interview by Pat Robertson, *The 700 Club*, CBN Studios, September 13, 2001.

32. Christopher Hitchens, quoted in John Amato, "Hitchens Slams Falwell's Life," May 15, 2007, www.crooksandliars.com.

33. James W. Haas, "The Real Barbarians," letter to the editor, *San Francisco Chronicle*, June 8, 2000.

34. Delli Carpini and Keeter, *What Americans Know About Politics*.

35. For a hilarious take-off on today's news, see *What They Call the News*, http://movies.msn.com/movies/JibJab.

36. Mary Ann Glendon, *Rights Talk: The Impoverishment of Political Discourse* (New York: Free Press, 1991).

37. David S. Meyer and Steven A. Boutcher, "Signals and Spillover: *Brown v. Board of Education* and Other Social Movements," *Perspectives on Politics* 5 (2007): 81–93.

38. A classic example in the literature is Jane Mansbridge's account of the failure of the proposed Equal Rights Amendment (ERA) to the Constitution. Had feminist groups been willing to compromise on such matters as unisex rest rooms and women in combat, where the American public was more conservative, the amendment would likely have passed. Jane Mansbridge, *Why We Lost the ERA* (Chicago: University of Chicago Press, 1986).

39. E. E. Schattschneider, *Two Hundred Million Americans in Search of a Government* (New York: Holt, Rinehart and Winston, 1969), 54.

40. Eric Hoffer, *The True Believer* (New York: Harper & Row, 1951), 80, 85, 86.

41. Diana Mutz and Byron Reeves, "The New Videomalaise: Effects of Televised Incivility on Political Trust," *American Political Science Review* 99 (2005): 1–15.

42. Diana Mutz, "Effects of 'In-Your-Face' Television Discourse on Perceptions of a Legitimate Opposition," *American Political Science Review* 101 (2007): 621–35.

43. Deborah Jordan Brooks and John G. Geer, "Beyond Negativity: The Effects of Incivility on the Electorate," *American Journal of Political Science* 51 (2007): 1–16.

44. Michael M. Franz, Paul B. Freedman, Kenneth M. Goldstein, and Travis N. Ridout, *Campaign Advertising and American Democracy* (Philadelphia: Temple University Press, 2007).

45. The decline in voting in national elections between the mid-1960s and mid-1990s was entirely concentrated in the independent-weak partisan-moderate segments of the population. Morris P. Fiorina, "Parties, Participation, and Representation in America: Old Theories Face New Realities," in *Political Science: State of the Discipline*, ed. Ira Katznelson and Helen V. Milner (New York: Norton, 2002), 536–38.

46. Molly Ivins, "The Blame Game," *http://underwire.msn.com/underwire/social/HiWire/31HWmolly.asp* (accessed August 8, 2000).

47. James Davison Hunter, "The Culture Wars Reconsidered," in *Is There a Culture War?* ed. E. J. Dionne, Jr., and Michael Bromartie (Washington, D.C.: Brookings, 2006), 27.

48. Dowd, a Bush reelection strategist, was explaining why Bush did not try to expand his electoral base. Quoted in Ron Brownstein, "Bush Falls to Pre-9/11 Approval Rating," *Los Angeles Times*, October 3, 2003.

49. Alan I. Abramowitz, "Disconnected, or Joined at the Hip?" in *Red and Blue Nation*, vol. 1, ed. Pietro S. Nivola and David W. Brady (Washington, D.C.: Brookings, 2007), 72–85.

50. An analysis of the rise in voting turnout in 2004 by Wattenberg concludes "Barring further extraordinary events such as those experienced during George W. Bush's first term, it is likely that the turnout increase of 2004 will prove to be a blip rather than the start of an upward trend." Martin P. Wattenberg, "Elections: Turnout in the 2004 Presidential Election," *Presidential Studies Quarterly* 35 (2005): 138.

51. Although Abramowitz does not cite it, the work most supportive of his position is a "back of the envelope" calculation that attributes at most a third of the increase in turnout between 2000 and 2004 to mobilization activities of the parties. See Daniel E. Bergan, Alan S. Gerber, Donald B. Green, and Costas Panagopoulos, "Grassroots Mobilization and Voter Turnout in 2004," *Public Opinion Quarterly* 69 (2005) 760–77.

52. Philip E. Converse, "Democratic Theory and Electoral Reality," *Critical Review* 18 (2007): 312–13.

53. Abramowitz, "Disconnected, or Joined at the Hip?" p. 84.

54. Delli Carpini and Keeter, *What Americans Know about Politics.*

55. Pew Research Center, "What Americans Know: 1989–2007," April 15, 2007, p. 1, *http://people–press.org/reports/display.php3?ReportID=319.*

56. Martin Wattenberg, *Is Voting for Young People?* (New York: Longman, 2006).

57. Prior, *Post-Broadcast Democracy.*

58. Andrew Kohut and Carroll Doherty, "What Was—and Wasn't—On the Public's Mind in 2007," Pew Research Center for the People & the Press, December 19, 2007, http://pewresearch.org/pubs/664/what-was-and-wasnt-on-the-publics-mind-in-2007.

59. Lawrence R. Jacobs and Robert Y. Shapiro, *Politicians Don't Pander: Political Manipulation and the Loss of Democratic Responsiveness* (Chicago: University of Chicago Press, 2000).

CHAPTER 3

1. Of course, by that time anyone who still sported a crew cut and wore a short-sleeved white shirt probably was a Republican.

2. A Gallup survey conducted in the autumn of 2005 reported that almost 40 percent of evangelicals who were surveyed did not believe that the Iraq war was justified; see Mark I. Pinksy, "Meet the New Evangelicals," *Los Angeles Times*, September 16, 2006, www.latimes.com/. On political diversity within the American evangelical community, see Christian Smith, *Christian America? What Evangelicals Really Want* (Berkeley: University of California Press, 2002).

3. George Stephanopoulos, "A Country Divided: Examining the State of Our Union," *20/20*, June 30, 2006, *http://abcnews.go.com/2020/story?id=2140483&page=1* (accessed July 5, 2006).

4. Daily Kos (www.dailykos.com/), arguably the most important liberal blog, boasts a half a million hits per day, about one-quarter of 1 percent of the voting-eligible public. Gallup provides survey-based evidence on blog readership. About three-quarters of the American public report using the Internet at some time. Of those, 9 percent report that they frequently read blogs—any blogs—whereas 66 percent report that they never read blogs. No matter how popular they may be among the political class, political blogs are barely on the radar screens of the American public. Lydia Saad, "Blog Readership Bogged Down," Gallup News Service, February 10, 2006, www.gallup.com/poll/21397/Blog-Readership-Bogged-Down.aspx.

5. In the summer of 2006, the so-called netroots, a virtual community of liberal Democrats organized around prominent liberal blogs, received widespread coverage for their role in upsetting incumbent Democratic Sen. Joseph Lieberman in a Connecticut primary election. Reportedly two of the more prominent liberal blogs, Daily Kos and MyDD, then had a combined readership of about a million people weekly. That figure is less than 0.5 percent of the national electorate and less than 1.5 percent of Democrats. Perry Bacon, Jr., "The Netroots Hit Their Limits," *Time*, September 24, 2006, www.time.com/.

6. In an exchange in a general interest magazine, James Q. Wilson expressed doubts about my description of a nonpolarized America, among other things asking whether I read political blogs and listened to talk radio. No, I do not, nor should anyone else looking for enlightenment as opposed to entertainment. A survey of the audience at a performance of *WWE Smackdown* undoubtedly would yield a more representative picture of the political views of Americans than would samples of political bloggers and callers to Rush Limbaugh. See James Q. Wilson, letter to the editor, *Commentary*, May 2006, 6.

7. Kai T. Erikson, *Wayward Puritans* (New York: Wiley, 1966), 12.

8. Fiorina, Abrams, and Pope, *Culture War?* 2nd ed. (New York: Pearson Longman, 2006), 27–29.

9. Gary Jacobson, *A Divider, Not a Uniter* (New York: Pearson Longman, 2007).

10. It also reflects the party sorting that we discuss in the next section of this chapter.

11. Philip Klinkner, "Mr. Bush's War: Foreign Policy in the 2004 Election," *Presidential Studies Quarterly*, 36 (2006): 281–96.

12. Jonathan Rauch, "On Foreign Policy, Shades of Agreement," *NationalJournal.com*, February 16, 2007, *www.nationaljournal.com/members/buzz/2007/socialstudies/021607.htm*.

13. Thomas Edsall, *Building Red America* (New York: Basic, 2006), 50–52.

14. For a wide-ranging collection of essays on swing voters, see William G. Mayer, ed., *The Swing Voter in American Politics* (Washington, D.C.: Brookings, 2008).

15. Alan Ehrenhalt, "Reagan–Mondale: A Polarizing Contest," *CQ Weekly Report*, August 25, 1984, 2067–68.

16. See John Cochran, "Democrats Polish Message, Renew Push for Swing Voters," *CQ Weekly*, July 31, 2004, 1857. Defining "persuadable" voters as those who have inconsistent policy preferences, Hillygus and Shields calculated that in 2004 persuadable partisans constituted a quarter of the voters and persuadable independents constituted another tenth. D. Sunshine Hillygus and Todd Shields, *The Persuadable Voter: Campaign Strategy, Wedge Issues, and the Fragmentation of American Politics* (Princeton, N.J.: Princeton University Press, 2008), 69.

17. The discussion in this section draws on research reported in Matthew Levendusky, "Sorting: Explaining Change in the American Electorate" (PhD diss., Stanford University, 2006), and summarizes the discussion in Morris P. Fiorina and Matthew Levendusky, "Disconnected: The Political Class vs. the People," in *Red and Blue Nation*, vol. 1., ed. David Brady, William Galston, and Pietro Nivola (Washington, D.C.: Brookings Institution, 2006), 49–71.

18. Although scholarly awareness of party sorting has been evident for some years and a number of excellent focused studies have appeared, until recently there has been relatively little work tracing the issues that are most closely associated with sorting, the groups in which sorting has most clearly occurred, and other specific features of the sorting process. One of the earliest studies to identify partisan sorting was Alan Abramowitz and Kyle Saunders, "Ideo-

logical Realignment in the U.S. Electorate," *Journal of Politics* 60 (1998): 634–52. For a discussion of party sorting on abortion, see Greg Adams, "Abortion: Evidence of an Issue Evolution," *American Journal of Political Science* 41 (1997): 718–37. For sorting on women's issues, see Kira Sanbonmatsu, *Democrats, Republicans, and the Politics of Women's Place* (Ann Arbor: University of Michigan Press, 2002).

19. Pew Research Center for the People & the Press, "Trends in Political Values and Core Attitudes: 1987–2007," March 22, 2007, *http://people-press.org/reports/display.php3?ReportID=312*.

20. Matthew Levendusky, *Choosing Sides: How Democrats and Republicans Became Liberals and Conservatives* (Chicago: University of Chicago Press, forthcoming).

21. On race, see Thomas Byrne Edsall and Mary D. Edsall, *Chain Reaction: The Impact of Race, Rights, and Taxes on American Politics* (New York: W.W. Norton, 1991). On cultural "wedge" issues, see Thomas Frank, *What's the Matter with Kansas? How Conservatives Won the Heart of America* (New York: Henry Holt, 2004).

22. Edward G. Carmines and James A. Stimson, *Issue Evolution: Race and the Transformation of American Politics* (Princeton, N.J.: Princeton University Press, 1989).

23. Geoffrey C. Layman, *The Great Divide: Religious and Cultural Conflict in American Party Politics* (New York: Columbia University Press, 2001).

24. The indexes consist of the average position taken by respondents on the items relating to an issue area. New Deal issues include these NES items: government provision of health insurance (VCF0806), government's role in securing everyone a good job and a standard of living (VCF0809), the government spending/services trade-off (VCF0839), the amount of government spending on the poor (VCF0886), and government spending on welfare (VCF0894). Racial items include whether the civil rights movement pushes too fast (VCF0814), whether the government should ensure school integration (VCF0816), whether students should be bused to promote school integration (VCF0817), support for affirmative action in hiring or promotion (VCF0867A), whether the government should ensure that African Americans receive fair treatment in jobs (VCF9037), and how much the government should help minorities (VCF0830). Cultural issues include attitudes toward abortion (VCF0837/VCF0838), toward school prayer (VCF9043), toward whether women and men deserve an equal role (VCF0834), toward laws protecting homosexuals from discrimination (VCF0876A),

toward homosexuals in the military (VCF0877A), and toward adoption by homosexuals (VCF0878). Defense issues include cooperation with the Soviet Union (VCF0841) and defense spending (VCF0843). All two- and four-point items were converted into seven-point scales.

25. While the stronger relationship between partisanship and New Deal positions is contrary to the claims of commentators such as Frank (in *What's the Matter with Kansas?*), it is consistent with recent research indicating that economic issues have shown no decline as an important cleavage in U.S. elections. See Andrew Gelman and others, "Rich State, Poor State, Red State, Blue State: What's the Matter with Connecticut?" *Quarterly Journal of Political Science* 2 (2007): 345–67; Stephen Ansolabehere, Jonathan Rodden, and James M. Snyder, Jr., "Purple America," *Journal of Economic Perspectives* 20, no. 2 (2006): 97–118; and Larry M. Bartels, "What's the Matter with *What's the Matter with Kansas?*" *Quarterly Journal of Political Science* 1 (2006): 201–26. The lack of sorting on the racial dimension is consistent with Abramowitz' critique of Carmines and Stimson's issue evolution thesis. See Alan Abramowitz, "Issue Evolution Reconsidered: Racial Attitudes and Partisanship in the U.S. Electorate," *American Journal of Political Science* 38 (1994): 1–24.

26. William A. Galston and Elaine C. Kamarck, *Politics of Polarization* (Washington, D.C.: ThirdWay, 2005); Ronald Brownstein, *The Second Civil War: How Extreme Partisanship Has Paralyzed Washington and Polarized America* (New York: Penguin, 2007).

27. Sanbonmatsu, *Democrats, Republicans, and the Politics of Women's Place.*

28. All but two of these items are seven-point scales. For simplicity, a Democrat takes her party's position if she takes a position to the left of the midpoint, and a Republican takes her party's position if she takes a position to the right of the midpoint. For the school prayer item, we assume that the Democratic position is one of the two more liberal answers, and the Republican position is one of the two more conservative answers. For the coding of the abortion item, see note 29 below.

29. Adams, "Abortion: Evidence of an Issue Evolution"; Fiorina, Abrams, and Pope, *Culture War?* 2nd ed., chap. 5.

30. The NES item gives the respondent four options: (1) By law, abortion should never be permitted; (2) The law should permit abortion only in case of rape, incest, or when the woman's life is in danger; (3) The law should permit abortion for reasons other than rape, incest, or danger to the woman's life but only after the need

for the abortion has been clearly established; and (4) By law, a woman should always be able to obtain an abortion as a matter of personal choice. The reported calculations assume that the official Republican position is that abortion should never be permitted or permitted only in cases of rape, incest, or a threat to the life of the woman, and the Democratic position is that abortion should always be allowed.

31. Chapter 5 of Fiorina, Abrams, and Pope's *Culture War?* (2nd ed.) shows that this conclusion does not depend on the NES survey item.

32. The GSS also asks about support for homosexual civil liberties (e.g., whether the respondent would allow a homosexual to teach in a college or university or give a speech in the local community; whether the respondent would allow a book written by a homosexual in favor of homosexuality to remain in a public library). Analyses of these items not reported here find the same patterns. *Culture War?* (2nd ed., chap. 6) also documents a similar pattern of growing tolerance for homosexuals in various spheres of American life. For the most recent data, see Lydia Saad, "Tolerance for Gay Rights at High-Water Mark," *Gallup News Service*, May 29, 2007, www.gallup.com/poll/27694/Tolerance-Gay-Rights-High Water-Mark.aspx..

33. There is always the further possibility that sorting may have occurred only for some demographic subgroups that cancel each other in the aggregate. To double-check the patterns (and nonpatterns) reported on the six cultural issues, Levendusky examined the percentage of respondents in various subgroups who supported their party's positions. He considered three obvious comparisons: men vs. women, Southerners vs. non-Southerners, and Whites vs. African Americans. Although subgroups differed in expected ways (women tended to be more liberal than men, Whites more conservative than Blacks), the differences were small and the general findings were the same. Sorting does not seem to differ much by demographic subgroups.

CHAPTER 4

1. I use the modifiers "not very" and "appreciably" only in recognition of the (unlikely) possibility that someone may find another survey somewhere that reports data showing more polarization than the databases relied on in this work.

2. The discussion that follows draws on and extends the discussion in two of my earlier essays, "Extreme Voices: A Dark Side of

Civic Engagement," in *Civic Engagement in American Democracy*, ed. Theda Skocpol and Morris Fiorina (Washington, D.C.: Brookings, 1999), 395–425; and "Parties, Participation, and Representation in America: Old Theories Face New Realities," in *Political Science: The State of the Discipline*, ed. Ira Katznelson and Helen Milner (New York: Norton, 2002), 511–41.

3. Morton Keller, *America's Three Regimes* (New York: Oxford, 2007), 174.

4. Walter Dean Burnham, *Critical Elections and the Mainsprings of American Politics* (New York: Norton, 1970); and David W. Brady, *Critical Elections and Congressional Policy Making* (Stanford, Calif.: Stanford University Press, 1988).

5. Richard L. McCormick, "The Party Period and Public Policy: An Exploratory Hypothesis," *The Journal of American History* 66 (1979): 279–98.

6. Michael McGerr, *The Decline of Popular Politics* (New York: Oxford, 1986).

7. Stephen Skowronek, *Building a New American State* (New York: Cambridge, 1982).

8. McCormick, "The Party Period," 298.

9. This distinction reflects a distillation of the empirically based debates that took place in the American politics literature during the 1950s and 1960s. It is not the same as Sabine's "two traditions," which are differentiated by the relative prominence given to liberty versus equality. George H. Sabine, "The Two Democratic Traditions," *The Philosophical Review* 61 (1952): 451–74.

10. One of the better known critiques was by Jack L. Walker, "A Critique of the Elitist Theory of Democracy," *American Political Science Review* 60 (1966): 285–95.

11. Joseph Schumpeter is most closely associated with this definition of democracy. See his *Capitalism, Socialism, and Democracy* (New York: Harper & Brothers, 1950).

12. See, e.g., Benjamin Barber, *Strong Democracy* (Berkeley, Calif.: University of California Press, 1984); and Amy Guttman and Dennis Thompson, *Democracy and Disagreement* (Cambridge, Mass.: Harvard University Press, 1996).

13. As in jurist Learned Hand's dictum that "even though counting heads is not an ideal way to govern, at least it is better than breaking them." Learned Hand, *The Spirit of Liberty*, 3rd ed. (New York: Alfred A. Knopf, 1960), 92.

14. There were, of course, important elements of participatory theory as well, such as the practice of instructing representatives to legislatures.

15. For an earlier statement of such arguments, see Robert Dahl, *The New American Political (Dis)Order* (Berkeley, Calif.: IGS Press, 1994).

16. Henry Clay was nominated by a convention in 1831, and President Andrew Jackson was renominated by a convention in 1832.

17. For overviews of the changes in the nomination process and the politics behind them, see James Ceaser, *Presidential Selection* (Princeton, N.J.: Princeton University Press, 1979); and Nelson Polsby, *Consequences of Party Reform* (New York: Oxford University Press, 1983).

18. David Mayhew, "Congressional Elections: The Case of the Vanishing Marginals," *Polity* 6 (1974): 295–317; and Andrew Gelman and Gary King, "Estimating Incumbency Advantage Without Bias," *American Journal of Political Science* 34 (1990): 1142–64.

19. Contrast Bernard R. Berelson, Paul F. Lazarsfeld, and William N. McPhee, *Voting* (Chicago: University of Chicago Press, 1954) with Warren E. Miller and J. Merrill Shanks, *The New American Voter* (Cambridge, Mass.: Harvard University Press, 1996).

20. Note the sharp rise in the number of roll call votes cast after the House adopted electronic voting. See Harold W. Stanley and Richard G. Niemi, *Vital Statistics on American Politics, 2003–2004* (Washington, D.C.: CQ Press, 2003), Table 6–5, p. 214.

21. Lawrence C. Dodd and Richard L. Schott, *Congress and the Administrative State* (New York: Wiley, 1979).

22. For a detailed account of this development, see Richard Stewart, "The Reformation of American Administrative Law," *Harvard Law Review* 88 (1975): 1669–1813.

23. J. David Greenstone and Paul Peterson, *Race and Authority in Urban Politics* (Chicago: University of Chicago Press, 1973).

24. Nancy Burns, *The Formation of American Local Governments* (New York: Oxford University Press, 1994).

25. Alan Ehrenhalt, *The United States of Ambition* (New York: Times Books, 1991).

26. Jeffrey Berry coined the phrase "advocacy explosion" in his textbook *The Interest Group Society* (Glenview, Ill.: Scott, Foresman, 1989). Kay Schlozman and John Tierney, *Organized Interests and American Democracy* (New York: Harper and Row, 1986); and Jack Walker, *Mobilizing Interest Groups in America* (Ann Arbor, Mich.: University of Michigan Press, 1991).

27. John G. Geer, *From Tea Leaves to Opinion Polls* (New York: Columbia, 1996).

28. After bottoming out in the 1960s, use of the initiative surged, although it should be noted that five states account for more than

half of all initiatives. See "A Century of Citizen Lawmaking," Initiative & Referendum Institute at the University of Southern California, www.iandrinstitute.org.

29. For a critical view of the initiative, see David Broder, *Democracy Derailed: Initiative Campaigns and the Power of Money* (New York: Harcourt Brace, 2000).

30. There is actually empirical evidence that, contrary to the assumptions of participatory democratic theorists, under many conditions, participation makes people more frustrated with rather than more supportive of the political system. See John R. Hibbing and Elizabeth Theiss-Morse, "Voice, Validation, and Legitimacy," in *Cooperation: A Powerful Force in Human Relations*, ed. Brandon A. Sullivan, Mark Snyder, and John L. Sullivan (Ames, Iowa: Blackwell, 2008), 123–42..

31. On the disparities in legislative representation, see Gordon Baker, *The Reapportionment Revolution* (New York: Random House, 1966), chap. 3.

32. On mothers' pensions, protective labor laws for women, and other "women's legislation," see Theda Skocpol, *Protecting Soldiers and Mothers* (Cambridge, Mass.: Harvard, 1992).

33. See Gerald N. Rosenberg, *The Hollow Hope: Can Courts Bring About Social Change?* (Chicago: University of Chicago Press, 1991).

34. Richard L. McCormick, "Ethno-Cultural Interpretations of Nineteenth-Century American Voting Behavior," *Political Science Quarterly* 89 (1974): 351–77. On the 1928 election, see Alan Lichtman, *Prejudice and the Old Politics* (Chapel Hill: University of North Carolina Press, 1979).

35. For a fuller discussion with sources, see Morris P. Fiorina et al., *The New American Democracy*, 5th ed. (New York: Pearson-Longman, 2007), chap. 4.

36. Richard Wayman, "Wisconsin Ethnic Groups and the Election of 1890," *Wisconsin Magazine of History* 51 (1968): 273. More generally, see Paul Kleppner, *The Third Electoral System, 1853–1892: Parties, Voters, and Political Cultures* (Chapel Hill: University of North Carolina Press, 1979).

37. William Reardon, ed., *Plunkitt of Tammany Hall* (New York: Dutton, 1963).

38. Morton Keller cited estimates that in New York State one in every eight voters was a federal, state, or local office holder. *Affairs of State: Public Life in 19th Century America* (Cambridge, Mass.: Harvard University Press, 1977), 239.

39. Terry M. Moe, "Political Control and the Power of the Agent," *Journal of Law, Economics, and Organization* 22 (2006): 1–29.

40. The locus classicus is Robert K. Merton, *Social Theory and Social Structure* (New York: Free Press, 1968):,125–34.

41. On campaigns past and present, see Richard K. Scher, *The Modern Political Campaign* (Armonk, N.Y.: Sharpe, 1997).

42. Clifford Brown, Lynda Powell, and Clyde Wilcox, *Serious Money* (Cambridge, England: Cambridge University Press, 1995); and Nolan McCarty, Keith T. Poole, and Howard Rosenthal, *Polarized America: The Dance of Ideology and Unequal Riches* (Cambridge, Mass.: MIT Press, 2006), chap., 5.

43. Larry Sabato, *Feeding Frenzy* (New York: Free Press, 1991).

44. David Mayhew, *Placing Parties in American Politics* (Princeton, N.J.: Princeton University Press, 1986), 20; and James Q. Wilson, *Political Organizations* (New York: Basic Books, 1973), chap. 3.

45. Barry Weingast, Kenneth Shepsle, and Christopher Johnsen, "The Political Economy of Benefits and Costs: A Neoclassical Approach to Distributive Politics," *Journal of Political Economy* 89 (1981): 642–64.

46. Michael McGerr, *The Decline of Popular Politics* (New York: Oxford University Press, 1986).

47. Sidney Verba, Kay Lehman Schlozman, and Henry E. Brady, *Voice and Equality* (Cambridge, Mass.: Harvard University Press, 1995), chap. 14. Cynics point out that many activists make their living managing or working for such organizations. Even if that is true, it is doubtful that activists choose organizations at random. Their ideological preferences point them toward certain issue areas.

48. James Sundquist, *The Decline and Resurgence of Congress* (Washington, D.C.: Brookings, 1981), 371

49. Quoted in Milton Rakove, *We Don't Want Nobody Nobody Sent* (Bloomington: Indiana University Press, 1979), 319.

50. It should go without saying that I mean nothing personal here. By "University-of-Chicago types," I refer to highly educated, ideologically motivated people who now constitute the bulk of the political class.

51. James Q. Wilson, *The Amateur Democrat* (Chicago: University of Chicago Press, 1962).

52. Aaron Wildavsky, "The Goldwater Phenomenon: Purists, Politicians and the Two-Party System," *Review of Politics* 27 (1965): 386–413.

53. Wildavsky, "Goldwater Phenomenon," 396.

54. Wilson, *Amateur Democrat*, 3.

55. Wildavsky, "Goldwater Phenomenon," 399.

CHAPTER 5

1. I recognize, of course, that some Democrats who represent Catholic constituencies continue to hold pro-life positions, but they are a minority in a party generally viewed as pro-choice. On how abortion activists sorted into the Democratic and Republican Parties, see Sanbonmatsu, *Democrats, Republicans, and the Politics of Women's Place*, chaps. 4–5.

2. Although as various commentators have pointed out, some states and localities had already recognized and begun dealing with the issue. Matthew A. Crenson, *The Un-Politics of Air Pollution* (Baltimore: Johns Hopkins, 1971); and Charles O. Jones, *Clean Air: The Policies and Politics of Pollution Control* (Pittsburgh, Pa.: University of Pittsburgh Press, 1975).

3. For a view of partisan sorting on environmental issues from a prominent Republican environmentalist, see J. Brooks Flippen, *Conservative Conservationist: Russell E. Train and the Emergence of American Environmentalism* (Baton Rouge: Louisiana State University Press, 2006).

4. Jones, *Clean Air*, chap. 7.

5. Charles R. Shipan and William R. Lowry, "Environmental Policy and Party Divergence in Congress," *Political Research Quarterly* 54 (2001): 245–63.

6. Harold W. Stanley and Richard G. Niemi, *Vital Statistics on American Politics, 2005–2006* (Washington, D.C.: CQ Press, 2006), 122–23.

7. On Dirksen's role, see Daniel B. Rodriguez and Barry R. Weingast, "The Positive Political Theory of Legislative History: New Perspectives on the 1964 Civil Rights Act and its Interpretation," *University of Pennsylvania Law Review* 151, no. 4 (April 2003): 1417–1542.

8. Reg Murphy and Hal Gulliver, *The Southern Strategy* (New York: Scribner's, 1971).

9. This contingency runs through the account of shifts in Republican electoral strategy between 1960 and 1968 in Hillygus and Shields, *Persuadable Voter*.

10. A standard finding in the literature is that mass opinion change generally occurs as a reaction to developments at the elite level. See, e.g., Edward G. Carmines and James A. Stimson, *Issue Evolution: Race and the Transformation of American Politics* (Princeton, N.J.: Princeton University Press, 1989), chap. 6.

11. An eighth is close on the horizon—the aging of the population—although its effects have not yet been felt.

12. In *How Congress Evolves*, Polsby provided a masterful account of how the rise of the Sunbelt changed the modern Congress. David Rohde was one of the first to point out the consequences of growing constituency similarity among congressional Democrats. See his *Parties and Leaders in the Postreform House* (Chicago: University of Chicago Press, 1991), chap. 3. Stonecash, Brewer, and Mariani emphasized the importance of Black empowerment in the South, immigration, and rising economic inequality for party sorting. See Jeffrey M. Stonecash, Mark D. Brewer, and Mack D. Mariani, *Diverging Parties: Social Change, Realignment, and Party Polarization* (Boulder, Colo.: Westview Press, 2004), esp. chap. 4.

13. The "South" category in figure 5.1 is the sum of the South Atlantic, East South Central, and West South Central census regions. The South Atlantic census region includes states like Maryland, Delaware, and West Virginia, which are not usually considered southern states. Moreover, there is some imprecision in the census figures because regional definitions also varied over time.

14. Polsby, *How Congress Evolves*, chap. 3.

15. David McCullough, *Truman* (New York: Simon & Schuster, 1992), 586–90; and Patricia Gurin, Shirley Hatchett, and James S. Jackson, *Hope and Independence: Blacks' Response to Electoral and Party Politics* (New York: Russell Sage, 1989), 36–38.

16. For a revisionist argument that Truman was deeply committed to the civil rights cause long before the 1948 election, see Michael R. Gardner, *Harry Truman and Civil Rights* (Carbondale: Southern Illinois University Press, 2002).

17. On the changing demographic bases of the parties, see Harold W. Stanley and Richard G. Niemi, *Vital Statistics on American Politics, 2005–2006* (Washington, D.C.: CQ Press), 122–26.

18. The term often is attributed to Kevin Phillips, *The Emerging Republican Majority* (New York: Arlington House, 1969), e.g., p. 38.

19. It was often said of Democrat Mendel Rivers, a long-time representative from South Carolina who served on and eventually chaired the House Armed Services Committee, that if he brought one more military base to South Carolina, the state would sink.

20. Calculated from Charles W. Boas, "Locational Patterns of American Automobile Assembly Plants, 1895–1958," *Economic Geography* 37 (1961): 218–30; and Thomas H. Klier and Daniel McMillen, "The Geographic Evolution of the US Auto Industry," *Journal of Economic Perspectives* 30 (2006): 2–13.

21. Polsby, *How Congress Evolves*.

22. On partisan change in the South, see Earl Black and Merle Black, *Politics and Society in the South* (Cambridge, Mass.: Harvard University Press, 1987), parts III and IV; and Donald Green, Bradley Palmquist, and Eric Schickler, *Partisan Hearts and Minds* (New Haven, Conn.: Yale University Press, 2002), chap. 6.

23. Warren E. Miller, "Party Identification, Realignment, and Party Voting: Back to the Basics," *American Political Science Review* 85 (1991): 561–62.

24. Morris P. Fiorina and Samuel J. Abrams, "Is California Really a Blue State?" in *The New Political Geography of California*, ed. Frederick Douzet, Thaddeus Kousser, and Kenneth Miller, (Berkeley, CA: Institute of Governmental Studies Press, 2008), 291–308.

25. Massachusetts has not elected a Republican to Congress since 1994, when Silvio Conte retired.

26. For a survey, see Jo Freeman, ed., *Social Movements of the Sixties and Seventies* (New York: Longman, 1983).

27. Betty Friedan, *The Feminine Mystique* (New York: Dell, 1963).

28. See Mary Frances Berry, *Why ERA Failed* (Bloomington: Indiana University Press, 1986); and Mansbridge, *Why We Lost the ERA*.

29. On the pro-life movement, see Kristen Luker, *Abortion and the Politics of Motherhood* (Berkeley: University of California Press, 1984).

30. For a detailed treatment of religion in American politics during the preceding generation, see Geoffrey Layman, *The Great Divide: Religious and Cultural Conflict in American Party Politics* (New York: Columbia University Press, 2001). I write "reemergence" because religion has long been intertwined with American politics, although it was relatively unimportant between the 1960 election and the rise of the religious right. The abolitionist movement had a strong religious base, of course. I have already noted in chapter 4 the pietist–liturgical conflicts of the nineteenth century. And Protestant-Catholic conflict was an important element of politics from at least the beginning of large-scale Irish immigration in the 1840s to the 1960 election. After sifting through all the competing claims about the 1927 election (urban vs. rural, wet vs. dry, immigrant vs. native), Allan Lichtman concluded that it was primarily Protestant versus Catholic. See his *Prejudice and the Old Politics* (Chapel Hill: University of North Carolina Press, 1979).

31. *Time*, April 8, 1966.

32. For an informative collection of essays on the changing worldwide religious landscape, see Peter L. Berger, ed., *The Desecularization of the World* (Grand Rapids, Mich.: Eerdmans, 1999). For

an argument that the secularization hypothesis is not (or will not be) as accurate a description of Europe as conventionally assumed, see Jytte Klausen, "The Re-Politicization of Religion in Europe: The Next Ten Years," *Perspectives on Politics* 3 (2005): 554–57.

33. Henry A. Plotkin, "Issues in the Presidential Campaign," in *The Election of 1980: Reports and Interpretations,* ed. Gerald Pomper and Marlene Michels Pomper (Chatham, N.J.: Chatham House, 1981), 51.

34. For a thorough analysis of the 1980 campaign and election, see Paul R. Abramson, John H. Aldrich, and David W. Rohde, *Change and Continuity in the 1980 Elections* (Washington, D.C.: CQ Press, 1982). For somewhat skeptical examinations of claims about the Senate losses, see John Ferejohn and Morris Fiorina, "Incumbency and Realignment in Congressional Elections," in *The New Direction in American Politics,* ed. John Chubb and Paul Peterson (Washington, D.C.: Brookings, 1985), 103–104; and Thomas Mann and Norman Ornstein, "The Republican Surge in Congress," in *The American Elections of 1980* ed. Austin Ranney (Washington, D.C.: American Enterprise Institute, 1981), 292–96.

35. Cited in Sinclair, *Party Wars,* 51.

36. As Gallup notes, when evangelicals are discussed in a political context, the term generally refers to White Protestant evangelicals. A majority of African Americans classify themselves as evangelicals, but they vote very differently from White evangelical Protestants. Less significant, some Catholics and even a few non-Christians claim to be "born again." Gallup reports that the percentage of White evangelical Protestants in the population is about 30 percent. Frank Newport and Joseph Carroll, "Another Look at Evangelicals in America Today," December 2, 2005, www.gallup-poll.com/content/?ci=20242&pg=1.

37. Kohut et al. also reported that surveys over the past several decades do not show any great increase in the number of self-reported evangelicals. Finke and Stark showed that the decline of mainline denominations and the rise of evangelical denominations were both evident as early as the 1940s. And although the data are fragmentary, they argued that this is part of a long-term process that has been going on since the birth of the republic. See Andrew Kohut, John C. Green, Scott Keeter, and Robert C. Toth, *The Diminishing Divide: Religion's Changing Role in American Politics* (Washington, D.C.: Brookings, 2000); and Roger Finke and Rodney Stark, *The Churching of America, 1776–1990* (New Brunswick, N.J.: Rutgers University Press, 1992), 245–49.

38. James Davison Hunter, *American Evangelicalism: Conservative Religion and the Quandary of Modernity* (New Brunswick, N.J.: Rutgers University Press, 1983); Matthew C. Moen, *The Transformation of the Christian Right* (Tuscaloosa: University of Alabama Press, 1992); and Christian Smith, *American Evangelicalism: Embattled and Thriving* (Chicago: University of Chicago Press, 1998).

39. Personal conversations with Gary Jacobson, Keith Poole, and Howard Rosenthal.

40. Of course, they might be explained by population movements into and out of the state, such as liberal Californians or Hispanic immigrants moving to conservative mountain states.

41. There is a lively debate over whether the United States has become more geographically polarized. See the exchange between Philip Klinkner and Bill Bishop and Robert Cushing in *The Forum, www.bepress.com/forum/vol2/iss2/.* Also see John H. Evans and Lisa M. Nunn, "Geographic Polarization in Politics and Social Attitudes," unpublished manuscript; and Edward L Glaser and Bryce A. Ward, "Myths and Realities of American Political Geography," *Journal of Economic Perspectives* 20 (2006): 119–44.

42. Levendusky showed that sorting is significantly more apparent among people who are more politically knowledgeable than average. *Choosing Sides,* chap. 4.

CHAPTER 6

1. For background see Richard Cortner, *The Apportionment Cases* (New York: Norton, 1970).

2. At the time, every New Jersey county had equal representation in the state senate. So Essex County with 923,000 residents had the same representation as Sussex County with 49,000. The California Constitution stipulated that no county could have more than one senator. Thus, Los Angeles County with 6 million residents had one senator as had the mountain counties of Mono, Inyo, and Alpine, which combined had 14,000 residents. All such arrangements were declared unconstitutional under *Reynolds.* See Gordon Baker, *The Reapportionment Revolution* (New York: Random House, 1966), 25–26, passim.

3. Equal representation of states in the U.S. Senate remains beyond the reach of the courts, of course, because of Article 5 of the U.S. Constitution.

4. For a survey of redistricting criteria, see David Butler and Bruce Cain, *Congressional Redistricting: Comparative and Theoretical Perspectives* (New York: Longman, 1992), esp. chap. 4.

5. David Brady and Douglas Edmonds. "One Man, One Vote—So What?" *Trans-Action* 4 (1967): 41–46; and Roger A. Hanson and Robert E. Crew, Jr., "The Policy Impact of Reapportionment," *Law and Society Review* 8 (1973): 69–93. More recent research has revised these earlier conclusions. Cox and Katz have argued that on the congressional level, the reapportionment revolution improved Democratic prospects outside the South and increased the advantage of incumbency. See Gary W. Cox and Jonathan N. Katz, *Elbridge Gerry's Salamander* (Cambridge, England: Cambridge University Press, 2002).

6. The seminal article in the politics-doesn't-matter genre was Richard W. Dawson and James A. Robinson, "Inter-Party Competition, Economic Variables, and Welfare Policies in the American States," *Journal of Politics* 25 (1963): 265–89.

7. See, e.g., Robert S. Erikson, "Reapportionment and Policy: A Further Look at Some Intervening Variables," *Annals of the New York Academy of Science* 219 (1973): 280–90.

8. Ansolabehere, Gerber, and Snyder found that although the reapportionment revolution may not have made public policy appreciably more liberal, aggregate state expenditures shifted away from counties that lost representation to counties that gained. See Stephen Ansolabehere, Alan Gerber, and James M. Snyder, Jr., "Equal Votes, Equal Money: Court-Ordered Redistricting and the Distribution of Public Expenditures in the American States," *American Political Science Review* 96 (2002): 767–77.

9. This table is based on the *Congressional Quarterly* (CQ) classification. In the CQ classification, "a suburban district is one in which at least 60 percent of the population lives within a defined metropolitan area but outside a central city. Similarly, an urban district is one in which at least 60 percent of the population lives inside a central city, while a rural district is one in which at least 60 percent of the population lives outside a metropolitan area (and outside towns of 25,000 or more). Where none of these categories accounts for 60 percent, the district is designated as mixed." Rhodes Cook, "Defining Congressional Districts: What Makes a Suburb a Suburb?" *CQ Weekly Online*, May 24, 1997, 1212–13, http://library.cqpress.com/cqweekly/document.php?id=wr10519970524–21suburbsdefine001&type=hitlist&num=3&. After the 2000 census CQ changed the threshold from 60 percent to a majority, so the most recent figures are not comparable to the earlier ones.

10. Robert E. Lang and Patrick A Simmons, "'Boomburbs;' The Emergence of Large, Fast-Growing Suburban Cities," in *Redefining*

Urban and Suburban America, ed. Bruce Katz and Robert E. Lange (Washington, D.C.: Brookings, 2003), 101–115.

11. In one of those striking then-and-now contrasts, federal policies encouraged residential segregation. The insurance underwriting manual stated "if a neighborhood is to retain stability, it is necessary that properties shall continue to be occupied by the same social and racial classes." Until 1950 the Federal Housing Administration (FHA) openly recommended restrictive covenants, and the agency practiced redlining of neighborhoods until the mid-1960s. On the FHA and Veterans Administration (VA) programs, see Kenneth T. Jackson, *Crabgrass Frontier* (New York: Oxford University Press, 1985), quotation on p. 208.

12. Ibid., 234–38.

13. Compare, e.g., William H. Whyte, Jr., *The Organization Man* (New York: Simon & Schuster, 1956), with Herbert J. Gans, *The Levittowners* (New York: Pantheon Books, 1967).

14. William Schneider, "The Suburban Century Begins," *The Atlantic Monthly*, July 1992, 33–44.

15. Angus Campbell, Philip E. Converse, Warren E. Miller, and Donald E. Stokes, *The American Voter* (New York: Wiley, 1960), 453–60.

16. A recent exception that finds a distinct suburban impact on political behavior is Juliet Gainsborough, *Fenced Off: The Suburbanization of American Politics* (Washington, D.C.: Georgetown University Press, 2001).

17. Richard F. Fenno, Jr., *Senators on the Campaign Trail* (Norman: University of Oklahoma Press, 1996).

18. Richard F. Fenno, Jr., *Home Style: House Members in Their Districts* (Boston: Little, Brown, 1978).

19. Ibid., 195–96.

20. Ibid., 85.

21. Ibid, 235.

22. Ibid., 187.

23. Ibid., 201.

24. Robert Putnam, *Bowling Alone* (New York: Simon & Schuster, 2000), chap. 3.

25. See, e.g., Everett Carll Ladd, *The Ladd Report* (New York: Free Press, 1999), esp. chaps. 3–4.

26. Jeffrey Berry, *The Interest Group Society* (Boston: Little, Brown, 1984), 20.

27. Kay Lehman Schlozman and Traci Burch, "Political Voice in an Age of Inequality," in *America at Risk: The Great Dangers*, ed.

Robert Faulkner, Marc Landy, R. Shep Melnick, and Susan Shell (Chicago: American Bar Foundation, forthcoming). The data were collected by Schlozman, Sidney Verba, and Henry Brady as part of a larger project on political equality.

28. Putnam, *Bowling Alone*, 157.

29. Theda Skocpol, *Diminished Democracy: From Membership to Management in American Civic Life* (Norman: University of Oklahoma Press, 2003). 13.

30. Ibid., 7.

31. Ibid., 25–30.

32. Ibid., 37.

33. Jeffrey Berry identified this characteristic of many public interest groups in the 1970s. See his *Lobbying for the People* (Princeton, N.J.: Princeton University Press, 1977).

34. Skocpol, *Diminished Democracy*, 226.

35. Ibid., 163.

36. Fenno, *Home Style*, xv.

37. "Every congressman also conveys a sense of identification with his constituents. Contextually and verbally, he gives them the impression that 'I am one of you'; 'I am like you': 'I think the way you do and I care about the same things you do'" (Ibid., 58).

38. James L. Sundquist, *Decline and Resurgence of Congress,* 371.

39. John Aldrich, *Why Parties?* (Chicago: University of Chicago Press, 1995).

40. The classic statement of the pluralist position is David Truman, *The Governmental Process* (New York: Knopf, 1951). In the 1950s Robert Dahl trained a school of pluralist political scientists at Yale University. See his *Who Governs?* (New Haven, Conn.: Yale University Press, 1961). Prominent critics of the pluralist school have included E. E. Schattschneider, *The Semisovereign People* (Hinsdale, Ill.: Dryden Press, 1975), esp. chap. 3; and Theodore Lowi, *The End of Liberalism,* 2nd ed. (New York: Norton, 1979), esp. chaps. 2–3.

CHAPTER 7

1. Of course, scaling methods like that developed by Poole and Rosenthal did not exist at the time, so the picture using then-prevailing methods would have presented a less clear picture.

2. David W. Brady and Hahrie C. Han, "Polarization Then and Now: A Historical Perspective," in *Red and Blue Nation*, vol. 1, ed. Pietro S. Nivola and David W. Brady (Washington, D.C.: Brookings, 2006), 119–51.

3. See the appendix.

4. Walter Dean Burnham, "The Changing Shape of the American Political Universe," *American Political Science Review* 59 (1965): 7–28; and Michael E. McGerr, *The Decline of Popular Politics* (New York: Oxford University Press, 1986).

5. Quoted in the preface and acknowledgements section; see note 6 of that section.

6. This section of the chapter extends the discussion in Morris P. Fiorina, "Parties as Problem Solvers," in *Promoting the General Welfare*, ed. Alan S. Gerber and Eric M. Patashnik (Washington, D.C.: Brookings, 2007), 237–55.

7. Morris P. Fiorina, "The Decline of Collective Responsibility in American Politics," *Daedalus* 109 (1980): 25–45. The article was written for a special issue that bore the title *The End of Consensus?* A number of the articles contained therein discussed the breakdown of consensus in various policy spheres. In light of the contemporary concern with the polarization of American politics, it may be that the fraying of a supposed earlier consensus is a perennial theme.

8. Morris P. Fiorina, "The Presidency and the Contemporary Electoral System," in *The Presidency and the Political System*, ed. Michael Nelson (Washington, D.C.: CQ Press, 1984), 204–26. A revision titled "The Presidency and Congress: An Electoral Connection?" appeared in Nelson's 2nd ed. (1988), 411–34; and a revision with the same title appeared in Nelson's 3rd ed. (1990), 443–69.

9. Although I came from a quite different intellectual tradition, I was very sympathetic to Ted Lowi's jeremiad against interest group liberalism. Theodore Lowi, *The End of Liberalism*, 2nd ed. (New York: W.W. Norton, 1979). With some qualifications, I still am.

10. The locus classicus is the midcentury report of the Committee on Political Parties of the APSA, "Toward a More Responsible Two-Party System." For a comprehensive account of the views of the earlier responsible party theorists, see Austin Ranney, *The Doctrine of Responsible Party Government* (Urbana: University of Illinois Press, 1962).

11. Indeed, I felt somewhat ambivalent when I learned recently that "The Decline of Collective Responsibility in American Politics" still is being reprinted in a widely used law school case book. See Daniel Lowenstein and Richard Hasen, *Election Law: Cases and Materials* (Durham, N.C.: Carolina Academic Press, 2004), 443–59.

12. Fiorina, *Divided Government*, 1st ed., 126–30; 2nd ed., 173–77.

13. Fiorina, *Divided Government*, 2nd ed., 136. During the first six years of the Bush administration, support for divided versus unified government was about equal. But as the administration's polit-

ical standing dropped, support for divided government rose. See Saad, "Support Up for Divided Government."

14. Fiorina, "Presidency and Congress," 1990, 465–66.

15. Aldrich, *Why Parties?*

16. For scholarly treatments of the Carter presidency, see Erwin Hargrove, *Jimmy Carter as President: Leadership and the Politics of the Public Good* (Baton Rouge: Louisiana State University Press, 1988); and Charles O. Jones, *The Trusteeship Presidency: Jimmy Carter and the United States Congress* (Charlottesville: University of Virginia Press, 1988).

17. Carter took office with the Democrats holding 276 of 435 House seats and 59 of 100 Senate seats.

18. James McGregor Burns, *The Deadlock of Democracy* (Englewood Cliffs, N.J.: Prentice-Hall, 1963).

19. Julius Turner, "Responsible Parties: A Dissent from the Floor," *American Political Science Review* 45 (1951): 143–52.

20. Late-twentieth-century seat swings were much smaller than in earlier eras. Midterm seat swings sometimes exceeded 90 House seats in the nineteenth century, and even in the New Deal period, the Democrats lost between 55 and 71 seats in three midterms. For a survey of the developments that led to the increased independence of presidential and congressional voting, see the articles in David Brady, John Cogan, and Morris Fiorina, eds., *Continuity and Change in House Elections* (Stanford, Calif.: Stanford University Press, 2000).

21. David Brady, Robert D'Onofrio, and Morris Fiorina, "The Nationalization of Electoral Forces Revisited," in *Continuity and Change in House Elections*, 130–48.

22. For differing accounts of the fate of the health care plan, see David W. Brady and Craig Volden, *Revolving Gridlock*, 2nd ed. (Boulder, Colo.: Westview Press, 2006), chap. 5; and Theda Skocpol, *Boomerang* (New York: Norton, 1996).

23. Denise Baer and David Bositis, *Politics and Linkage in a Democratic Society* (Englewood Cliffs, N.J.: Prentice-Hall, 1993), appendix.

24. Quoted in Jim VandeHei and Michael Fletcher, "Bush Says Election Ratified Iraq Policy," *Washington Post*, January 16, 2005. On electoral mandates generally, see Patricia Conley, *Presidential Mandates* (Chicago: University of Chicago Press, 2001).

25. "Pushing the Limit," *New York Times*, May 19, 2002; "While Farmers Milk Public for Billions More," *USA Today*, May 15, 2002; and "Bush the Anti-Globaliser," *The Economist*, May 11, 2002.

26. David Nather and Rebecca Adams, "The Real Crisis Waits Its Turn," *CQ Weekly*, February 21, 2005, 446–51.

27. The APSA report does recognize the potentially positive effect of higher stakes—increasing popular interest and participation in politics. See, e.g., ASPA's Committee on Political Parties, "Toward a More Responsible Two-Party System," p. 65. The report seems less cognizant of the potential negative effects of high-stakes politics.

28. At the start of the 109th Congress, Speaker Hastert declared that he would bring no proposal to the floor of the House that did not have a majority in the Republican Conference.

29. "Roll call votes on the House floor, which are supposed to take 15 minutes, are frequently stretched to one, two or three hours. Rules forbidding any amendments to bills on the floor have proliferated, stifling dissent and quashing legitimate debate. Omnibus bills, sometimes thousands of pages long, are brought to the floor with no notice, let alone the 72 hours the rules require. Conference committees exclude minority members and cut deals in private, sometimes even adding major provisions after the conference has closed." Norman Ornstein and Thomas Mann, "If You Give a Congressman a Cookie," *nytimes.com*, January 19, 2006, www.nytimes.com/2006/01/19/opinion/19ornstein.html.

30. For an overview, see Donald R. Wolfensberger, "Pols Apart," *The Wilson Quarterly* 28 (Autumn 2004), 49–59.

31. Norman Ornstein and Thomas Mann, eds., *The Permanent Campaign and its Future* (Washington, D.C.: American Enterprise Institute and the Brookings Institution, 2000).

32. In a famous 2003 article, John DiIulio, a prominent political science professor and Bush administration appointee, was quoted as saying "There is no precedent in any modern White House for what is going on in this one: a complete lack of a policy apparatus. . . . What you've got is everything—and I mean everything—being run by the political arm." Quoted in Ron Suskind, "Why Are These Men Laughing?" *www.ronsuskind.com/newsite/articles/archives/000032.html* (accessed March 23, 2007). Reacting to the appointment of Karl Rove, President Bush's chief political lieutenant, as deputy chief of staff, a high-level policy post in which he coordinates the work of the Domestic Policy Council, the National Economic Council, the National Security Council, and the Homeland Security Council, Paul Light, a senior scholar of the executive branch, noted that, "It codifies the fact that policy is politics, and politics is policy." Quoted in Mark Sandalow, "Bush Gives Policy Post to Shrewd Kingmaker," *San Francisco Chronicle*, February 9, 2005.

33. As Baer and Bositis pointed out, the APSA report was largely silent on race.

34. Writing about a completely different subject, Mayhew also observed that major midcentury political scientists saw American politics largely as a conflict between the economic haves and have-nots. David Mayhew, *Electoral Realignments* (New Haven, Conn.: Yale University Press, 2002), 153–56.

35. Burns, *Deadlock of Democracy*, 336.

36. APSA's Committee on Political Parties, "Toward a More Responsible Two-Party System," 20.

37. Such exceptions would include the fight over silver coinage among late-nineteenth-century Democrats and the Regular v. Progressive split among Republicans in the early twentieth century.

38. Duncan Black, *The Theory of Committees and Elections* (London: Cambridge University Press, 1958); and Downs, *Economic Theory of Democracy*.

39. Gerber offered an interesting explanation: under some conditions a strategy that maximizes probability of election may produce no gain (indeed, even a loss) of votes. See Alan Gerber, "Does Campaign Spending Work?" *American Behavioral Scientist* 47 (2004): 541–74.

40. Notably, after *losing* the popular vote in 2000, the Republican administration governed as if it had won a mandate.

41. APSA's Committee on Political Parties, "Toward a More Responsible Two-Party System," 1

42. On the difference between compromise on a single issue and compromise across a bundle of issues, see Fiorina, *Divided Government*, 121–24.

43. Americans may prefer Madisonian supermajoritarianism. Mark Mellman reported a recent poll in which, by a two to one margin, respondents preferred that Supreme Court Justices "should have to get the support of at least 60 of the 100 senators" rather than 51. Mark Mellman, "Why Not Require 60 Votes?" *The Hill*, March 16, 2005.

44. Downs, *Economic Theory of Democracy*. Technically speaking such a platform is not in equilibrium, but with more than one issue dimension equilibria rarely exist. Parties still have to take positions—out of equilibrium or not.

45. As the APSA report commented, "A program-conscious party develops greater resistance against the inroads of pressure groups." APSA's Committee on Political Parties, "Toward a More Responsible Two-Party System," 19.

46. Ibid., 22.

47. Amy Goldstein, "Foster: White House Had Role in Withholding Medicare Data," *Washington Post*, March 19, 2004. Fortunately for the country the costs have not proved to be as large as initially estimated, although the crisis in Medicare still looms on the near horizon.

48. Dan Eggen, "Justice Staff Saw Texas Districting as Illegal," *Washington Post*, December 2, 2005.

49. See the special issue on Social Security in the online journal, *The Economists Voice*, www.bepress.com/ev/vol2/iss1/.

50. Steven Schier, *By Invitation Only* (Pittsburgh, Pa.: University of Pittsburgh Press, 2000).

51. Steven Rosenstone and John Mark Hansen, *Mobilization, Participation, and Democracy in America* (New York: Macmillan, 1993), 162–69.

52. Steven Ansolabehere and Shanto Iyengar, *Going Negative* (New York: Free Press, 1995); and Ted Brader, *Campaigning for Hearts and Minds* (Chicago: University of Chicago Press, 2006). For other, more skeptical, views see the multi-author exchange on negative advertising in the *American Political Science Review* 93 (1999): 851–909. The latest addition to the literature is Michael M. Franz, Paul B. Freedman, Kenneth M. Goldstein, and Travis N. Ridout, *Campaign Advertising and American Democracy* (Philadelphia.: Temple University Press, 2008).

53. Preliminary calculations by Marc Hetherington indicate that 60 percent of the increased turnout between 1996 and 2004 is due to the mobilization activities of the parties. Personal communication, March 12, 2007. And as noted in chapter 2, one group of scholars calculated that mobilization activities may have accounted for one-third of the increase in turnout between 2000 and 2004. See Bergan, Gerber, Green, and Panagopoulos, "Grassroots Mobilization and Voter Turnout in 2004."

54. I am unpersuaded by research that purports to show that party in the electorate has resurged to 1950s levels. Morris Fiorina, "Parties and Partisanship: A 40-Year Retrospective," *Political Behavior* 24 (2002): 93–115.

55. In 25 states that record party registration, Election Data Services reports that between 2000 and 2004 independents and third-party registrants showed a 21 percent increase compared with 7.4 percent for Democrats and 5.5 percent for Republicans. I thank Zachary Courser of Claremont-McKenna College for calling these figures to my attention.

56. Eric M. Uslaner, *The Decline of Comity in Congress* (Ann Arbor: University of Michigan Press, 1993).

57. Marc J. Hetherington, "Turned Off or Turned On? How Polarization Affects Political Engagement," in *Red and Blue Nation*, vol. 2 ed. Pietro S. Nivola and David W. Brady (Washington, D.C.: Brookings, 2008), 1–33; and Sarah A. Binder, "Consequences for the Courts: Polarized Politics and the Judicial Branch," in *Red and Blue Nation*, vol. 2, 107–33.

58. David Mayhew began the discussion in *Divided We Govern* (New Haven, Conn.: Yale University Press, 1991). One of the most recent contributions to this continuing debate is Sarah A. Binder, *Stalemate: Causes and Consequences of Legislative Gridlock* (Washington, D.C.: Brookings, 2003).

59. Keith Krehbiel, "Comment," in *Red and Blue Nation*, vol. 2, 93–105.

60. David W. Brady, John A. Ferejohn, and Laurel Harbridge, "Polarization and Public Policy: A General Assessment," in *Red and Blue Nation*, vol. 2, 185–216.

61. Nils Gilman, "What the Rise of the Republicans as America's First Ideological Party Means for the Democrats," *The Forum*, 2 (2004), www.bepress.com/forum/vol2/iss1/art2/.

CHAPTER 8

1. Fiorina, Abrams, and Pope, *Culture War?* 2nd ed., 209.

2. See, e.g., Edward R. Tufte, "The Relationship between Seats and Votes in Two-Party Systems," *American Political Science Review* 67 (1973): 540–54.

3. Summarizing very broadly, in 1977 Ferejohn concluded that redistricting had little to do with the mid-1960s electoral changes. Much later Cox and Katz disagreed, finding that it had a disparate effect on Republican and Democratic incumbents. Ansolabehere and Snyder disagreed again, showing that the incumbency advantage grew in offices whose constituencies were not subject to redistricting. See John A. Ferejohn, "On the Decline of Competition in Congressional Elections," *American Political Science Review* 71 (1977): 166–76; Gary W. Cox and Jonathan N. Katz, *Elbridge Gerry's Salamander* (Cambridge, England: Cambridge University Press, 2002); and Steve Ansolabehere and James M. Snyder, Jr., "The Incumbency Advantage in U.S. Elections: An Analysis of State and Federal Offices, 1942–2000," *Election Law Journal* 1 (2002): 326.

4. Gary C. Jacobson, *The Electoral Origins of Divided Government* (Boulder, Colo.: Westview Press, 1990), 94–96; and Fiorina, *Divided Government*, 14–18.

5. Beginning with *Shaw v. Reno* (1993), of course, the Supreme Court has held that weirdly shaped districts do have some limits.

6. For a survey of relevant research, see Thomas Mann, "Polarizing the House of Representatives: Does Gerrymandering Matter?" in *Red and Blue Nation*, vol. 1, 263–83. For a conclusive refutation of the hypothesis that redistricting has contributed significantly to contemporary Congressional polarization, see Nolan McCarty, Ketih T. Poole, and Howard Rosenthal, "Does Gerrymandering Cause Polarization?" manuscript, August 6, 2007.

7. Poole and Rosenthal, *Ideology and Congress*, 103–107.

8. Mann, "Polarizing the House of Representatives," 274–80.

9. This position is by no means universally held by political scientists. For dissenting views, see Justin Buchler, "The Statistical Properties of Competitive Districts: What the Central Limit Theorem Can Teach Us about Election Reform," *PS: Political Science and Politics*," 40 (2007): 333–37; and Thomas Brunell, "Rethinking Redistricting: How Drawing Uncompetitive Districts Eliminates Gerrymanders, Enhances Representation and Improves Attitudes toward Congress," *PS: Political Science and Politics* 39 (2006): 77–85.

10. Curtin Gans, "2006 Primary Turnout a Record Low—15 Percent of Eligibles Vote," http://domino.american.edu/AU/media/mediarel.nsf/b0af33083b8462d085256a1d00572a4b/c4906adb098c248285257202008ibf9a?OpenDocument.

11. On the lack of major differences between presidential primary and general election voters, see Barbara Norrander, "Ideological Representativeness of Presidential Primary Voters," *American Journal of Political Science* 33 (1989): 570–87; and Alan Abramowitz, "Don't Blame Primary Voters for Polarization," *The Forum* 5 (2008), www.bepress.com/forum/vol5/iss4/art4/.

12. Bruce Mehlman and Alex Vogel, "Flip-Flopping in the Age of YouTube," *The Politico*, May 8, 2007, www.politico.com/news/stories/0507/3889.html.

13. *California Democratic Party et al. v. Jones*, 530 U.S. 567 (2000). In addition both the Alaska and Washington State Supreme Courts had recently determined that their state's blanket primaries were constitutional. These states, too, had to change their primary process after the Supreme Court ruling.

14. E. E. Schattschneider, *Party Government* (New York: Farrar &Rinehart, 1942), 1.

15. *California Democratic Party et al. v. Jones*, 6.

16. Wendy K. Tam Cho and Brian J. Gaines, "Candidates, Donors, and Voters in California's Blanket Primary Elections," in *Voting at*

the Political Fault Line, ed. Bruce E. Cain and Elisabeth R. Gerber (Berkeley: University of California Press, 2002), 174–76.

17. For a survey of the campaign finance scene since McCain–Feingold, see Michael J. Malbin, ed., *The Election after Reform: Money, Politics and the Bipartisan Campaign Reform Act* (Lanham, Md.: Rowman & Littlefield, 2006).

18. Hillygus and Shields, *Persuadable Voter.*

19. Helped along in part by the tone-deafness of congressional Democrats who appeared more concerned with the welfare of their public employee union allies than national security in the debate over establishing a Department of Homeland Security.

20. Thomas Edsall, *Building Red America* (New York: Basic, 2006), 50–52.

21. Political scientists consider the Perot voters as a classic swing group. In the 1992 House elections they cast a majority of votes for Democrats. In 1994 they swung more than 2:1 to the Republican side. Paul R. Abramson, John H. Aldrich, and David W. Rohde, *Change and Continuity in the 1992 Elections,* rev. ed. (Washington, D.C.: CQ Press, 1995), 312, 331.

22. In 2006, swing-state tracking polls in the last month of the campaign reportedly had the number of swing voters varying from 22 to 29 percent. Craig Charney, "Why Dems Won," *nypost.com,* November 10, 2006, www.ppionline.org/ndol/ndol_ci.cfm?kaid=85&subid=900184&contentid=254103. An interesting situation emerged in the May 2007 French presidential election when the standard right versus left plus the National Front competition was muddied by the facts that the Socialists nominated a woman for the first time in French history and there was a strong centrist candidate as well. In consequence, polls reported that more than 40 percent of the French electorate was undecided the week before the election.

23. Pietro S. Nivola, "Can the Government Be Serious?" in *Agenda for the Nation,* ed. Henry J. Aaron, James M. Lindsay, and Pietro S. Nivola (Washington, D.C.: Brookings, 2003), 485–525.

24. Morris P. Fiorina, Samuel J. Abrams, and Jeremy C. Pope, "The 2000 U.S. Presidential Election: Can Retrospective Voting Be Saved?" *British Journal of Political Science,* 33 (2003): 163–87.

25. The discussion that follows draws on and extends the discussion in Morris P. Fiorina, "A Divider Not a Uniter—Did It Have to Be?" in *The George W. Bush Legacy,* ed. Colin B. Campbell, Bert A. Rockman, and Andrew Rudalevige (Washington, D.C.: CQ Press), 92–111.

26. Campbell's definition of the "base" (strong and weak partisans plus independent leaners who do not place themselves in the exact center of the ideological scale) is extremely generous. In particular, an independent may say she leans toward a particular party because *in that particular election,* she likes that party better than the other.

27. For explanations of and excuses for the 2000 performance of forecasting models, see recaps in *PS: Political Science and Politics,* March 2001, and in the May 2001 issue of *American Politics Research.*

28. As he did in his 2007 State of the Union Address—too little, too late.

29. The McKinley coalition expanded well beyond the smaller Republican coalition that contested elections in the 1874–1896 "period of no decision." In 1896 the Republicans succeeded in taking a significant chunk of the industrial working class away from the Democrats. See James L. Sunquist, *Dynamics of the Party System,* rev. ed. (Washington, D.C.: Brookings, 1983), chap. 7.

30. Jim Rutenberg, "Ex-Aide Says He's Lost Faith in Bush," *nytimes.com,* April 1, 2007, www.nytimes.com/2007/04/01/washington/01adviser.html?pagewanted=print.

31. One of the most telling indicators is that a series of recent books trumpets warnings about the coming theocracy. Whenever academics and public affairs commentators reach agreement about a subject, it is almost certainly about to change and make their analyses obsolete. For a review essay on recent antitheocratic books, see Ross Douthat, "Theocracy, Theocracy, Theocracy," *firstthings.com,* August/September 2006, www.firstthings.com/article.php3?id_article=130.

32. Lexington, "Trouble in the Family," *The Economist,* March 3, 2007, 40.

33. Albert Hunt, "Letter from Washington: Evangelical Christians Feared, but Multifaceted," *International Herald Tribune,* April 15, 2007; John Dickerson, "A Weak Reed: Why Christian Conservatives Are Souring on the GOP," *slate.com,* June 28, 2006, www.slate.com/id/2144601/; and Mark I. Pinsky, "Meet the New Evangelicals," *latimes.com,* September 16, 2006, www.latimes.com/writers/mark-i-pinsky.

34. "Evangelicals Urge Pullback from Politics," Reuters News Release, May 7, 2008.

35. For replies to such elderly reproaches, see Betsy Reed, "Race to the Bottom," *The Nation,* May 19, 2008; and Caille Millner, "When Can I Call Myself a Feminist Again?" *San Francisco Chronicle,* May 5, 2008.

36. As sociologists and demographers have pointed out, the traditional family with working father and stay-at-home mother is a generalization of a relatively short period of modern history.

37. It creates some tensions in the Democratic Party as well, although not as severe as on the Republican side. Some economists believe that immigration, especially illegal immigration, exerts downward pressure on the wages of unskilled and low-skilled native workers, who tend to be Democrats. In addition, Democratic local and state officials are on the fiscal firing line when it comes to providing social services to immigrants. Hence, some of them naturally show less sympathy to immigrants and immigration than the bulk of the party.

38. John B. Judis and Ruy Teixeira, *The Emerging Democratic Majority* (New York: Scribner, 2004).

39. Samuel P. Huntington, *Who Are We? The Challenges to America's National Identity* (New York: Simon & Schuster, 2004). Using the standard historical indicators—English acquisition, citizenship, intermarriage, homeownership—recent immigrants from Asia and Latin America are following the same path as earlier waves of European immigrants. Gregory Rodriguez, quoted in Patrick McDonnell, "Immigrants Quickly Becoming Assimilated, Report Concludes," *San Francisco Chronicle*, July 7, 1999.

40. On immigration generally, see Philip Martin and Elizabeth Midgley, "Immigration: Shaping and Reshaping America," *Population Bulletin*, 61 (2006). On English acquisition specifically, see Douglas S. Massey and Frank D. Bean, "Linguistic Life Expectancies: Immigrant Language Retention in Southern California," *Population and Development Review* 32 (2006): 447–60.

EPILOGUE

1. Quotations from E. J. Dionne, Jr., "Democrats Won with Votes on Loan," *realclearpolitics.com*, November 9, 2006; Chuck Todd, "Congress Gets a Case of the Blues," *nationaljournal.com*, November 8, 2006; David Ignatius, "A Move Back to the Political Center?" *realclearpolitics.com*, October 18, 2006; E. J. Dionne, Jr., "Rising Radical Center," *washingtonpost.com*, October 24, 2006; and Mort Kondracke, "Democrats, GOP Should Heed Voters' Call for Moderation," *realclearpolitics.com*, January 4, 2007.

2. Craig Charney, "Why Dems Won," *nypost.com*, November 10, 2006.

3. Quoted in Jim VandeHei, Mike Allen, and Jonathan Martin, "Republicans Fear 2008 Meltdown," *The Politico*, May 29, 2007.

4. Jacob Weisberg, "Karl Rove's Dying Dream," *nypost.com*, November 2, 2005.

5. Quoted in Jim Rutenberg, "Gingrich Lambastes President and Rove," *nytimes.com*, May 30, 2007.

6. Morris P. Fiorina, "A Divider, Not a Uniter—Did It Have to Be?" in *The George W. Bush Legacy*, eds. Colin Campbell, Bert A. Rockman, and Andrew Rudalevige (Washington, D.C.: CQ Press, 2007).

7. Michael Barone, "Talkin' 'Bout My Generation," *National Review Online*, July 23, 2007.

8. Ellen Goodman, "Obama Can Unite, but Can He Fight?" *Realclearpoltics.com*, December 7, 2007. First published in the *Boston Globe*.

9. Daniel Henninger, "1968: The Long Goodbye," *Realclearpolitics.com*, November 15, 2007. First published in the *Wall Street Journal*.

10. Lexington, "The 40-Year Itch," *The Economist*, January 5, 2008, 30.

11. Ibid. In late 2007 as the Iowa caucuses approached, Hillary Clinton inadvertently provided a humorous illustration of Obama's point. Responding to Obama's enlistment of Oprah Winfrey in the campaign, Clinton responded with Barbara Streisand—your father's entertainer in the view of many Americans.

12. Andrew Sullivan, "Goodbye to All That," *The Atlantic.com*, December 7, 2007.

13. William Jelani Cobb, "As Obama Rises, Old Guard Civil Rights Leaders Scowl," *washingtonpost.com*, January 13, 2008.

14. V.O. Key, Jr., "A Theory of Critical Elections," *Journal of Politics* 17 (1955): 3–18; Walter Dean Burnham, *Critical Elections and the Mainsprings of American Politics* (New York, Norton: 1970); and James Sundquist, *The Dynamics of the Party System: Alignment and Realignment of Political Parties in the United States* (Washington, D.C.: Brookings, 1973).

15. See the essays in *The End of Realignment? Interpreting American Electoral Eras*, ed. Byron E. Shafer (Madison: University of Wisconsin Press, 1991); and David Mayhew, *Electoral Realignments: A Critique of an American Genre* (New Haven, Conn.: Yale University Press, 2002).

16. David W. Brady, *Critical Elections and Congressional Policy Making* (Stanford, Calif.: Stanford University Press, 1988).

17. John H. Aldrich and Richard G. Niemi, "The Sixth American Party System: Electoral Change, 1952–1992," in *Broken Contract?*

Changing Relationships between Americans and Their Government," ed. Stephen C. Craig (Boulder, Colo.: Westview Press, 1996).
   18. Fiorina, *Divided Government,* 1st ed.

APPENDIX

   1. James Snyder, "Artificial Extremism in Interest Group Ratings," *Legislative Studies Quarterly* 36 (1992): 319–45.
   2. Technically speaking, to avoid "artificial extremism" the bills that are proposed must produce a uniform distribution of cutting points between the bill and the status quo. Krehbiel and Woon provided a thoughtful consideration of problems in selecting among the roll call votes that occur. Keith Krehbiel and Jonathan Woon, "Selection Criteria for Roll Call Votes," September 2005, Stanford GSB Research Paper No. 1943.
   3. Stanley Bach and Steven S. Smith, *Managing Uncertainty in the House of Representatives* (Washington, D.C.: Brookings, 1988); Steven S. Smith, *Call to Order: Floor Politics in the House and Senate* (Washington, D.C.: Brookings, 1989); and Gary W. Cox and Mathew D. McCubbins, *Setting the Agenda: Responsible Party Government in the U.S. House of Representatives* (New York: Cambridge, 2005.
   4. Poole and Rosenthal have argued that the slippage is empirically insignificant. *Ideology and Congress,* 68–69. Snyder and Krehbiel disagree (personal conversations). For the most current research dealing with these questions, see the articles in the special issue of *Legislative Studies Quarterly* 33 (2008).
   5. Jason M. Roberts and Steven S. Smith, "Procedural Contexts, Party Strategy, and Conditional Party Voting in the U.S. House of Representatives, 1971–2000," *American Journal of Political Science* 47 (2003): 305–17. For additional evidence consistent with changing agenda strategies, see Gary W. Cox and Jonathan N. Katz, "Gerrymandering Roll Calls in Congress, 1879–2000," *American Journal of Political Science* 51 (2007): 108–119; and Cox and McCubbins, *Setting the Agenda.*
   6. Robert Van Houweling, "Legislator's Personal Policy Preferences and Partisan Legislative Organization" (PhD diss., Harvard University, 2003).
   7. Keith Krehbiel has been the most persistent poser of this question.
   8. Barry Weingast and Daniel Rodriguez, "The Positive Political Theory of Legislative History: New Perspectives on the 1964 Civil Rights Act and Its Interpretation," *University of Pennsylvania Law Review* 151 (2003): 1417–1542.

INDEX

Page numbers for tables and graphs are in *italics*.